Hi Rita,

Hope you enjoy this
book —

Cheers,

Aloysius - Datch

13/02/2017

Homeward Bound

Anju and Ivy D'Souza and the Story of Early 20th Century Goan Migrants

Aloysius D'Souza

2017

Homeward Bound: Anju and Ivy and the Story of Early 20th Century Goan Migrants

© 2017 Aloysius D'Souza smhsdatch@gmail.com +91-9657126048

Published in 2017 by

Saligao 403511 Goa, India. http://goa1556.in, goa1556@gmail.com
+91-832-2409490
in association with

The Margao (Rua Abade Faria) bookshop with a difference

Distributed by:

GoaBook.Club

Making Goa books accessible via mail-order.

Project co-ordinated by Frederick Noronha
Cover design by Bina Nayak binanayak@gmail.com
Printed in India by Brilliant Printers Pvt. Ltd, Bangalore
http://www.brilliantprinters.com
Typeset with LyX, http://www.lyx.org. Text: Bitstream Charter, 10/14.2.

ISBN: 978-93-80739-84-7   Price Rs 400

This book was assisted with a Government of Goa (Directorate of Art and Culture) grant of Rs 23,000 which helped to meet part of the costs of publication.

Contents

This book, about the lives of
my Mum and Dad in Burma and India,
is dedicated to Goans everywhere
to whom that small little area on the
west coast of India called Goa is home.
All Goans, like me, in our
innermost thoughts sing:
'Be it ever so humble
There is no place like home (Goa)'

Introduction

S YLVESTER Philip D'Souza went west to Canada in 1918 in search of gold, but lost his fortune. A year later his son Anju D'Souza went east to Burma, and discovered a golden land.

Anju – my father – followed other Goans to Burma to find a different way of life. He was moulded into a person totally different from people of his age in Goa and Bombay.

Dad would regale us with stories of his adventures through the various stages of his life. My daughter, Deepika, kept prompting me to record his stories with a tape recorder or similar device, which I never did. But many of his stories are so vivid that, even today, I can visualize Dad telling them. Deepika and Dad's friends will remember many of the stories and incidents I now recount.

But these are more than just the stories of one family. This book seeks to record stories of a generation and more, in times when Goa was undergoing very rapid change. This is the story of Goa, of a period many would recall wistfully.

Special thanks for all the encouragement goes to my daughter, Deepika, who bugged me to write her Grandfather's story. And to Ulrike, my cousin Leo's, daughter, who read my early notes and put them in some order and structure so that I could proceed to fill in the details. Her uncles, Alex, Rudi and Eddie, helped me with background on Uncle Salu and Aunt Bemvinda. On my mother's family side, her elder sisters' (Flory and Bella) grandchildren, Martha, Marilyn and Corrine, provided me with details about the Cheron family of which I was not aware.

My sincere thanks go to Neela D'Souza for reading my early draft and giving me valuable suggestions. Definitely, my heartfelt thanks are due to Frederick Noronha who turned all my notes and photographs into a publishable book and who also suggested applying to the Government of Goa, Department of Art and Culture, for a grant to publish this book. An important aspect of bringing out this book is the financing of its publication and for this I owe my grateful thanks to the Government of Goa, Department of Art and Culture for their grant of Rs. 23,000 which covered part of the costs.

Aloysius D'Souza
December 16, 2016

Bombay (Cumballa Hill)
Goa (Alto Porvorim)

In Nachinola... and Rangoon

L EOPOLDINA Souza e Sequeira was, for all practical purposes, a World War I widow; but she had her three children with her when her husband went to France in 1917. Now with World War II coming to the east, was she to lose all three of her children in the Japanese bombing of Rangoon?

Bom Jesu Feast, January 1, 1942. Nachinola, Bardez, Goa:

Leopoldina had just been informed at Mass that Rangoon had been bombed by the Japanese. This had happened just before Christmas 1941, and that hundreds of people had been killed. Her son Anju and his family, her daughter Bemvinda and her family, and her younger son Gerry, were all in Rangoon. She had no news of them and indeed had reason to be worried.

She had no news either of her husband, Sylvester Philip, from the other end of the world in Montreal, Canada. He had gone with the Maharaja of Tekari[1] in 1917 to join the Allied Forces in France during World War I. When the war ended he did not return but instead went on to Canada where gold had just been discovered.

Now, World War II in Europe was going badly for the British. Goans had heard that ships crossing between North America

---

[1] Tekari (or Tikari) Raj was a *zamindar* family of the Bhumihar community in South Bihar. They controlled 2,046 villages on their estate, which covered a 7,500 square kilometres area, near the town of Gaya.

and England, and also those coming around the Cape of Good Hope to India, had been sunk by the Germans. Seamen, including many Goans, had been killed. Leopoldina fervently prayed: "*Bom Jesu* (Good Jesus), on this your feast, please bring my family safely through this war."

Enquiries with the parish priest and with village seniors, including Dr Jose D'Souza, whose brother was in Brazil, brought no further news. Leopoldina immediately went to Saligao, hoping that her mother, whose brother and eldest son were also in Burma, and other families there having relatives in Burma, may have the latest information. Beyond confirming that Rangoon had been bombed, nobody had further information though.

All they could do was wait and pray.

Rangoon, Burma, December 23, 1941 10 a.m.

ANJU and me were standing out in the street in front of our house watching the 'air show'. A few AVG (American Volunteer Group) P40 Tomahawks and RAF Buffalo planes were taking on a Japanese air armada of over a hundred planes, which was flying over Rangoon bombing and machine gunning the city.

Ivy, in a white dress, her face almost as white as her dress, arrived in a rickshaw. With her was my sister, Iza. Ivy and immediately shouted that we should get into the inspection pit in the garage.

From downtown Rangoon she had come running down the centre of the road, when a *rickshaw-walla* stopped and told her to get in and he would take her wherever she wanted to go. He ran down the centre of the road with a Japanese plane flying just above them, machine gunning people on either side of the road. The gunner could apparently not get his gun to bear on the rickshaw directly below him. On route, Ivy picked up my sister, Iza, from Grandma Cheron's house on 50th Street.

Ivy bundled all of us, including the *rickshaw-walla*, our cook and his wife, into this inspection pit and insisted we stay there until the all clear was sounded. Miss Strong and her servants refused to come down from the first floor and take shelter.

When the sound of planes overhead faded into the distance, although no 'all clear' was heard, we ventured out. Our cook complained that all the lunch had got burnt. Anju discovered that he had a wound on the back of his hand from a bit of flying shrapnel. We picked the shrapnel off the ground and noticed that it had changed colour; we were worried that it carried some form of poison.

Down our street, the sailors' home next to Biddy's house was on fire. Bereft of fire hoses, the men from our street set up a bucket brigade and doused the houses on either side and at the rear. They wanted to prevent the fire from spreading and letting the house burn down. The Fire Brigade was too busy in other parts of Rangoon and could not respond to all the fire calls.

Further devastation was lying in wait nearby. Just before the bombing, Eddie D'Cruz, his pregnant wife Connie, mother-in-law, little daughter Winsome, and her nanny, had entered their home from the hospital and were relaxing in their sitting room on the ground floor. Their concrete building received a direct hit. The bomb came straight through the upper two floors and exploded right in their midst. All were instantaneously killed, except Eddie who was blown out onto the road with arms and legs amputated, shouting for help. He died even before he could reach the hospital.

At the other end of Rangoon, Diego's wife, Agnes, who had delivered her baby on December 21 at the Dufferin Hospital, found that one of the wings of the hospital had taken a direct hit and was in flames. She raced down from the third floor carrying her baby and hid under one of the beds on the ground floor. She came home that evening. A week later the baby was christened Noelynn. With all the distractions, Fr St Guilly entered 'Roselyn' in the baptism record. Everyone called her Noelynn till the family returned to post-war Rangoon in 1945 and obtained a copy of the baptism record required for school admission.

Uncle Hippolito's (Myingyan D'Souza) family was in Rangoon in December 1941 when the Japanese bombed the city. At the *gharry* (horse carriage) stand next to their house, the horses still harnessed to the carriages were dead – standing upright – with no visible wounds. Obviously it was a case of death by shock from the bombs that exploded near them. Uncle Hippolito, Aunty Ancy and Hilda, Irene and Isabelle immediately left for Myingyan. This was in the Mandalay division, some 580 kms away. Arist, Alphonse and George could not leave Rangoon because of their work.

The marbled floors of the ballroom, banquet room and corridors of the Rangoon City Hall were slippery with blood. Bodies of those already dead and many others seriously wounded were brought in from the streets. There must have been many more dead in the bombed buildings, but this became apparent only on subsequent days.

The British Burmese Government was totally unprepared for the Japanese invasion. A detailed analysis of this unpreparedness is given in James Lunt's *Imperial Sunset* (London: MacDonald, 1981), specifically in Chapter 16 titled 'Burma Rifles'.

After attacking Pearl Harbour on December 7, 1941, over the radio the Japanese kept promising 'Christmas presents from above' to the children of Burma. During this period many of Anju's friends, who had volunteered as Air Raid Patrol (ARP) Wardens, wearing their tin helmets, would go down the streets at night checking if the black-out at each house was total. If they saw a chink of light, they would knock on the door and insist that the curtains be properly drawn, or thick brown paper be pasted over glass windows. We had fitted conical card-paper shades over all hanging lights, so that their light was directed downwards.

As precaution against bomb blasts, we pasted paper Xs over all glass windows. This was meant to prevent potential flying splinters of glass cutting people inside or outside the house, office, shop or school. We had been told to head for underground shelters, if available, or the inspection pits in garages at homes.

But, no actual drill or rehearsals had been carried out. People were totally unaware of how to act in the event of a bombing or strafing by enemy planes.

That evening, after doing a quick tour around Rangoon, Anju and Ivy decided to lock up and shift to the bungalow which John Menezes had hired near Kokine Lakes. With us were our cook and his wife and our two dogs, Patch and Mitzy. Grandma Cheron and Clare, Amy and Mayrose decided to stay on in Rangoon as Diego could not leave the bakery and Agnes needed to be near medical help.

We joined Mrs. and Mr. John Menezes with Eric and Leslie early that evening. While the adults organised themselves, Iza, Eric and I with the dogs enjoyed investigating the large garden. For us, city bumpkins, having a large garden with lots of plants was a totally new experience. We discovered 'onions' in the flower beds. When we dug some up and showed them to the elders, we were informed that they were lily bulbs and not onions that could be eaten. Behind the bungalow there was a grove of banana trees; the ones which had fruited and were due for chopping were up-rooted and replanted as camouflage over the trench which had been dug. I discovered that the inside white stem of the banana plant was what was used in *mohinga*[2].

After this hectic day we all went to bed early, but not for long. The siren sounded and we were bundled into blankets and carried into the trench. In spite of entreaties from the ladies, the men remained outside to see what was happening. Rangoon was again being bombed. Although we were close to Mingaladon Airport, the Japanese apparently did not target the airport, probably preserving it for their own future use. Some Japanese planes were shot down and the pilots baled out. But immediately on landing they were attacked by locals and killed. Their mouths were said to have been pried open and their gold teeth yanked out.

---

[2] Mohinga is a rice noodle and fish soup from Myanmar and is an essential part of Burmese cuisine. It is considered by many to be the national dish of Myanmar.

Next day, Christmas Eve, more friends joined us. This included Arist, George and Alphonse, Mario and Francis Manricks, Mr. Gilda, the Parsi teak trader from Bombay, and Mrs. and Mr. Sequeira. Arist remained glued to the radio to hear what was happening by way of the Japanese invasion and British counter moves. Mr. Gilda saying his prayers on the verandah every morning, in his long thin muslin vest with his tape in hand, was a scene totally new to us.

Even though there was a chapel near by, there was no question of attending Midnight Mass as one could not drive at night. We attended Christmas Mass in the morning. After Mass we visited Mrs. and Mr. Pimenta who had shifted out of Rangoon to a house quite close, with the main Rangoon water supply pipeline in between. Their dog, a spaniel, had given pups and they had one pup left. It promptly played with me and I got on very well with the pup. On asking if I could have the pup, I was told that it was Edigio's and he had to decide whether or not to give it away. We left without the pup.

We visited Grandma Cheron and family in Rangoon and brought back our Christmas presents which Santa had delivered to our 52nd Street house. I got a small sailing boat with sails, which I promptly deployed in the little pond at the bungalow, and a Meccano set. Iza got a toy porcelain tea set. Between us we got a pair of roller skates. Later, these would be the only toys that came to India with us.

While driving through Rangoon, there was the awful smell of death as many dead bodies still remained under the debris of bombed buildings. Streets were almost totally empty of pedestrians.

By that evening the exodus from Rangoon started – by road, rail and with some even trekking. A lucky few were able to get berths in the British-India Steam Navigation (BISN) Company ships to either Calcutta or Madras. Very few were able to fly out from Rangoon. But some Europeans and government officials were advised to go by train to Mandalay from where planes were taking passengers to Calcutta.

During the days after Christmas, the two cars driven by Anju and John Menezes would leave for the city every morning with all the men folk. They would be back well before dusk since they were not allowed to use their headlights while driving at night. They brought news of people leaving Rangoon, some going to India by ship but many going up-country to sit out the Japanese bombings. No one expected that the all-conquering British would be driven out of Burma.

Mrs. and Mr. Pimenta came with Edigio to wish Ivy and Anju on their wedding anniversary, December 28. Edigio had brought the pup, whom he had named Nelson. He handed over the pup to me with detailed instructions on how to look after him. He was actually crying when handing Nelson over. I thanked him and promised to look after Nelson.

Almost every night, but definitely on moonlit nights, Japanese bombers came over and bombed Rangoon. Consequently, we spent most nights in the trench.

As far as we youngsters were concerned this was a wonderful holiday. During the days, we investigated the neighbourhood, discovering Chinese market gardeners who grew the special vegetables used in Chinese food.

By mid-January Rangoon was almost empty. Still, the smell of death was everywhere. No one walked about the streets. There was little traffic, and most shops closed; but Cheron Bakery remained open. When Anju went into town and stopped anywhere he was immediately surrounded by a pack of dogs, who came up to him, sniffed him and then moved off with the most mournful of expressions. These dogs had been abandoned by their masters and mistresses, but apparently continued to hope for their return.

No arrangements had been made to evacuate the civilian population, a large proportion being Indian labourers and their families. Most of these refugees, probably a million or more, trekked out through the jungles and hills of upper Burma into north eastern India. There is no count of how many of these refugees died on this trek and from the subsequent stresses and illnesses.

No active men were being allowed to leave Rangoon. Diego persuaded Grandma Cheron, together with Agnes with Noellyn, and Clare, Amy and Mayrose to leave by ship for Calcutta. At the jetty to see them off on January 16, we watched a large number of friends and acquaintances leave with tearful good-byes to their men-folk and prayers that they would meet soon.

One group of civilian refugees, who trekked from Rangoon, reached Myitkinya in the Kachin State, Burma on May 6, 1942. They were told to report to the airstrip for a flight to India. The Japanese decided otherwise and bombed the two planes already loaded with wounded servicemen and civilians. They also strafed the airstrip. The massacre at Myitkyina airstrip is just one of the many barbarous acts of the Japanese during WW II.

Civilian refugees who reached the Assam border between Burma and India were greeted and given food, clothing and medical care by volunteers, mostly managers of tea estates with their wives and staff. They were then sent by rail to Calcutta, where they were temporarily accommodated in transit camps in Loreto Convent, Middleton Row and St Xavier's School, Park Street. From Calcutta these civilian refugees moved on to other parts of India where they had relatives and friends.

British and Indian troops, who were posted in Burma, found themselves ill-equipped to face the onslaught of the 'super' Japanese soldiers. They were forced to retreat leaving behind a large number of their colleagues – either dead or captured – and virtually all their artillery and vehicles. The Japanese considered anyone who surrendered beyond contempt. They immediately either killed them by sword or bayonet or tortured them to death in case they felt they could get useful information from them.

The 17th Indian Division, including a Gurkha Battalion, which had been sent south to prevent the Japanese from reaching Rangoon, found themselves outflanked and were forced to retreat along the railway line. Their last stand was to be at the railway bridge over the Sittang River (about 260 kms from Rangoon), but due the confusion the bridge was blown up before our troops had crossed over.[3]

One of the causalities at the Sittang River crossing was Major Sam Manekshaw. He was machine gunned in the abdomen by the Japanese. Due to the severity of his wounds, he was not expected to live and hence his Commanding Officer, Major General David Tennant (Punch) Cowan pinned his own Military Cross onto Major Manekshaw as a tribute to his gallantry during this action.

The Japanese drove the British out of Burma in less then six months, from December 1941 to May 1942.

The British Army consisted of few British regiments together with Indian and Gurkha regiments with General William 'Bill' Slim in charge. It had to prepare to meet the Japanese offensive to over-run India entering from Assam and Arakan, with the possibility of a Japanese amphibious invasion along the Bengal-Orissa coastline. Simultaneously they were preparing for the re-occupation of Burma using whatever equipment they could scrounge for the Fourteenth Army, unofficially referred to as the "forgotten army". General Bill Slim's motto, which he imparted to his staff officers and to regiments in the Fourteenth Army was: "God helps those, who help themselves."

None of these troops had been trained for the jungle warfare they would have to encounter when resisting the Japanese attack or advancing into Burma. In fact, some of these troops had been sent to India to rest and recuperate (R & R) from the desert war in the Middle East and North Africa, and were posted to the Burma front without further training or being re-equipped. Some training in jungle lore and warfare was imparted to few British and

---

[3]   See Battle of Sittang Bridge on the Wikipedia: It was part of the Burma campaign during World War II, and fought between February 19-23, 1942. A decisive victory for Japan, it resulted in heavy losses for the British Indian Army, which was forced to retreat in disarray. Brigadier Sir John George Smyth, V.C., who commanded the British Indian Army at Sittang Bridge, called it "the Sittang disaster".

Indian soldiers in the jungles of the Central Provinces (now Madhya Pradesh). One of the experts imparting this training was Jim Corbett, famous as the saviour of the Terai hill tribes from marauding man-eating tigers and leopards.

British attempts to re-occupy Burma started with a limited but not very successful offensive into Arakan (on the west coast, now called Rakhine) towards the end of 1942. Fighting well-trained, well-equipped and entrenched Japanese armies, adept in jungle warfare, General Slim had first to boost the morale of his once badly defeated army.

The Fourteenth Army, now consisting of British, Indian, Gurkha, West African, East African and American troops, supported by the RAF and the American Air Force, gradually got the upper hand. On May 2, 1945 Rangoon was re-occupied by a single pilot of a Mosquito aircraft of RAF 221 Group – all the Japanese having fled. Unfortunately, there does not appear to be any record of the name of this pilot. The Fourteenth Army came in from the north. An amphibious force from Ceylon and Akyab, supported by carrier-borne aircraft, came up the Rangoon River on the same day. Mopping up isolated Japanese troops continued for the next few months.

Thus it took the Allies about 30 months to re-occupy Burma.

In the Service of the Maharaja

A NJU, my father, was 97 years young. A week before his death, I discussed with him how we should celebrate the completion of his century. A little earlier, we had read how Queen Mary (Queen Elizabeth II's mother) had celebrated her 100th birthday in hospital with a bottle of champagne smuggled in by her loyal butler.

However, that was not to be. I left Goa for Bombay on Monday evening and I was informed the following Saturday, June 17, 2000, that Anju had died at 12:30 hours. Anju was perfectly okay that morning and had started work to prepare pork *vindaloo* for the weekend. Anju died almost instantaneously of a massive haemorrhage in his brain. Thus ended a life spanning almost a century, started in Goa, moving through Bombay to Burma, back to Bombay and finally home to Goa.

Ivy, my mother, had shared Anju's experiences for more than fifty years up to her death on April 9, 1981. Ivy would normally awake around 7 a.m. and get their breakfast ready. Anju, who awoke around 5.30 a.m., would have by then made and drunk his large mug of tea. That morning when he finished watering the plants and other chores around the house he was surprised to find that Ivy was not yet up. When he called out and there was no response, he went to check on her. He put his hand under the mosquito net and found her cold. Anju got a shock; she had died in her sleep.

Ivy's was the sobering influence on Anju's exuberant and optimistic way of life. In the almost 20 years after her death, Anju would miss her when needing to take some decision or other. In the months before his death, Anju had mentioned to me a number of times that he had seen Ivy in his dreams and she was beckoning him to come join her, which he finally did on June 17, 2000.

Anju was born on November 10, 1903, at his maternal grandparents' home in Arrarim, Saligao, Goa. He was christened Angelo Maria D'Souza and was the first child of Leopoldina Isabelle D'Souza e Sequeira and Sylvester Philip D'Souza of Nachinola. Anju was brought back to the village of Nachinola, about eight kilometres away, to the new house which had just been completed that year. His sister, Bemvinda, was born in Goa on August 22, 1911, and their brother, Gerald (Gerry), was born in Calcutta on September 24, 1915.

Grandad Sylvester Philip (SP) was working for the Maharaja of Tekari (in today's Gaya District of Bihar) who had an estate close to Calcutta. After Bemvinda was born, Grandad brought the family to Calcutta with Lino Correa (of Nachinola) and Francis Braganza (music shop) as neighbours. They lived in a house in Collin Lane (near the New Market), which had a banyan tree growing out of one wall. Anju claimed that this house was haunted and here they lost one baby brother, born before Gerry.

Anju, who had attended primary school at Saligao (probably the church school), was admitted to St Joseph's School (run by Irish Christian Brothers) at Bow Bazar, Calcutta.

His classmates teased him that he was a girl since his name was 'Maria'. He approached Brother Michael to delete Maria from his name; instead Brother Michael changed Anju's name in the school records to Angelo Michael D'Souza. Anju studied at St

Joseph's till the Fifth Standard, until Granny Leopoldina moved back to Goa in 1917.

During school holidays the family would stay at the Maharaja's estate outside Calcutta. Also staying at the estate was Mr. Dickson, the Maharaja's driver, probably imported from England with the car, as was the custom then. Mr. Dickson's son, about the same age as Anju, was his good friend. As was to be expected, Anju and his friend got up to various pranks, one of which Anju was very happy to relate:

> Early in the morning, bread was brought to the estate by the baker in a big basket. He balanced the basket on his head and held a stout *danda* (bamboo) in which three discs of metal were inserted. This he would bang on the ground to announce his arrival.
>
> Young Dickson and I planned to pinch some buns from the bread basket as the baker passed under the main arched gateway to the estate. It was not that we were hungry, but just for the thrill of it.
>
> Accordingly, we perched ourselves on the two gate posts, not visible to anyone approaching from the road, so that by leaning forward we could pick the buns without the baker seeing us. As the baker passed, both of us leaned forward, lost our balance and fell into the bread basket. The baker gave quite a yell. Both of us got up, ran and slipped back into our beds and pretended to be fast asleep.
>
> SP, Dickson and members of the staff came to investigate but could find no trace of the two *chokras* who had dropped on to the baker. SP suspected that I must have been one of the *chokras*, but when he checked and found me fast asleep, they concluded that they must have been two urchins from the neighbourhood, who had run away. The baker was compensated for the damaged bread and he went on his way.

However, the Maharaja, who was at his window on an upper floor, had watched the whole incident. After all the hubbub had died down, he called the two of us and told us that he had seen what we had done. He warned us that we could have hurt ourselves badly, in addition to hurting the baker. After telling us not to get up to such tricks again he sent us packing. But he was a good sport and did not inform either Mr. Dickson or SP.

In 1917, the Maharaja led a company to France to join the British forces fighting the Germans in World War I. Grandad SP went with him, leaving Granny Leopoldina with Anju, Bemvinda and baby Gerry in Calcutta.

Granny could not manage on her own in Calcutta so she took the three kids and went back to Nachinola, Goa. Anju and Bemvinda continued their schooling at Saligao. They stayed with their Grand Mother, who was known as *Baabi Consu*, and was quite an enterprising lady. Among Anju's favourite relatives in Saligao was his cousin, Eudocina, his mother's sister's daughter. She had lost her mother while still a baby and her father had re-married; so Anju felt it necessary to share his joy in life with his motherless cousin.

After WW I ended on November 11, 1918, Grandad SP with a French friend, Evarist, decided to go to Canada where gold had just been discovered. Some time later he wrote to Granny Leopoldina that his efforts to find gold were not successful and he had lost all he had invested. Gerry heard Granny read out and translate the letter. When he went to the church school the next morning he informed everyone: *"Papa bangarache baint budlo"* (Papa has drowned in a gold well).

That afternoon, a surprised Granny saw the parish priest together with the curate in full dress vestments (normally worn only in church for high Mass) coming up to the house. She promptly dressed to meet these personages. They were surprised that Granny Leopoldina was not wearing black nor did she seem to be mourning her loss. On meeting her, they conveyed their sympathies over the 'death' of her husband. She was stunned and asked where they had heard this news. They pointed to Gerry and quoted him. Granny had to explain that Grandad had not fallen into the well and drowned, but that all his funds had gone down the gold mine in which he had invested without any recoverable gold being found.

Grandad Sylvester thereafter took a job as conductor with the Canadian Pacific Railway going from Montreal to Vancouver, almost 5,000 kms. He was away from his home in Montreal for ten days on each trip. He corresponded with Anju while Anju was in the Army. A photograph of his letter and not his actual letter would be delivered to Anju. This was because it was believed that spies could send coded messages the size of a full-stop in written or typed letters. Thus, by taking a photograph of the original letter, these hidden reports, if contained, could not be deciphered. He also sent post cards of various sites, including that of the Oratory of St Joseph in Montreal.

When I visited Montreal in 1972, I tried to locate Grandad's address, but that area had been re-developed and I was not successful. I did visit the Oratory of St Joseph. My cousins, Leo and Alex Rodrigues, who migrated to Toronto, Canada, in the early 1960s had also tried to trace Grandad's address, but also without success.

Uneventful Bombay...
Golden Burma

F UNDS were not coming regularly from Grandad, so Anju decided to come to Bombay in 1918 to find a job. Knowing how to read, write and speak English and being tall and personable, he got a job as a clerk with Bombay Tramway Co. (the predecessor to the BES&T) at their Colaba office. He shared a small flat at Dhobi Talao with three friends from Saligao. One of Anju's flat mates was Tommy Emar, who went on to become a noted businessman and philanthropist in British East Africa and is now remembered for the football gold cup tournament that was held in his name. Each paid their cook four *annas* (a quarter Rupee) for each day's shopping. In return, they each got two non-vegetarian meals, breakfast and evening tea. The cook obviously also fed himself, and maybe others too. Such was the cost of living in those times.

While working at Bombay Tramways, there was a strike by drivers and conductors. So the English officers took over the driving while Anju and other clerks acted as conductors on the electric trams running from the Colaba tram terminus to Kingsway Terminus at Dadar. They had police protection on the trams, but could not stop and get down anywhere for fear of being attacked by the strikers.

There was no food at either terminus. While passing through Parel, Anju spied a *bajjia-walla* who had just fried a large tray of assorted *bajjias*. He jumped down from the running tram, grabbed the tray and ran back and boarded the running tram. All this with the *bajjia-walla* shouting and waving behind him. The English officer promptly paid the *bajjia-walla* for the *bajjias* and for the tray and they enjoyed these fresh and crisp *bajjias* with other hungry officers and colleagues when they got to the Kingsway terminus.

Anju's sojourn in Bombay was obviously not very eventful, as he never mentioned much about his stay or his job, except for this *bajjia-walla* anecdote.

Burma – The Golden Land

Meanwhile, Granny Leopoldina's brother, who had a provision store in Myitkyina[4], Upper Burma, heard of their problems and offered Anju a job at his shop. Early in 1919 Anju went to Burma and started working for his uncle. Always independent, Anju could not cope with his uncle's orders and after a short time left him to start a provision store of his own.

While looking for a place at Meiktila in which to locate his shop, he came across a bungalow which was said to be haunted. Frightening noises were heard at night. Anju investigated and found that a branch of a tree was over-hanging the bungalow. When there was any breeze, the branch scraped the corrugated roof of the bungalow, producing these 'mysterious' noises. During the day nobody noticed these noises, but in the silence of the night the sounds were heard and were attributed to ghosts. Anju did not tell anyone, but approached the land-lord, who was very happy to offer his large 'haunted' bungalow at a very low rent. Immediately after shifting into the bungalow, Anju got the over-

---

[4] Myitkyina has been an important trading town between China and Burma since ancient times. It is today the capital city of Kachin State in Myanmar, located 1,480 kilometers from Yangon. In Burmese it means 'near the big river', and Myitkyina is on the west bank of the Ayeyarwady River. It is the northernmost river port and railway terminus in Myanmar.

hanging branch cut and thus laid the 'ghost' to rest.

On the ground floor he opened his shop, Meiktila Provisions and Liquors, and had his residence on the upper floor. He had an odd job man to help him in the shop as well as with his house-keeping and cooking.

As there were no refrigerators, ready-to-eat food in those days consisted of canned or bottled meat, fish, butter, cheese, sauces and jams. Anju had to carefully check for breakages or damage in transit, and clean up the residual undamaged items in a case before putting the stocks on the shelves for sale. Usually, extra labels were included in each case for just such an eventuality. Groceries like rice and *dals* came in sacks. Beer and liquors were in bottles packaged in wooden crates.

American oil drillers from Yenangyaung (a city on the Ir-rawaddy River, 363 kms from Yangon) and the Chauk (a town and river port in north-central Burma) oil-fields would come and buy their provisions. If they were late, as the roads were most primi-tive, they would stay the night upstairs, with Anju's 'cook' provid-ing some dinner. Bedding, which Anju provided, consisted of a straw mat laid on the wooden floor with a pillow and a light sheet as cover.

Because of the rough terrain over which they travelled, their cars did not last very long. No repair facilities were available at Meiktila and hence when their cars gave trouble they aban-doned them and bought new cars. These men did not want a standard car with body; they wanted only the front bench seat with no canopy and a large strong wooden box mounted behind the driver to carry their tools. Anju got himself appointed as the Ford Motor Co.'s agent for Upper Burma to cater to this business. Thereafter, these oil-drillers not only bought their cars from Anju but also all their provisions. When they came to Anju's stores, they filled their large tool box with provisions of which a major part consisted of crates of beer and liquors.

Anju was doing pretty well and was able to send funds by postal money order regularly to Granny in Goa. He also managed to keep up payments on Grandad SP's insurance policy, which SP was unable to pay from Canada.

In 1927 Ford Motor Co. stopped production of their Model T car. The demo car, which Anju owned, represented a major part of his capital. When Ford refused to take this back or give Anju the new model – no one was willing to buy the old model – Anju was forced to give up Ford's agency.

Further, Anju had trustingly stood guarantor for a 'friend' who had borrowed some money from a money-lender. When that 'friend' did not repay the loan, Anju was forced to pay up the principal plus the substantial interest thereon. This brought to an end Anju's career as a businessman. He sold all his stock, collected outstandings and left for Rangoon to find something else to do.

He also swore that he would never go into business again. Incidentally, he was most upset when I gave up a salaried job in 1973 to start a business of my own.

Chance Meetings That Shape Your Life

O N the train to Rangoon, Anju met an Englishman, the manager of Sun Life of Canada Insurance Co., who asked him what he was doing. When Anju mentioned that he was on his way to Rangoon to find a job, this gentleman suggested he meet him and he would train him to be an insurance salesman.

On arrival in Rangoon, Anju approached his two direct relatives – Uncle Sequeira of Myitkyina (his mother's brother) and Uncle Hippolito D'Souza of Myingyan (his grand-mother's brother). Uncle Sequeira was not at home, but his wife, Ismen, told Anju quite bluntly that she would kick his ass and definitely wouldn't offer him her place to stay. Myingyan Uncle Hippolito and Aunty Ancy were far more hospitable and invited Anju to stay with them until he found a job. Anju slept in the boys' bedroom together with Arist, Alphonse and George. When they slept late on Sundays, Uncle Hippolito would stalk back and forth outside the bedroom loudly declaiming: 'Early to bed, early to rise, maketh a man healthy, wealthy and wise'.

Anju approached Sun Life Assurance Company of Canada and the gentleman, whom he had met on the train, took him in hand. In a few months, he transformed Anju into a first class insurance salesman. Anju had already picked up Burmese and could converse quite comfortably with the elite as well as the commonman. Anju toured the length and breadth of Burma selling insurance policies to Burmans, including the *saophas* or *sawbwas* (the Burmese equivalent of India's *maharajas*), Englishmen, Americans (including his friends the oil-well drillers), Anglo-Burmans, Anglo-Indians and Goans.

He would regularly visit the Shan States, particularly at the time of the *Bawgyo* festival at which all the *saophas* of the Shan States as well as those from Kayan (famous for their 'giraffe necked' women), Chin, Ka Chin and Karen tribes would gather. Many of these *saophas* had sons who were educated in Rangoon and in some cases in England and could speak English fluently. Sun Life extended special policies, intended for Englishmen and other Westerners, to these English-educated *sawbwas* and consequently Anju secured many high value policies.

Places like Myitkyina, Bhamo, Mogok, Bawdwin, Shwebo, Monywa, Mandalay, Maymyo, Lashio, Kengtung, Myingyan, Thazi Junction, Taunggyi, Meiktila, Pyinmina, Toungoo, Prome, Henzada, Bassein[5], Tharrawaddy, Thaton, Martaban, Moulmein, Amherst (now Kyaikkami) and Tavoy were familiar names that rolled off Anju's tongue – all associated with some experience or other.

He would buy a first class railway ticket which permitted him to travel on all routes of the Burma Railways up to a specified number of miles. Anju found that there were many Goans in these up-country towns working with the Burma Railways and the Posts & Telegraphs Department. Some also had established provision stores and bakeries. In addition some Goan young men, like Dr Victor D'Cruz, Sunny Machado and Albert Menezes, were in Government service and had been posted up-country, where they had few friends with whom to spend time after work. All these welcomed Anju's visits and introduced him to other government officials and friends, to whom Anju could sell insurance

---

[5] Currently called Pathein, a port city and the capital of the Ayeyarwady Region, Burma. Not to be confused with the place with a similar name, north of Bombay (Mumbai).

policies. Anju thus kept widening his circle of friends and insurance prospects.

I remember Anju telling us of an English gentleman, Commissioner of a district, whom Anju called on one evening. As he was about to knock, Anju heard this gentleman say: "Now darling, you stay where you are; don't get up to any mischief. I shall be back in a couple of minutes."

Anju thought that this gentleman had a lady guest and felt that he should not disturb him. He was just turning away without knocking, when the gentleman came to the door and, seeing Anju, welcomed him in. Anju remonstrated that he did not want to disturb him as he had a guest to whom he was just speaking. The gentleman pointed to his lit cigarette in the ash tray and said, "I was speaking to her".

On another occasion, Anju dropped in on a friend, who was just sitting down to lunch. He was promptly invited to lunch with him. When lunch was served, the roast chicken had only one leg. Feeling slightly embarrassed, this gentleman asked his cook what had happened to the other leg. The cook blandly replied that this chicken had only one leg. The boss asked his cook to show him a live chicken with only one leg. After a while, the cook called softly him, "*Saheb*, come see chicken with one leg." On going into the backyard the cook pointed to a chicken sleeping with her head tucked under her wing while standing on one leg. *Saheb* clapped his hand, the chicken promptly put down its second leg and ran off. The cook was quick to say: "But *Saheb*, you did not clap your hand at table, otherwise the chicken would have put down its second leg."

Refrigerators had not reached Burma yet, nor was ready-dressed poultry available. When unexpected guests arrived a live chicken would be caught, killed, dressed and cooked within at most an hour. It would get served up with locally grown vegetables and salad. Chicken was the standard menu in all *dak* bungalows or government guest houses. On his tours Anju usually had nothing but chicken for lunch and for dinner. Consequently, chicken, which was considered a delicacy for festive occasions in most homes, was virtually taboo in our home.

In some jungle areas where chickens could not be bred, Anju was served up a variety of other types of meat, including crow and monkey. (During the war at the Burma Front, troops were taught survival skills while in the jungle, which included eating the flesh of snakes or lizards raw, as it was not advisable to light a fire in the jungles which would attract Japanese snipers.)

During one expedition in the jungles, Anju and his friends stopped for rest at a small Burmese house. With true Burmese hospitality, they were served tea by their host. One of Anju's friends asked their host for some milk to add to the black tea. This was procured and served up in a small jug. Anju, when entering this house, had seen a mother nursing her baby and guessed from where the milk had come. He declined, saying that he preferred black tea, but the others were happy to drink 'milked' tea, as he would narrate later.

Anju qualified as a member of the Macaulay Club of Sun Life Assurance Company of Canada 'which comprises leading representatives of the company for the period July 1, 1933 to June 30, 1934'. This carried a prize of five gold sovereigns (which Ivy subsequently converted into jewellery), a gold carriage clock, and an Underwood portable typewriter (which I still have).

Anju teamed up with Prudence Balthazar Noronha and together they became known as 'The Insurance Twins'. When not touring various parts of Burma they lived in a double storied bungalow in Jogoan on the outskirts of Rangoon. They had a 'Madrasi' cook and his wife acted as housekeeper. Anju occupied the ground floor while Prudence occupied the first floor. When they were home this bungalow was a favourite home away from home for many of Anju's friends, mainly Goan bachelors from Rangoon. Anju invested in a Morris tourer with a collapsible top for going to and from Rangoon. Their cottage was close to Burma Railway quarters at Kemmendine where many Anglo-Indian and Anglo-Burman families lived. Young ladies from this colony were attracted to Anju and Prudence, actually not so much for them, but because of the car which could get them into town and back for the various club dances and other functions. Local trains did not ply at night. Anju recounted one story about these young ladies:

> Four girls from the railway colony came with us to Rangoon for a dance. Ivy and other Goan girls were also at this dance, but when they saw us with these Anglos, they pretended not to know us. But these Anglos, while at our table, danced with their boy-friends and forgot about us. We found other partners and had a good time, but decided to teach these young ladies a lesson. On the way home, at around 5 a.m., when well out of town, I suddenly stalled the engine and stopped. I got down and looked under the bonnet and tinkered around a bit, then declared that I could not repair it. There was no alternative but to push the car till we got home or found some mechanic (a forlorn hope at those wee hours of the morning). I sat at the wheel and the girls in their long evening gowns and Prudence and the other two boys with us 'pushed' the car. I say 'pushed', because only the girls were actually pushing. The three guys were leaning on the car pretending to push, since they were in the know. I watched the girls in the rear-view window and saw that they were really sweating. So, after about half an hour, I suddenly turned on the ignition and the car started. We said: 'Oh the car has started. Now get in quickly and we shall get you home.'

After that I paid more attention to our Goan girls.

On another occasion, Anju and Prudence reached Rangoon early one evening after a very successful tour. After reporting to the office and handing over the paper-work and premia, they decided to celebrate. They finished their celebrations at around 5 a.m. next morning and decided to visit the Cheron home since Anju was by then courting Ivy.

On arrival, Ivy opened the door to these two exuberant guys and was not too impressed. However, when Mrs. Cheron came to meet them, Anju cooked up a story of a derailment and delayed arrival at Rangoon and that they had had no dinner, and so on. He told his story with such a straight face that Ma Cheron believed him and immediately made a large mug of Ovaltine – the milk flavoring product made with malt extract sugar and whey – for each of them. Keeping down the *Ovaltine* after all the whiskeys and other drinks which they had consumed was quite a feat. Since that time we could not persuade Anju to drink *Ovaltine*.

Anju narrated how he and his friends, as bachelors at Jogoan, used to go for early morning walks around the countryside. On one such jaunt they came across a *mohinga-wala*. Not having had any breakfast, each decided to eat a bowl of *mohinga* with all the add-ons. After they finished, each put his hand into his pocket and suddenly realised that no one had brought along any money. One of them suddenly hugged his stomach and pretended that he was going to throw up. One after the other, they all followed his example. The *mohinga-wala* picked up his pots and ran for dear life. They could not stop laughing at their ruse, but subsequently they felt very guilty for having cheated this poor man of his day's earnings, since he was sure to have thrown away the rest of his stock. After reaching home, they got the car, placed money in their pockets and went in search of this *mohinga-wala*. But he was nowhere to be found. Probably he was hiding from them and was more afraid when he saw them approach in a car.

Anju incidentally remained with Sun Life Assurance of Canada till the Japanese bombing.

Love... and Marriage

A NJU finally popped the question and Ivy accepted. There must have been quite some opposition from Grandma Cheron, since Ivy was a graduate and he had passed only the Fifth Standard. (But, like Mark Twain, I discovered after my post-graduation in management studies that Anju with his experience knew considerably more about life than I had learned in college or from text books. He was educated in the college of hard knocks.)

Banns read at St Mary's Cathedral announced that Angelo Michael D'Souza, bachelor, was to wed Ivy Victoria de Souza, spinster. The wedding was fixed for December 28, 1932. Granny Leopoldina arrived from Goa in time for Christmas with a copy of Anju's baptism certificate, which gave his name as Angelo Maria D'Souza. Fr St Guilly, the parish priest, on seeing it, informed Anju that he would not solemnise the wedding as Anju's name was different from that announced in the banns. Anju replied, "Okay, we shall get married by the registrar." Fr St Guilly was thoroughly upset, particularly since Ivy was one of his favourite parish helpers, and agreed to officiate at Ivy and Anju's wedding. (When Anju later narrated this story he would imitate Fr St Guilly's French accent.)

On the wedding day, Anju came in from Jogoan well in time and sent Gerry in the car to pick up his bride. In the car were some wedding presents which had arrived at Jogoan, and had to be delivered to the Portuguese Club. Gerry reached the club, handed over the presents and got involved with decorating the hall.

A good hour later, one of Anju's friends passing the Club saw the car and asked Gerry if he had already reached Ivy to St Mary's. Gerry promptly raced off to 50th Street to pick up Ivy and reach her to St Mary's Cathedral.

In the meantime, Fr St Guilly was getting more and more agitated over the non-arrival of the bride. Finally, he came to Anju and told him that if Ivy did not arrive within five minutes, he would proceed with the wedding without the bride. Fortunately, Ivy arrived just then. (Anju long afterwards wondered how Fr St Guilly could proceed with the wedding without the bride!)

Photographs were taken after the wedding on the side steps of St Mary's. In these are Ivy and Anju with the three bride's maids, Clare, Amy and Mayrose, and the three best men, Prudence, Diego and Gerry. The photograph showed to advantage the best-men's run of the mill suits but the beautiful dresses of the bride's maids were covered up. The original photograph and photo album were left behind in Rangoon when we were evacuated. Fortunately, Ivy's Aunt, Umbalina, at Salvodar do Mundo had a framed copy which she gave Ivy. This photograph now hangs in our Porvorim house.

At their wedding reception, the favour which was affixed to the men's coat lapels was a chicken wishbone painted silver, with a bow of silver silk ribbon. I do not know how many guests there were at the reception, but assuming a reasonable figure of two hundred, I often wondered how many chickens were roasted in order to make these favours.

Anju and Ivy never told us about their honeymoon. Ivy did mention going to stay at the Jogoan bungalow, where she found that Anju's cook and his wife were taking Anju and Prudence for a royal ride. When she started checking up on them, they resigned. To the best of my knowledge, Ivy and Anju, with Prudence living upstairs, continued living at Jogoan till after Iza was born on August 31, 1933. Prudence married Denise about a year after Ivy and Anju. He and his wife continued to live upstairs. With no domestic help and their men touring for long stretches of time, Ivy and Denise finally shifted to Rangoon in 1934. I was born on December 16, 1934.

Ivy's sisters – Clare, Amy and Mayrose – fondly remember the week-ends and holidays spent with Ivy and Anju at Jogoan. Gerry also spent his holidays with Ivy and Anju.

Kerosene Lamps and *Mangaad*

I N 1935, Anju took Ivy and the two of us children from Burma to Goa for a holiday. Once, while sitting in the verandah of our Nachinola house, Ivy and Anju, with light only from a kerosene lamp, spotted bright shining eyes in the compound, which Anju claimed were those of a tiger. This may have been true, since we have dense jungle behind our house.

During this holiday, both Iza and I contracted whooping cough. The only locally available remedy was the juice of the fruit of a cactus plant which grew in Lino Correa's compound. Ivy got her hands thoroughly pricked while collecting these fruit which she squeezed and fed to the two of us.

Since this was the first visit of Anju with his wife to Nachinola, Granny Leopoldina organised a *bhicariche jevonn* (a meal for the beggars, a form of thanksgiving) where the poor (not necessarily beggars) were invited to a festive lunch. Anju and Ivy had to sit in the middle and join in the meal. I remember Ivy mentioning that she felt highly embarrassed at this function. Each and every guest would extoll the newly weds and call down blessings on them. I am sure that Ivy did not understand all that these people said in Konkani. I guess Anju must have proudly shown off his wife and two kids to all the relatives in Goa.

Anju remembers the return journey to Burma for the *mangaad* (mango preserve) he agreed to carry to a friend in Rangoon sent by that friend's doting mother. She had packed the *mangaad* in a Carr & Co. rectangular cream cracker biscuit tin; she must really have packed the *mangaad* down. Anju put this tin wrapped in old newspapers (there were no ubiquitous plastic bags at that time) in his suitcase along with his clothes. At Castle Rock, the British Customs post on the Goa border, when Anju opened his suitcase for the Customs check, he was dismayed to find that the tin had burst and there was *mangaad* all over his clothes – lovely and delicious to eat, but ooh so messy and sticky. The clothes carried a yellow stain after several washes, in spite of the *dhobi's* most vigorous bashing.

Somehow totally lost on Anju was all the effort put into squeezing tree-ripened mangoes, which were then placed in a large copper vessel with lots of sugar and continuously stirred over a low wood fire for hours to get the perfect consistency without burning. He never ever agreed to carry *mangaad* again, even though he enjoyed eating it when Granny made some.

Life in Rangoon

D URING the Christmas season all the dry fruit, which would go into plum cakes and Christmas puddings, would be spread on the dining table at Grandma Cheron's house. There, it would undergo cleaning, removing of stalks and seeds, and then get soaked in rum for at least a fortnight before being put into the cake batter.

During one of these dry fruit cleaning sessions, my sister Iza, who was just fifteen months old, was placed on the table, while Ma Cheron and her daughters cleaned the dry fruit. Iza kept stuffing currants into her mouth. Her next stool was red and everyone got a fright as they jumped to the conclusion that Iza had developed bloody dysentery. When the stool was inspected by a more experienced elder lady, they were told that this was just undigested red currants.

My earliest personal memory is of the first floor of Biddy's house on 52nd Street. Like most houses in Rangoon, this house was built completely of teak with wooden walls and floor. Living downstairs was a cantankerous old lady, who, every time I ran across the floor, would bang with a pole on her ceiling and Ivy would force me to sit still or tip-toe around. As punishment I remember being put on a high stand meant for an evergreen plant in a brass pot, from which I was afraid to jump down.

On another occasion I was rocking back and forth in my small chair, while Ivy and Anju were playing Bridge. I lost my balance, fell and banged my forehead on the corner of the piano leg and got a nice big cut, the scar earned from which I now use as my identifying mark on my passport.

We employed a South Indian couple, the husband as our cook and the wife as the housemaid. This cook was always grumbling and being short and bent we christened him Grumpy after one of the seven dwarfs in the movie *Cinderella*. One day, when Ivy and Anj was totally lost on Anjuu had both gone out, Iza and I were left in the care of Grumpy and his wife. They made the two of us sit on the lowest steps of the outside staircase, where Grumpy entertained us with Indian and Burmese songs and dances. Ivy and Anju, on their return, were pleasantly surprised to find that Grumpy was not always grumpy.

After working with us for years, Grumpy and his wife left for Madras to join their family. We employed another *'Madrasi'* couple. Grumpy returned to Burma some months later but was very sick and was admitted to hospital. Anju could not go to see him immediately. When he did reach the hospital a couple of days later, he was informed that Grumpy had died. Anju never forgave himself for not going to visit Grumpy immediately and giving him what help he might have required.

When Anju was with us, particularly on Sundays, he would call the *mohinga-walla* and we would each have a bowl of *mohinga* or *kaukswe*. I still savour the memory of these snacks and look forward to anyone who offers to make them; but with *ngapi* not easily available, the taste is not the same. (Recently, Deepika was able to convince one of her colleagues who lives in Port Blair to bring us some real *ngapi*, brought by Burmese fishermen visiting the Andamans and Nicobar Islands.) *Ngapi*, pungent pastes made of either fish or shrimp in Burmese cuisine, has a very strong, almost off-putting, fish smell. But to someone who is born or lived in Burma, this smell is delicious.

Another smelly food was the *durian*, which resembles a small jack-fruit. When ripe, you can smell it a mile off. Anju tells of a train journey to Rangoon. Prudence and Anju were in a first class compartment for four, with two berths empty. At Mandalay, a Burmese government official got into this compartment carrying, among his baggage, a basket of *durians*. This gentleman spotted a friend in another compartment and joined him, leaving his baggage behind. The owner of the fruit did not return till nightfall. After putting up with the smell for awhile, Anju and Prudence pushed the basket out of the running train, left the windows open to dispel the smell and went off to sleep. Next morning on arrival at Rangoon they detrained, picked up their own baggage and were going away when this gentleman turned up to claim his luggage and found his basket of *durians* missing. He asked them where it was, and they replied that they knew nothing of it, and suggested that it may not have put on the train at Mandalay.

Burmans believe that *durian* is a strong aphrodisiac. Anju used to say: "When the *durians* ripen, the *loungyis* come down."

(From Rangoon in 1948, Anju used to send me parcels of tuck containing *durian* preserve among other goodies when I was at school in Mount Abu. Normally, when anyone receives a parcel of tuck, all one's 'friends' hang around, hoping to get a share. No one would come near my parcel. Recently Deepika brought me beautifully packed *durian* preserve from Bangkok. But the processing had reduced the smell considerably and this *durian* preserve did not taste as good as I remembered.)

While living at Biddy's house, I used to get very high fevers and go into convulsions immediately after Anju left to go on tour. After various treatments did not cure me, our doctor suggested that I be taken for a holiday to some place far away from Rangoon. Biddy urged Ivy to shift out of this house, since while staying in this house after her daughter Catherine was born, she had lost three sons; only after shifting to another house Gerard was born and survived. She felt there was some sort of a curse on the house, which applied only to sons born while staying in that house.

After our holiday in Taunggyi (some 450 kms from Rangoon,

with a driving distance of over 630 km), the capital of the Southern Shan States, we returned to Rangoon to Miss Strong's house, further along 52nd Street. I remember Biddy's house was brown like Grandma Cheron's house, made of varnished teak, but Miss Strong's house was painted white. Miss Strong lived upstairs and we stayed on the ground floor. I seem to remember that our front door which opened from the road direct into our sitting room was always open throughout the day. It was closed only at night.

Iza and I had a small table with matching chairs, at which we had our meals. Iza was a fussy eater and would dawdle over her food until she got a shout from Ivy. I finished my food as fast as I could put it down – in anticipation of the *p-u-ding-dign-in-ging-ging*. Our cook would normally make a separate bowl of jelly, blancmange or custard for each of us and a larger mould would be served to the elders. Having finished my food, the cook would give me my bowl of pudding, which I would promptly polish off.

Iza, still dawdling over her food, would usually not want to finish her share of pudding and, without waiting for an invitation, I would finish her share too. Then Ivy, Anju, and guests, if any, would sit for dinner. Iza and I were expected to go off and do something else. But I would keep an eye on the progress of the dinner and return when the pudding was being served. Seeing me so to say with my tongue hanging out, Anju would give me his share. What was left was the cook's share, but usually he too would give that to me. Thus I ended up eating most of any pudding that was prepared for the family.

In those days the rules of fast and abstinence laid down by the Catholic Church were far more strict. We were not expected to eat any kind of meat on Wednesdays and Fridays in Lent and also on Christmas Eve and the eve of the Feast of Our Lady's Assumption. Adults had also to fast on all Fridays of Lent and on Christmas Eve. On Fridays of Lent, Iza and I would have our dinner as usual, including our pudding. Then, when Ivy and Anju were having their 'fasting dinner' of hot-cross buns and coffee, I informed them that I was also fasting and demanded my share of a hot-cross buns and coffee.

Once, Anju came home on a Friday evening in Lent and informed all of us that he would not even have the prescribed light meal. Ivy was quite impressed by Anju's sacrifice, until a few days later, one of Anju's friends dropped in and asked him, "Anju, what were you doing at Mughal Street (now Shwe Bon Thar Street) last Friday evening?" Anju had obviously had a really good meal of some meat dishes and could not possibly have eaten anything more that Friday evening.

On a holiday or Sunday afternoon, Anju would take a nap in an easy chair in the sitting room. To keep us quiet, he would tell us to pull out his grey hair – at that time relatively few – and would agree to pay us one pice (one sixty-fourth of a Rupee) for each grey hair extracted. After his nap, he would count the number of grey hair each of us had pulled, kept very carefully separate, and reward us the correct number of pice. He would then call the *chana-walla* (seller of roasted chick peas) and buy a measure for each of us and for himself. He instructed us that we must take off the skins and then eat the *chana*. Iza would very carefully peel her *chana* and keep the peeled *chana* aside. Anju and I would eat our *chana* quickly, skin and all, and then while chatting with her and hearing her stories, we would help ourselves to Iza's peeled *chana*. When she finally finished peeling all her *chana* she would turn to start eating the peeled *chana* and then cry, "Mummy see, Daddy and Aloysius have eaten my *chana*." (Years later in Bandra, if there were fried prawns for lunch or dinner, Ivy would ensure that all four of us got an equal share. Iza would keep her share at the side of her plate to be savoured last and eat her food, talking all the time. Anju and I would surreptitiously pinch prawns from her plate and at the end she would discover that most of her share of prawns had disappeared. She was never too sure whether or not she had eaten them.)

Miss Strong had two large dogs, while we had two smaller ones, Scottish terriers, Patch and Mitzy. We got ourselves a lovely small kitten. To ensure that it stayed in our house, we were told to give it the grease-proof wrapper of the *Polson* butter packet to lick. The butter would get on to its paws and then its own smell with the butter would be on the wooden floor of the house, and the kitten would recognise this house as its own.

We had fun with the little kitten; Patch and Mitzy had also become friends with it. Suddenly Miss Strong's dogs came down the stairs at top speed, and, since our doors were always open, charged into our house and went for the kitten. The kitten very quickly jumped up on to a high shelf, with our two dogs doing all they could to get the other two dogs away. The kitten tried to go higher but misjudged and fell down to be immediately torn to pieces by those big dogs. After they killed the kitten they went off for their walk and left the two of us and our two dogs crying over what was left of the kitten. We have never tried to keep a cat as a pet again.

Iza loves to remind me of a visit to the Rangoon zoo. I had lovely curls at that time. The big attraction there was Darby and Joan, a chimpanzee couple, who would have formal tea at a little table with proper crockery with cakes and (maybe) tea. I went very close to the monkey's cage to get a better view. One monkey from an adjoining cage caught and pulled out a big bunch of my hair. After that Ivy was forced to give me a proper boy's hair cut. Since then I always wear my hair short; no problem with dressing my hair either.

I loved to help anyone and everyone. That included Anju servicing his car in the garage, which had a pit so that you could go under the car to clean and grease all the joints. Or Gerry, as he did odd jobs around the house. Even when we went to Grandma Cheron's house I was helpful. They did not entrust me with cleaning the raisins and other dry fruit, as I ate more than I cleaned. Clare (*Kela* to me) was a seamstress. She had a hand operated Singer sewing machine and invited me to turn the handle. I did so – nice and vigorously – and Aunty *Kela's* thumb once even got stitched to the fabric.

Living in Rangoon was fun. The streets were parallel and consecutively numbered. There was little or no traffic, only a few cars and *rickshaws* (pulled by a man). Our evening outing was a walk down the street wishing and chatting with friends as we passed, usually to Grandma Cheron's house on 50th Street and possibly on to Cheron Bakery at the corner of 49th Street. Opposite Grandma's house lived the Ferraz family, with a large number of kids some our own age. At the corner of our street the D'Cruz family lived; only Bertram was about our own age. Mr. D'Cruz's eldest son, Eddy, was married and had his own flat in a new brick building nearby. They had a daughter, Winsome, maybe just about a year old, who became a good friend of mine. Since I called her 'little monkey' she retaliated by calling me 'monkey'. Her favourite game was to play peek-a-boo with me over her nanny's shoulders. While walking down these streets you could hear children practising the piano – most houses had pianos. Girls usually learnt to play the piano and boys learnt to play the violin.

Visits to other families especially at birthdays and anniversaries contributed substantially to our social life. At house parties guests would gather round the piano and join in old favourites like *'In the shade of the old apple tree', 'I'm forever blowing bubbles', 'After the ball', 'The Isle of Capri', 'O my Darling Clementine'*. I remember singing *'London's burning, London's burning, Call the engines, Call the engines, Pour on water, Pour on water'* continuously until stopped. Anju had his own favourites, like *'I have a pair of arms and nobody using them now...'* and one for which he was most in demand but for which there had to be quite some prior alcohol intake *'Foola-mange'* sung with his glass containing alcohol balanced on his head with body movements and hand action. I was never able to understand how that glass balanced on his head. (During Bombay's Prohibition, he could not make the glass balance with any non-alcoholic drink.)

Amy (Ivy's younger sister) was teaching at the girl's school at

Syriam, the major port linked by history to the Portuguese some 16 kms from Rangoon. She would leave for Syriam by launch every Sunday evening around 17:00 and come back for the weekend arriving by launch on Friday around 19:00. (I do not think she had to cook for herself, because when she got married in 1943 she knew nothing of cooking.) For us the walks to the jetty, not too far from our house on 52nd Street, on Friday and Sunday evenings were looked forward.

Opposite our house there was a Burmese family with children our age with whom we were quite friendly. Burmans are very friendly and when you visit them. They are most hospitable and would offer you whatever food they had in their house. Anju told us that in order not to embarrass any family he would always say that as he had just eaten a meal, he would appreciate a glass of water. This would not put a strain of their resources.

Castes, Clubs, Christians

T HERE are no castes among Burmans and people mixed socially without any restrictions. Englishmen and other Westerners, Anglo-Burmans, Anglo-Indians and Goans were members of the same clubs. (Only after we came to India did we discover 'castes' among Indians and <u>even among Goan Christians!</u>

In Bombay too we came across clubs where only White people of every social strata could become members. Even White non-members, including those from the lowest strata of seamen, were permitted entry while no Indian, no matter how high his social status, could become a member. Surprisingly this did not change with Independence in 1947 but only much later around 1970.)

On really festive occasions, like Christmas and New Year's Eve, dances were held in all the clubs across Rangoon. After bringing in the New Year in your own club (for which you had paid the entrance fee) most of the couples would go off to wish their friends at their clubs and join them for a while. No additional entrance fee was charged when visiting such other clubs.

At parties and dances liquor flowed freely, but I do not remember seeing anyone drunk; happy, yes, and full of *joie-de-vive*. There were the inevitable scraps after a dance over some real or imagined slight, but these were soon patched up. The antagonists shook hands and repaired to the bar for a final 'one for the road'.

In 1938, R. J. Pimenta (my future father-in-law) was appointed manager of Oriental Insurance Co. for the whole of Burma. He was the first non-Englishman appointed to such a senior position. The Goans of Rangoon were rightly proud of Mr. Pimenta and invited him to be chief guest at their next Portuguese Club function. Mrs. and Mr. Pimenta led the grand march. Mrs. Pimenta, who was much younger than her husband, was a good dancer and every young gallant vied for her as partner.

At the Portuguese Club (and possibly at other clubs at that time) an essential item was the 'Palais Glide' and the 'Lambert Walk'. The wooden floor of the club would reverberate with the entire group stamping during these events. At the Portuguese Club the specialty was *mandos* and *dulpods* (Goan folk songs and music) which were sung and danced with the men holding their handkerchiefs. Goan ladies did not wear saris for functions at the Portuguese Club but dressed as per the current European fashion in floor-sweeping ball gowns.

Dances in those days were whole night events, starting at around 21:00 and ending at about 05:00. Either on their way in or back to Jogaon, Anju and his friends (ladies and gents) would stop at Moghul Street for a late dinner or an early breakfast. The restaurants here remained open round the clock. Immediately as the car drew up, the waiters would put a plank across to act as a table and spread a table cloth. They would serve the food on this plank, so that the ladies did not have to get out of the car. The men would meanwhile eat their fill in the restaurant.

On one such occasion while the ladies were being served, another young man, not of their group, passed some comment to which Anju took objection. When that guy challenged Anju, Anju promptly biffed him on the chin and knocked his dentures loose. The guy had to go down on all fours to find his dentures. Amy and Mayrose would love to get Gerry to retell this story, since he would get down on all fours to show how that guy went off searching for his dentures.

After one such Saturday night dance, Anju and his pals decided to go straight to St Mary's Cathedral for Sunday Mass. Like good Catholics they went and sat in a pew right up front. When Mass started they noticed that the candles on the altar were dancing and so were the priest and altar-boys. When shaking their heads did not clear their vision, they nudged each other and decided to leave the church. In order not to be noticed, they bent double, crawled out of their pew and crawled out of church on all fours. (As will be recalled at that time the priest offered Mass with his back to the congregation otherwise he might have stopped the proceedings and made a wonderful sermon about these young men.) It took Anju and his friends quite some time to live down this escapade.

At around five, I remember taking part in a variety entertainment at the Portuguese Club. My partner for *'Hands, Knees and Boomps-a-Daisy'* was Celine Pinto, a pretty but frail girl my own age. We were the couple closest to the front edge of the stage. When we sang out "Boomps-a-Daisy" I bumped Celine so vigorously that she flew right off the stage, fortunately into the arms of a gentleman standing just there.

Picnics at the Royal Lakes, with swimming and boat rides, are fondly remembered. The young men wore swimming suits which covered their chests, not just swimming trunks. Felix or Earnest had slipped off one shoulder strap 'a la Tarzan'.

We spent one holiday at Amherst, a seashore south of Rangoon. Ivy, Clare, Amy and Mayrose, Iza and myself were holding hands and dancing in fairly shallow water. Gradually, unnoticed by any of us, we were being drawn into a whirlpool. Gerry spotted this. Without making a fuss, he and Anju joined our circle, joined in the banter and slowly pulled us away from the whirlpool. Only after we were safe on dry land, did they tell us of the danger.

At Amherst I discovered *tuktoos* (local name for geckos or large lizards named for the sound they made). They were all over the walls and ceiling and emitted this distinct call. They would suddenly jump forward, catch and then swallow moths and other insects (some almost as large as themselves). These *tuktoos* were very different from the lizards who crawled on our walls and ceiling in Rangoon.

Huge wooden vats half buried in the sand above high water mark were part of beach furniture. Fishermen filled one basket of tiny fish and prawns (not marketable) and one basket of sea salt alternately, until the vat was full. They would batter down the lids and leave these vats in the heat and rain for three to six months. When they opened these vats, the solid mass floating at the top was *ngapi* and the liquid was *ngapi-down*. Both these are essential flavouring in most Burmese food.

On the shoreline there were bushes with thorny leaves and red berries, reminding one of Christmas.

We did go to films, earlier the Charlie Chaplin silent films and also Westerns (with cowboys and Red Indians). But after watching a few I began to notice that the background scenery was almost the same and the Indians were always being chased. These were silent movies and the background music played by the live orchestra was also usually the same. Later there were movies like *Cinderella, Snow White and the Seven Dwarfs* and *The Wizard of Oz*. We quickly learnt the songs from these movies.

While we celebrated Christian feasts, Christmas and Easter, with European, Anglo-Burman and Goan friends, we also celebrated Burmese festivals specially the water festival. I remember only once celebrating Diwali. We were invited by Anju's insurance company doctor, Dr. Basu, a Bengali, to his home for Diwali. I was served a large *thali* filled with various Indian sweetmeats, which I, very regretfully, could not finish. My suggestion that we ask them to pack the balance for me to eat at home drew frowns.

During *idapour* or *Thingyan,* the Burmese water festival which normally coincided with Easter, all the families (not only the Burmans) on the street joined in throwing clean water on each other and on friends from other areas who arrived on bicycles or cars to join in the fun. One Easter, we had as house guests , Mr. and Mrs. Sequeira, who had just arrived from Goa. We were dressed for Easter Mass, when our neighbours came to pour water on us. Anju explained that we were on our way to Mass, but would definitely join them on our return. On our way to church, one of the Burmese boys rode on the foot board of our car and shouted ahead to prevent others throwing water on us. Immediately after getting home, we all, except Mrs. Sequeira, changed and joined in the fun. In spite of entreaties, she refused to change and join all of us. A couple of Burmese boys then came into our sitting room and thoroughly drenched her. The new dress she was wearing was of some material which shrank, leaving her thoroughly embarrassed.

Rangoon was very clean and eating out was safe. The usual Burmese dishes like *hingyo, letho, kaukswe* and *mohinga* had fish, prawns and *ngapi* as essential ingredients. The food stalls at Moghul Street served up mostly Muslim dishes like *kababs and kormas* (to be eaten with *parathas)* and *biryani*, made with chicken, mutton or beef. Chinese food like chow mein, various dumplings and crisp spring rolls usually had pork and noodles as the main ingredients. Indian sweets like *rasagoollas* and *sandesh* were milk based, but were not as popular as cakes and pastries, at least not in our home. For take-aways, food was packed in the large outer cabbage leaves, which had not been used as ingredients, or banana leaves.

Rangoon was a planned city reclaimed from swamps of the Irrawaddy delta. The rest of the delta region was infested with mosquitoes and malaria was a scourge to all posted to those regions. Surprisingly, Rangoon was free from mosquitoes. I do not recall ever using a mosquito-net. (In contrast mosquito-nets were essential in Mount Abu, Bombay and Porvorim, Goa. In Calcutta also we did not require mosquito nets.)

Where Goan choir-masters found jobs readily

The 1920s were the era of silent movies. But background music had to be provided. Goans – with their basic Western music education from the *misteros* (choir-masters) in village churches back home – found jobs very easily. Balbino d'Athaide (Grandma Cheron's brother) and Salvador 'Salu' Rodrigues (Anju's future brother-in-law) both came to Rangoon to play background music for the silent films.

Sometimes a musical score accompanied the film and the musicians had to play as per the score. But often, they were shown the film and then played music they considered appropriate. These jobs kept them busy only in the evenings; they were free for the rest of the day. They took up teaching music or dealing in and repairing musical instruments to supplement their income.

By the 1930s talkies had made silent movies obsolete and to most Goan musicians their bread and butter jobs disappeared. Some of these musicians had formed bands which performed at dances and social events. Hotels and clubs employed them to provide lunch or dinner music. Dances on weekends and occasions like Christmas or New Year's Eve also offered employment to these bands. But musicians led a precarious hand-to-mouth, uncertain existence. Teaching music and dealing in or repairing musical instruments offered a more regular income.

Good-bye Burma: a departure by sea

A FTER the initial bombing of Rangoon and the evacuation of most people from Rangoon, we stayed on. Mrs. Pimenta and family would not leave without Mr. Pimenta who would leave only if allowed to carry the records of Oriental Insurance. These meant bulky ledgers with bank records, there were no computers with data on compact discs at that time. Similarly Ivy would not leave without Anju.

Finally, the Portuguese Consul told all Goans that the last ship for civilians (women and children only) was the *Chilka* scheduled to leave on February 6, 1942. Mr. Pimenta and Anju forced all of us to leave together on this ship.

Accordingly, early that morning, Ivy with one suitcase with our clothes, Iza and I each carrying a small bag with our toys, hugged and kissed our dogs, Mitzy, Patch and Nelson, and got into Anju's car for the jetty. *En route* we stopped to tell Diego that we were leaving and I hugged and was kissed goodbye by his two dogs. Mrs. Pimenta with John, Helmana, Lourdes, Jimmy, Edigio and the twins, Rozaria and Celina, in their car also came with two suitcases between all of them. We boarded the ship before noon and were told that the ship would leave around 17:00. At about 13:00 the sirens warned of a Japanese air raid. Anju and Mr. Pimenta had to leave the jetty and seek shelter. We remained on board and prayed. Fortunately the Japanese did not bomb the dock area that day. After the all clear, Anju came back with a pillow case full of biscuits and toasts and the largest jar of Horlicks he could get.

We had been allotted space on deck just large enough for us to sleep one up against each other with hardly any space to turn over. There were about 2,500 persons on board this ship which normally accommodated only 250 passengers. The ship left the jetty around 17:00 and slowly moved down the Rangoon River to the sea. But we did not seem to move far out to sea since we could see land all the way till we came to Calcutta – seven days sailing for a normal three day voyage. No lights were allowed on board and we had to have our dinner well before dark. Not that there was much to eat as the ship's galley could only serve us boiled rice, which we ate with Crosse & Blackwell mustard pickle, carefully rationed out. The twins survived on Horlicks, hot water was plentiful from the galley and Mum had carried her 'Horlicks Mixer'. (Mrs. Pimenta carefully saved this empty Horlicks jar. I remember seeing it at her Poona flat till just before her death in 1991. Our Horlicks mixer continued to be used by us until one day when using it in Goa the bottom neatly came out; obviously the steel plunger operating over the years had worn down the glass bottom and it got finally cut through. The plunger still remains at 75, Defence Colony.)

We boys – Jimmy, Edigio and I – went around investigating the ship and discovered Salu and Gerry. They had managed to get onto the ship, hid somewhere, and only came out when the ship was well at sea. As they could not persuade the cooks to give them any food, instructions being to serve only women and children, they joined us and shared whatever food Ivy was able to persuade the cooks to give us.

At one stage John got lost and Jimmy and I had quite a job searching for him. The ship's officers were very friendly and showed us around the bridge and explained some of the equipment there. They also told us that the reason for hugging the shore was because there were Japanese submarines in the Bay of Bengal. (On her return voyage from Calcutta to Rangoon, the *Chilka* was torpedoed by a Japanese submarine.)

After seven days we reached Calcutta. On the jetty we spotted Clare, Amy and Mayrose. They had been meeting every ship from Burma to welcome friends and relatives. They took Ivy, Iza and me to Grace Antunis' small fat at Chandni Chowk. They had managed to borrow the empty room between Grace's and the flat next door. All nine of us with our luggage squeezed into this small room. Mrs. Pimenta and children were met and taken care of by the Oriental Insurance staff.

Grandma Cheron, Agnes with Noellyn, Clare, Amy and Mayrose left by train for Bombay on February 16. At Bombay, Agnes and Noellyn were met by her brother, Nasciment Couto, who then took them to Goa to stay with her mother at Ranoi, Quitula in the village of Aldona. Grandma Cheron, Clare, Amy and Mayrose went on to Karachi and stayed with Bella and Raymond Lobo.

Ivy did not know where to go and wanted to stay on in Calcutta till Anju came from Rangoon. Mrs. Pimenta suggested we go to Goa. Oriental Insurance arranged for all our tickets through to Margao.

We were lucky to get out of Rangoon by ship. For those forced to trek out the experience was horrendous; Mr. Pimenta, Uncle Hippolito and his family, Uncle Albert and his family have tried to blank out those memories. John (Pimenta) who is five years older than me does not want to recall our departure from Rangoon.

That was the last I saw of Burma, though Anju and my sister, Iza, did go back after the war. But the memories live with me, especially of her wonderful people and their delicious food. We keep alive these happy memories by experimenting with our own version of Burmese cuisine and visiting any restaurant which claims to serve up genuine Burmese food to compare it with our own memory of that dish.

The moment anyone mentions that he or she or their relatives were from Burma there is immediately a bond of friendship established. I would love to revisit Burma, but I am afraid that today's reality will totally destroy all the beautiful memories I have of that country.

Goa in the 1940s

F ROM Calcutta to Goa, we must have changed trains at Kalyan and Poona though I have no recollection of this. At the British Customs post, Castle Rock, we had to detrain and take all our luggage to their counters for checking and then back into the train for our onward journey. We passed the Dudh Sagar waterfalls and were amazed at the flow of white water, just like milk (*dudh*). At Collem, the Portuguese authorities were far more thorough. All baggage was transferred into a room and fumigated. The compartments were also fumigated. After this, we were permitted to re-board the train.

We were passing through beautiful countryside when Iza suddenly put her fingers over Ivy's eyes and said, "Mummy, don't look, those men have no clothes on." She herself continued looking at men wearing only *kashties* (minimal loin cloths) working in the fields of Goa.

Mrs. Pimenta's brothers met us at the Margao Railway Station and took us to their home at Consua, where we stayed for a few days. We were given the use of their large guest bedroom with a big canopied double bed. On the window sill there was a beautiful porcelain jug with matching wash basin and soap-dish with cover. Under the bed was a matching porcelain chamber pot. Since there were no electric lights, this chamber pot was used at night to avoid having to go to the toilet which was at the other end of the house. Early morning one of the maids came and filled the jug with hot water for us to wash our faces and she took away the chamber pot. (When Hazel and I announced our engagement in 1965, Mrs. Pimenta's brother, Jose, who had inherited this house and property, asked me what I would like to have as a wedding present. I requested that porcelain set. He was amazed that I had remembered it after more than twenty years, but sadly he could not bring himself to give away the priceless heirlooms.)

Opposite their home was a fairly well wooded hill-side. We boys went right up the hill. We were told that there were some wild animals in these woods. One evening, Mrs. Pimenta's brother, Nonato, took his gun, went hunting and came back with hares to be cooked. This same brother kept us enthralled with his magic tricks.

Mrs. Pimenta's father, Dr. Mesquita, was hard of hearing and used an ear-trumpet. John would go right up to the old man who was bent with age and shout into the ear trumpet to get him to hear anything. Dr. Mesquita had a small museum filled with specimens preserved in alcohol in glass bottles. From these specimens it was obvious that Dr Mesquita had carried out many surgical operations – amazingly with no anaesthesia except *feni* and with only washing of hands and scrupulous cleanliness as asepsis. (When Hazel and I personally checked in December 1986, the specimen bottles were still there, but sadly with little or no alcohol in each, but the greater loss was that all of Dr Mesquita's notes beautifully hand-written in a series of note books had been devoured by white ants.)

There was a baby grand piano in the house, badly out of tune. This had been bought so that Mrs. Pimenta, as a young girl, could learn to play the piano. The piano was brought in from Bombay on a *pathmari* (sailing boat); the first one to be bought had sunk with the *pathmari* in which it was being transported. While the loss of the piano was noted no one seemed to remember whether or not the sailors on the *pathmari* had survived. There was no insurance and Dr Mesquita had to buy a second piano, which arrived safely. As young girls were not expected to travel to and fro, the piano teacher came to their home from Margao twice a week. He walked a distance of about nine kilometres each way and was paid fifty coconuts for each visit.

At their house we had our first experience of a piggy toilet. Theirs was a six-seater model and one had to climb three or four steps to reach the seats, which were fairly high above ground level, so we did not realise that there were pigs down below.

They had quite a herd of cows. One calf had died at birth. To persuade the mother to continue giving milk, they had stuffed the skin of this calf and she would lick it while the herdsman milked her.

They had an alcohol still to distil cashew *feni* during the February-to-April cashew season and coconut *feni* during the balance of the year. (At a later visit I discovered Jose Mesquita's method of quality control for *feni*. He would take a round of their compound ending at the *feni* still, where a small snifter glass was kept. This he would fill straight from the outlet of the still and taste it while still hot. He claimed he could gauge the alcohol content in this way. His wife had to be alert because if he kept tasting the *feni* too many times, his judgement would be affected. So she had to ensure that lunch was ready on time.)

One large ground floor hall was used for storing the produce from their fields: boiled paddy spread over the floor for drying, tamarind was being cleaned. Other activities were also being carried out but I did not at that time understand their significance.

Green Fields, Two Ferries... and Nachinola

A FTER a few days we left Consua for Nachinola. This trip, through beautiful green fields (due to the winter paddy crop) and across two ferries in which the car crossed the rivers Zuari and Mandovi, is forever engraved in my memory. Somehow all my trips over this road in the years since 1942 do not measure up to my memory of that first trip.

On reaching Nachinola we were tearfully greeted by Granny Leopoldina (in a cotton sari, which we associated only with ayahs in Rangoon). She had been told by Bemvinda who had arrived in January that we had all been left behind in Burma. Salu and Gerry had arrived a week before us and had told Granny that we were on our way but that Anju was not with us.

Life in Nachinola was totally different from anything we had experienced till then, particularly the silence. After the experience of bombing and machine gunning in Rangoon, Goa was wonderfully peaceful. However, Iza and I, while playing in the garden, got quite a fright one afternoon to hear the siren. We bolted into the house to take shelter; but it was only the seller of bangles, whose long drawn out call, to our overly sensitized ears, resembled the sound of the siren.

There were no electric lamps. Small *pontis* (bottles filled with kerosene fitted with a tin cap through which a cotton wick protruded) provided very dim, smoky, reddish light. In the sitting room we had a large kerosene wick lamp with a white globe. It was possible to read in the light provided by this lamp and all of us studied around this table. We moved from room to room carrying a *ponti*. Kerosene being in short supply, lamps could not be kept lit in each room. Fortunately none of us was afraid of the dark.

There was no running water. Water had to be drawn by pulling up copper *quasaws* or *cousaus* (vessels with narrow mouths designed so that the rope noose could be put around the neck) from the well which was 54 feet deep. Quite some skill was required to get the *quasaw* to fill in the well and then strength and alertness to pull it to the surface. Granny Leopoldina encouraged us to draw water from the well by allowing us to use the small *chimboos* (small brass *quasaws*). The workmen and their wives who lived in our out houses used earthen *quasaws* as they could not afford the brass ones. One had to be extra careful when using these earthen *quasaws* as they could easily break if lowered too quickly or when drawing them up, if one pulled too vigorously and the pot began to swing and banged against the side wall of the well and was smashed. Water had to be drawn and filled into the *morkhi* (large copper vessel in which water is heated) for our baths and filled into the *gurgulet* (earthern pot with a spout, shaped like a cockerel). From this we would pour water into glasses to drink. Water from our well has a taste all its own and even now when I visit the Nachinola house I prefer well water rather than any sweet or fizzy drink.

One full *quasaw* was placed in the dining room on the window sill into which had been carved a sort of wash basin. In this we washed our faces and our hands; the dirty water flowed through a wooden trough to plants in the garden.

We had baths in a small cubicle in the kitchen. To bathe, we had to draw water in small *chimboos* (copper vessels) from the *morkhi* (large copper vessel) under which dry leaves had been burned to heat the water. We youngsters were not allowed to enter the kitchen when any lady was bathing, as she had to stretch out to draw water from the *morkhi* and exposed her upper torso. During the summer and in the rains we youngsters and the men had our baths near the well with water drawn directly and poured over us. Bathing with water freshly drawn from the well was most invigorating, but if there was a breeze it could get quite chilly.

A few months later our well had to be cleaned. This was done every two years. A man went down into the well using a rope and the footholds carved in the walls of the corner opposite that where the pulley for drawing water was located. Being 54 feet deep, the man entering the well had to be very skilled. Our well was served by a perennial spring and never dried. At midsummer, around June, the water level would be about 24 inches – or two feet – but due to silt accumulation, the actual depth of clear water was about 18 inches. Water was first drawn up and all available vessels – *morkhis, quasaws,* etc – were filled, since after cleaning it would take at least two days for the water level in the well to be such that we could draw clear water again.

The first priority was to catch the fish which lived in our well to control various larvae. These were caught and placed in an open bucket filled with clear well water. This bucket was carefully drawn up and placed at a safe distance away from where all of us were moving about.

Inside the well, the sealed *caju feni* jars were checked and moved to the further side of the well, and the oldest jars were pulled up. Then the process of emptying the well of water and sediment could commence.

This was a tedious job. First a basket was repeatedly lowered into which dead leaves, twigs, pieces of broken earthen *quasaws,* etc were filled. Then an open bucket was lowered and the man in the well churned up the water and filled the bucket, taking particular care to get out as much of the silt as possible. While we were drawing and throwing away buckets full of the silt-laden water, the spring kept feeding fresh clean water into the well. Granny would monitor the water coming out of the well and only when she was satisfied that most of the silt had been removed, would she direct that the bucket with the fish be lowered into the well and the fish freed to swim in the now clean and clear water. After this, the man came up from the well to a well-deserved large tot of *feni*, to take the chill out of his body.

I do not remember the kitchen in Miss Strong's house, but I am sure we did not use firewood, but probably charcoal. At Nachinola we used firewood for cooking. The kitchen would get quite smoky if the wood was allowed to smoulder. However, we quickly learned how to blow through a hollow bamboo to make the firewood burn vigorously. But this was not always encouraged by Granny. Sometimes she would want the food on the *chula* to cook slowly. If the fire was too strong and the *burkhalo* or *kundli* (earthernware cooking vessels) had very little contents in it, the pot would crack with the heat. Granny Leopoldina used two sets of *chulas*, one at floor level, which she and the servant girl used most of the time. This had two stones on either side and the rear was the *don* (large earthern vessel with a broad mouth). Into this went all the food scraps, which were not fed to the dog or cat, and the water in which rice had been cooked. Granny would add rice or wheat bran and oil cake to this; the mixture was fed to the pigs twice a day.

There were another two *chulas*, built onto a stone and cement platform alongside, which Ivy and Bemvinda used for heating milk and making coffee or tea, as they could not squat on the floor. An advantage of using the *chula* on the floor was its proximity to the *morkhi*, the heat from the cooking fire to some extent heated the bath water which was always tepid and never cold.

Granny Leopoldina and Marianne, the maid whom Ivy had employed, did almost all the work involved in preparing and cooking our food by sitting on low stools or the *bankin* a couple of inches off the floor. They cut the vegetables, cleaned the fish and cut the meat by sitting astride the *addo*, which also had an attachment for scraping coconuts. Grinding of *masala* was done in the *vaan or gor-go-ro,* where all the ingredients, red or green chillies, shredded coconut, whole coriander and cumin seeds, turmeric, ginger, garlic, onions, etc, were gradually ground into a paste by rotating the central stone pestle in the large circular stone mortar. Grinding *masala* in the *vaan* looks very easy, but when I tried to do it, the ingredients just went round and round without getting pulverised. The taste of *masala* ground in the *vaan* or on a flat grinding stone used in other parts of India, is totally different from *masala* ground in an electric liquidiser or food processor.

After using the same ingredients and following the recipe exactly, no food cooked on today's gas or electric ranges tastes as good as that cooked in earthenware vessels over a wood fire.

(My brother-in-law, Jimmy Pimenta, who lives in Toronto, Canada, took back with great care earthen *kundlies* and tried his hand at cooking Goan food over his gas range in Toronto. Being a scientist he explained that cooking in a *kundlie* actually amounted to cooking at the boiling point of water (100°C) and not at the high temperatures generated by gas or electric stoves or in a pressure cooker. But there was still a vast difference in taste, probably the lack of wood smoke flavour. This old method of cooking saves far more of the nutrients in food.)

In Rangoon we had meat (usually beef) at almost all our meals with fish once or twice a week. At Nachinola, beef was rarely part of our diet. On the road to our church, there was a small building, erected by the *Comunidade,* which was the butcher's shop. He came every Saturday with at most two young bulls. He would slaughter and butcher one and sell this fresh meat to the villagers from Nachinola and adjoining villages. If all the meat was sold and there were still customers he would slaughter and butcher the second animal. People who bought meat would be given bones for soup and for their dogs free of charge. The intestines of these animals would be cleaned and dried and were available for sale to those who required them for making Goa sausages *(choris).*

Since there were no refrigerators, all the meat had to be

cooked the same day. Spices and vinegar were used both to give taste and to preserve the meat. In fact, most meat (beef and pork) dishes tasted much better on the second day and thereafter – if it lasted that long. The dish was taken out from the meat-safe and heated, we helped ourselves and the balance went back into the meat-safe to be taken out and reheated before being served at the next meal. I do not think this cooked meat was ever served cold.

Normally food for the day included breakfast, bread and coffee, at around 07:00, then *kanji* (overcooked rice with the water) with pickle or *kalchi corrie* (yesterday's dried curry) or Goa *jaggery* at 11:00, lunch between 12:00 and 13:00 consisting of rice with prawn or fish curry with a vegetable dish and fried fish or prawns. Meat (beef or pork) would be on the menu maybe on Sunday or some feast. Tea was between 15:30 to 16:00 with some snack usually made with *jaggery,* and dinner around 20:00 of some gravy dish with bread or *chappatis* (either from wheat or rice or *nachni* flour). On special occasions *sannaas* (rice flour batter fermented with toddy made into cakes and steamed) or *vorre* (small *chapattis* deep fried) would be additional. The normal Goan rice (large reddish grains) could not be used for *pullao,* for which special white rice was purchased. In place of *kanji* for us youngsters, Granny would make *teezaan* (porridge) from *nachni* (finger millet, *ragi*) flour sweetened with *jaggery* which was far more nutritious. Afternoon snacks included *gorshe* (new rice cooked with jaggery and flavoured by *haldi* leaves), *paatoyo* (ground rice flour paste spread on a *haldi* leaf with coconut and jaggery stuffing and then steamed). Granny Leopoldina loved to experiment with snacks and I was a willing guinea-pig, who enjoyed whatever she cooked.

Granny would eat with us at the dining table, but if we were not at home, Granny and Marianne would sit on their *bankins* in the kitchen to eat their food. The cat and dog would sit alongside and being fed scraps of food from their plates, in addition to a plateful of the same food doled our separately in their individual plates. Only on days when we bought beef, the dogs would get rice cooked with beef bones.

The third bedroom adjoining the kitchen had been converted by Granny into a store room. Here she had large *burnees* (earthenware jars with large mouths) containing Goa jaggery, rice, wheat flour, *nachni* (finger millet), tamarind, *bindel* and *binda-che-sola* (both byproducts from the *Garcinia indica* wonder tree), *ambe-che-sola*, whole red chillies, whole turmeric *(haldi)*, and other spices. In a large *bahn* (a round enclosure made with bamboo matting resting on the floor) raw paddy was stored. From this some quantity was removed from time to time, boiled in a *morkhi*, dried initially on the *angan* (courtyard) and then on the floor of the sitting room. We were encouraged to walk through the drying paddy dragging our bare feet through the paddy, so that the paddy got stirred up and damp paddy got brought to the surface. The paddy was thoroughly dry after five or six days. It would then be sent to the mill to be husked. (Subsequently, I visited a large commercial organisation where paddy was boiled in large quantities and dried using circulating scoops which threw the wet paddy from a height. I suppose because the boiled paddy was not thoroughly dried due to high atmospheric humidity, the rice when husked had a peculiar smell.)

One day when I looked into the paddy *bahn* I saw a large black snake coiled comfortably and fast asleep. I walked out quietly and called Granny, who then told me that this was a sort of house snake (not domesticated, but not poisonous) which ate rats and was thus the protector of our paddy. When paddy had to be drawn from the *bahn* they would bang on the bamboo sides and with this noise the snake would climb out on to the rafters and disappear. This snake, probably when chasing a rat through the rafters, fell into our well. There was quite a furore among our Hindu workers and they very quickly made arrangements for one of them to go into the well to get the snake into a basket and then drawn out.

We also had another 'house' snake – a cobra – which I discovered in 1964. This one lived in a hole in the *durrig* (wall) next to our well. He would come out exactly at 16:00 every afternoon and cross our front compound diagonally to the place where our original small gate had been (this was walled up in 1948). Then, he would go along the wall through the new large gate into the fields to catch his requirement of food. Granny's dog, Betty, would announce his exit from his bolt hole by barking and, keeping a safe distance from him, follow him till he left the compound. He would occasionally lift up his hood to warn Betty.

When I noticed this I told Granny and she told me that this was our house snake. As long as we did not do anything to it – like throwing stones, etc – it would not harm anyone from the house, she assured. There are stories about such house snakes in various houses in Goa.

(Years later in 1984 when we were putting in the floor of our factory in New Bombay employing local workers, there was suddenly a shout of '*Saap, saap*' (snake, snake) and every one was running away. I went to see what was causing the ruckus and saw a large black rock snake. The workers had taken up sticks and stones to kill the snake. I stopped them and explained that this was not poisonous and lived on rats and other small rodents. These workers were amazed that I had stopped them from killing this snake when some of them probably worshipped snakes. I had to explain to them that snakes kept the rat population in control, which in turn saved us from losses. Thereafter, they would strike the stone foundation, in some hollow of which this snake was living, and after he left, they would commence work. He still lives somewhere in our compound and we have no problem with rats.)

There were no flush toilets, only piggy toilets then. Ours was a two seat design – two people could use the toilet at the same time, but Iza and Bella would only go into the toilet if Leo and I kept guard to chase away the pigs. The smaller kids used a chamber pot inside the house, which was then emptied into the piggy toilet.

We had a whole new environment to explore – the garden in

which Granny Leopoldina grew cucumbers, *tendlis* (jerkins) and lady fingers – and a rose garden which was her particular domain. Granny encouraged us to eat a few of the small cucumbers when we were sent to collect them for lunch or dinner. Leo and I with great delight discovered a small sand pit under the coffee plant at the foot of the garden from which we dug up ginger, and got a whack each, since this was ginger kept as seed for planting the next season. In this same sand pit we found turmeric *(haldi)* kept for seeding. There is another form of *haldi* (turmeric) – *amba haldi* grown for medicinal use and dug up only when required.

(Years later while on holiday, I was riding a hired cycle and fell and sprained by right hand. After returning the cycle and walking home my wrist was already starting to swell. Somehow I managed to eat lunch, without, I thought, drawing Granny's attention. After lunch I reclined in one of the deck chairs in the verandah and fell asleep. I was suddenly awakened to a cool feeling on my right hand, which had now swollen into almost a balloon. Granny was applying a greenish paste – *amba haldi* ground in vinegar and *feni*. Within fifteen minutes of applying this paste, the swelling had gone down and the pain had disappeared. I was able to use my right hand quite normally.)

She had grown, what we considered a type of cactus, which has now been identified as *aloe vera*. One of the thick fleshy leaves of this plant was put into the embers of the fire. Then Iza's finger with a whitlow (boil under the nail) was inserted into this hot leaf and bandaged in place. In about four hours, the pus from the boil had been drawn out and Iza's finger was almost normal.

Granny Leopoldina had various other plants growing in the garden which had medicinal value. People from Nachinola and surrounding villages would come to her for these herbal medicines. She would freely distribute these herbal medicines (leaves, bark, roots and fruit) with detailed instructions for their use.

She never called in a doctor to treat any of our illnesses or those of her animals. For colds and coughs and for tummy upsets, the panacea was *caju feni,* with hot water and sour lime sweetened with either honey or sugar. In fact, during the rains, all of us from the smallest to the oldest lined up to be dosed with a small glass of *feni* with some spices and sugar candy added. This was Granny's prophylactic against colds and coughs.

Then we had trees to climb and fruits to pluck. Mango, jack fruit, pomelo in our own compound and *caju* and *jamun* trees and *kanta or karaunda* bushes on the surrounding hills. Many trees were infested with red ants, whose bites were really painful. The village workers, who climbed the mango or jackfruit trees to pluck the fruit, claimed that tying a live red ant in their *kashtie* kept other red ants from biting them. I cannot vouch for the truth of this statement.

February was the *caju* season so we helped Granny Leopoldina collect *caju* (cashew) fruit, separate the seeds and put this fruit in the big stone trough in which the *caju* juice was squeezed out. Since Granny was interested in the juice, we were permitted to pick *cajus* from other people's property, provided we took only the fruit, leaving the *caju* nut on the ground for the owner to collect.

This juice was allowed to ferment and was later taken to the *caju feni* distillery on the hillside behind our church. This was a government-supervised distillery and Granny paid a fee according to the quantity distilled. The first distillate contained low alcohol content and was called *urrack.* Anju and Gerry enjoyed this as it was light, like beer or wine. This *urrack* was re-distilled to get *feni.* There was some sort of measurement to evaluate the alcohol content of this *feni.*

Feni (both *caju* and coconut) from the current year's production was given to the workers at the end of their day's shift together with their wages for the day plus a measure of uncooked rice. *Feni* was measured out in a *koti* (half of a coconut shell, which had been cleaned of all the fibres and polished). Each worker had his own *koti.* There was obviously a premium for the bigger *kotis.*

The current year's production of *feni* was not for home consumption or for serving to guests. Granny Leopoldina would fill large ceramic jars (with screw caps) with the current year's production of *caju feni*, probably about eighteen to twenty bottles in each jar, add her own mixture of spices with dried orange peel, screw down the caps and seal the jars with cement – the year was inscribed into this cement seal. These jars would be very carefully lowered into our well, in which the water level never went below the top of these jars. (This, of course, entailed the lowering of one of our workers into the well to properly place the jar away from any possibility of being hit by a *quasaw*.)

As and when needed, she would pull up one jar which had been in the well for at least five years. This mellowed *caju feni* was preferred by Anju and quite a number of his friends to the finest of imported whiskeys or other alcoholic products, which at that time were available for as little as a few Rupees per bottle.

As a reward for our 'work' of helping collect caju fruit, we were allowed to roast *caju* seeds. We soon discovered that if we were not careful the juice from the shell burnt our skin which went grey and subsequently peeled. If we wiped our mouth or face with hands wet with *caju* shell liquid, our lips and facial skin got burnt and turned grey and finally peeled. Thus there was plenty evidence if we roasted *caju* seeds on our own. (*Caju* shell liquid is now an important raw material; and machines which drum-roast *caju* nuts are designed so that the *caju* shell liquid is recovered.)

In our compound we had *bael* fruit trees. The fruit when ripe was yellow, it had a strong outer shell, which when cracked open yielded a soft orange pulp with seed pods in a sort of glutinous substance. This orange pulp had to be carefully scraped out, without breaking the seed pods. We could eat this pulp as such or add it to water and make a refreshing drink. This fruit as well as the leaves of the tree was in great demand as a remedy for various stomach ailments. A sort of preserve is also made of the pulp, *bael muramba,* which is sold as herbal medicine. Even the dry shell is used as medicine.

In addition to mango and jack fruit trees found in most com-pounds, Granny had grown papaya, banana and guava, so we en-joyed a variety of fruits more or less throughout the year. We col-lected quite a lot of *jamun* from the trees in the jungle behind our house and Ivy made some *jamun* wine. I subsequently dis-covered that *jamun* is very good for those suffering from diabetes. One problem with *jamun* and *caju* juice, they permanently stain your clothes, so we were careful to use only old clothes if we were going to collect these fruit.

After a few days, Bemvinda, Salu with Bela, Leo, Louis and Alex left for their own house in Olaulim. Gerry stayed on.

Battling a *Regidor*

ANJU, who had been shipping teak from Rangoon for strategic use in India, was allotted a berth on the last ship, loaded with teak for the British Government, which sailed just before Rangoon fell to the Japanese on March 8, 1942. Before leaving Rangoon he brought our three dogs, Patch, Mitzy and Nelson, to Diego's shop so that they would continue to be fed. They instinctively knew he was going away and jumped right back into the car. He had to leave the car on the dockside. Surprisingly, Diego's two dogs jumped up with their front paws on his shoulders and licked his face in farewell. Diego never mentioned what he did with all five dogs when he left Rangoon a couple of days later.

Anju landed at Madras and then came on by rail to Goa. He arrived about a month after we had reached Nachinola. When he arrived we were truly thankful and Granny Leopoldina organised a *ladainh* in thanksgiving, which the whole village of Nachinola attended. This was my first experience of *ladainh* when the Litany of the Saints is sung and various prayers offered in Konkani and Latin at our local *vaddo* chapel. After the *ladainh*, every one was served boiled gram (chick peas) with pieces of fresh coconut. And for the men, a *kotti* (coconut shell cleaned and polished) full of cashew *feni,* which each swallowed at one gulp.

After the initial detailing of his experiences and catching up on our news, Granny Leopoldina gave Anju a detailed account of what had transpired in Goa during his and Gerry's absence in Burma. The *regidor*, a local village official in Portuguese times who was our neighbour and Anju's childhood friend, had taken for granted that Anju and Gerry would settle in Rangoon. He assumed that they would never return to Goa, as had their own father and many others who had left Goa to seek their fortunes in India (Karachi, Calcutta and Bombay) or Africa or Canada or Brazil. Consequently, he took it for granted that Granny would have no male members to support her.

When the Nachinola *Comunidade* (village community) had allotted our house plot, they had specified that the access road be broad enough for a bullock cart to negotiate. However, when building the *durig* (a primitive wall of odd shaped stones packed with mud) to surround the village-owned paddy fields in front of our house, this official very carefully built the *durig* within the allotted pathway. Since a *durig* is about half a metre wide at the base, the path left was too narrow to allow passage of a bullock cart.

Granny Leopoldina complained against the *regidor* to higher authorities in Mapuça. Her frail woman's voice could not prevail against that of the *regidor*. Further, all applications and verbal appeals had to be made in Portuguese. Granny Leopoldina learnt the Portuguese language and took the case to the highest authority in Panjim. In spite of her limited Portuguese and appearing herself without help of any *advogado* she managed to win her case. The *Comunidade* and *regidor* were instructed to rebuild the *durig* leaving a clear pathway wide enough for a bullock cart to pass. This decision had been given early in 1941, but the *regidor* had yet to issue instructions to have the present *durig* demolished and rebuilt.

Two or three evenings after Anju arrived, Iza and I , playing in the garden, noticed that Anju was marching up and down the driveway obviously in a temper (he rolled his tongue down and inward when he was angry). Gerry had a little earlier taken a stick and gone around our front neighbour's house and took up station hidden by the *durig* on the further side on our branch road. The *regidor* and his friend, one D'Souza, used to go for a *passoi* (stroll) every evening, returning along the road in front of our house. Apparently the plan was to let them pass our house and then Anju would walk down our driveway and Gerry would pop out from behind the opposite *durig* and, having the *regidor* between them, confront him and obtain an explanation and an apology. As soon as these two passed the entrance to our driveway, Anju called out in Konkani, "Antu, I would like a word with you." They looked back, saw Anju striding down our driveway with walking stick in hand and saw Gerry in front. They immediately took to their heels, jumped over the *durig* into the field opposite and raced for home shouting in Konkani "Help! Help! They are coming to beat me!" They raced by a round-about route and entered the *regidor's* house by his back door. Anju and Gerry went to the *regidor's* front door (his house is about 200 metres from our house) and knocked, but the *regidor's* would not show himself.

The next day, Anju and Gerry approached the village *Comunidade* office and officially called for details as to when the wrongfully built *durig* would be demolished and rebuilt (it had to be done before the monsoon in June). Other *Comunidade* members assured Anju and Gerry that this work would be immediately carried out and completed well before the monsoon. This was done and this *durig* still stands, leaving a clear driveway through which cars can enter our Nachinola compound by the new big gate.

I was informed by Granny Leopoldina of an earlier feud between our two families. The *regidor's* great-grand-father and Anju's great-grand-father were neighbours and friends. For some occasion, Anju's great-grand-father, borrowed five hundred Portuguese coin equivalent to the British Indian half Rupee. Not being literate, he had signed some paper with a couple of crosses, witnessed by other villagers, who were also not literate. Anju's great-grand-father died. After a couple of years, Anju's great-grand-mother, having collected five hundred coins, went to pay back this debt. She was shocked when old creditor showed her the paper signed by her husband stating that he had sold their house and property to him for this amount and that there was no question of any loan to be repaid. Anju's great-grand-mother made a loud wailing noise (as is done when someone dies) and cursed the old man. Shortly thereafter, there was an influenza epidemic and the old man and his grand-son died on the same day and were buried in the same coffin, the baby being placed on his grand-father's legs.

Our original house, probably of stones plastered with mud, is no longer traceable, but the stand of teak trees in the compound (well over fifty trees) remains untouched till today. They are worth a fortune, but no one will come forward to buy and cut down these trees. Anju's grand-father, Manu *Irmao*, built the new house and it was completed in 1903, just in time for Anju to be brought home from Saligao. (These family feuds were forgotten over the years and when we went down for holidays the *regidor* and D'Souza would drop in to greet us and for a convivial drink.)

To celebrate Easter and our safe return from Burma, Granny Leopoldina had one of our pigs killed on Wednesday during Holy Week. The village pig-catcher was called. With his dogs, he chased and caught the pig and tied its legs together. The pig was carried with a stout bamboo between its tied front and back legs. It squealed so loudly that all the other pigs ran away. Then the pig-catcher slit its throat and collected the blood in a *vati* (earthenware bowl), into which Granny had added vinegar. He then burnt straw over the pig's carcass to rid it off the hair. He brushed it down with more straw. He then washed the pig with hot water and using a cut-throat razor shaved off the remaining hair from the whole carcass, including the tail, leaving a little tuft at the very end. He now cut the pig open and removed the intestines and internal organs. Our family could at most consume about ten kilos, so the pig man had in advance secured orders from other people for various quantities of pork. It was interesting to see that each buyer got a piece of the liver, heart, kidneys and ear. He gave Granny the proceeds from this sale of meat, after deducting his fee.

The intestines were thoroughly cleaned and prepared into *booch* (a highly spiced dish with vinegar, almost a pickle). Liver, heart, kidneys and pork meat were boiled and cut into small cubes, which together with the coagulated blood, was converted into *sorpotel* with a mixture of spices ground in vinegar. *Feni* was added for better preservation. All the utensils used were earthernware, as vinegar would corrode metal vessels. These two dishes would not be served immediately, but would be heated twice each day and put back into the store-room for a minimum of three days and only then served. By this time, the *masala* had thoroughly been absorbed into the meat and also the spices had mellowed.

Easter lunch was *sannaa, vorem ani maas* (fermented and steamed rice cakes, deep fried wheat small *chapattis* and meat). In our house, unlike in most Goan houses, we would also have a salad either of onions leeks, mint leaves, cucumber, tomatoes, green chillies with fresh sour lime and salt as dressing or of slightly green pineapple with finely cut green chillies and salt. Virtually everything (except a few spices) was home grown.

A large portion of pork meat, cut into one inch cubes, was marinated in spices with vinegar and *feni* and left for two or three days, being stirred up morning and evening. These pieces of pickled pork were then stuffed into clean and dry cow's intestines and tied at intervals to make Goa's famous *churacaos* (sausages). These sausages were put on sticks and dried in the hot sun, with us youngsters appointed to guard them against crows, kites and dogs. Small hand mirrors were placed around the perimeter of the *angan* (courtyard). Kites and crows diving to tackle these sausages would get reflected sunlight into their eyes and would be forced to abort their dive (a similar principle to searchlights being used to distract enemy bombers and fighters during the Battle of Britain). These sausages were brought in each evening and taken out next morning for about five days. After that these bamboos were strung up in the kitchen where the sausages continued to be cured with the normal kitchen smoke. These sausages were so well preserved that they could be kept for over a year, right through the monsoon, without deteriorating.

The brain was made into a separate dish which was not so heavily spiced. Large pieces of pork (the legs) were roasted (*asaad* and *bafaad*) with light spicing. Finally all the bones were cooked into *aar-baar* (also heavily spiced). These dishes were for immediate consumption.

During the intervening period, we visited Salu and Bemvinda in Olaulim, Balbino and family in Salvador do Mundo, Great Granny and other relatives in Saligao, Diego and Agnes in Quitula, Aldona. All of these villages are located within the *taluka* or *concelho* (sub-district) of Bardez, within a range of 5-15 kilometres away.

Great Granny (Granny Leopoldina's mother) was over 90 years at that time and her hands trembled so much that when she brought *koondlies* (earthen cooking pots) to the table, she would spill the curry. But when Anju poured her a wine glass full (really full to the point of brimming over) of *feni*, she would convey the glass to her lips without wasting one drop.

Great Granny had grown a plum tree just outside her bedroom window. Nurtured by her with great care and regular application of organic manure, this tree used to be loaded with fruit. Flying foxes (large fruit bats) would come at night from far away to feast on these plums. So Great Granny installed up in the tree an empty kerosene tin with a small wooden bar suspended inside to act as a sort of bell. When she heard the flapping of the flying foxes or their shrill calls, she would wake and pull on the ringer to make a noise and drive them off. She used to make a very good wine from these plums. As *Baabi Consu*, she was well known in

Saligao for managing on her own with no support from husband or son.

I looked forward to visiting Great Granny because she always had something special for us. My only problem was using the toilet. As was normal in Goa, this was away from the house and could be seen from the village road that ran alongside. If you were going to the toilet you had to carry a *chimboo* (small metal pot) with water, which clearly announced your destination to anyone passing on the road. Inevitably, someone would pass just then and would enquire in Konkani *"Tu cumaon voita?"* (Are you going to the toilet?) This is basically just a form of greeting, but to me it was mighty embarrassing. (So much so that when Iza and Frank decided to settle in Goa after returning from Burma, I told them not to choose Saligao as their place of residence.)

Anju stayed with us till Easter, then he and Gerry went to Bombay to look for jobs.

In 1943, while we were living at Nachinola, Ivy had to take Great Granny to the Ribandar Hospital, as she had a huge growth on her knee, which was successfully removed. She died at the age of 97 in 1948.

Great Granny had a relative whom we called *Jacku Mumptee* (Joaquim Sebastian Coelho). I have never found out how he was related to us. He developed a special soft corner for me and whenever I was in Goa for my holidays, he would somehow find out and come walking all the way from Saligao to Nachinola with *belio* (finger-shaped pieces of black jaggery), which was then a speciality of Saligao. This form of *gur* is no longer available, in fact sugarcane has ceased to be cultivated in Saligao and consequently there is no production of *belio* either.

Trekking Out of Burma

A T Saligao we had been informed that Aunty Ancy with Hilda, Arist, Alphonse, George, Isabelle and Irene had reached Poona. They had trekked out from Burma.

After the first bombing Uncle Hippolito and the ladies shifted to Myingyan (in Mandalay, central Burma, some 580 kms from Rangoon), leaving Arist, Alphonse and George in Rangoon. When the news was broadcast that Rangoon would soon fall, Arist, Alphonse and George also went to Myingyan.

Since the Japanese were on the verge of entering Rangoon, they decided to travel overland to India. They had to carry Uncle Hippolito, who was paralysed, in an easy chair. Initially they had transport and *coolies* to help carry Uncle. Gradually as the route got steeper and deteriorated into a jungle path, they had great trouble carrying Uncle. Also *coolies* were difficult to find.

For quite some distance Arist, Alphonse, George with some help from the ladies, carried Uncle. Finally they reached the Indian border and were put onto a train. They reached Poona, where Aunty Ancy's sister was living, and there Uncle Hippolito died. After recouping for about a fortnight in Poona they came on to Goa. We met them towards end of May.

Mr. Pimenta also trekked out of Burma. He started out by car from Rangoon with all of Oriental's ledgers and quite some cash. At Mandalay he had to ditch the car as the Ava Bridge to the road north had been destroyed. He met Hugh Nazareth, who then travelled with him onwards. In spite of all the difficulties encountered *en route*, he brought out the company's records. He reached the Indian border and then came on to Bombay and there handed over all records to his head office. With these records Oriental could effectively settle insurance claims relating to losses in Burma. For this service he was awarded a citation of appreciation in a silver casket, which the family treasures.

(Along the route the sights of dead and dying and bodies being devoured by dogs and carrion were such that Mr. Pimenta could never subsequently bear to watch meat being cut or smell raw meat. When Mrs. Pimenta was cooking meat, he was exiled to the front verandah of their Poona bungalow or he would go upstairs and read his newspapers.)

On arrival in Goa, after completing his work at Bombay, Mr. Pimenta came all the way to St Xavier's School, Moira, to meet Ivy and personally thank her for assisting his wife and children. Only Edigio came with him, as John, Helmana, Lourdes and Jimmy were at school.

Job-Hunting in Bombay

A FTER this short holiday, Anju and Gerry left for Bombay to look for jobs. On reaching Bombay, Anju and Gerry took up residence at Mrs. Rocha's Boarding House at Sitaram Building, Crawford Market. They would study 'Situations Vacant' columns in the *Times of India* each morning and then write job applications and promptly deposit them in the 'Replies' box at the Times of India building.

Gerry was the first to get a response – from Killick Nixon, the firm once known for its construction equipment, for an engineer to be posted at their Western India Plywood factory at Dandeli, close to Londa, which was on the rail route to Goa. He appeared for the interview. With his U.K. certificate and experience at Dalla Boatyard and B.O.C. (Burmah Oil Company), Syriam, he was immediately appointed. This suited him fine as he could spend short holidays in Goa.

Anju experienced some difficulty in securing a suitable job. Then he spotted an advertisement from the British Army calling for men with experience of Burma and with knowledge of the Burmese language to be given short term commissions in the British Indian Army. They were to be posted to the Burma Front in anticipation of the re-entry of the British into Burma. He personally applied to Army H.Q. at Colaba. There he met a number of friends from Burma. After a short interview all of them were appointed as Viceroy's Commissioned Officers with the rank of Second Lieutenant and were told to report for duty the next morning. However, the Army was not ready and each morning they reported to Army H.Q., signed the muster and drew their TA/DA and then were free to loaf till the next morning. They were given an advance and told to go to the specified tailor and get themselves outfitted with proper uniform and kit.

One morning after signing the muster, they boarded a bus from the Colaba Bus Station to the Crawford Market and climbed to the upper deck. At Electric House, a very presentable and well endowed young lady climbed to the upper deck and the young men noticed that she was wearing an aeroplane pendant on a chain around her neck. They commented to each other *in Burmese* about her beauty and mentioned that the plane had a beautiful landing ground. Just before reaching Victoria Terminus (VT), the young lady got up and turning to them thanked them *in Burmese* for the compliments paid to her. Anju and his pals would have liked to be invisible at that moment.

When they got their uniforms and were issued their revolvers, four of them decided to celebrate. In full uniform they went to 'Coronation Darbar' (the closest equivalent in Bombay to Rangoon's Moghul Street) at Grant Road for a drink and dinner. They were ushered into a 'family room'. They had relaxed and each took off his Sam Browne belt with revolver in the holster and hung it on the hooks in this family room. They ordered their drinks and meals. The food took a long time coming, but the drinks were promptly served and kept coming. After being served three or four times, Anju noticed a hand appearing over the top of the partition from the next family room and groping for the Sam Browne belts. He immediately shouted and got up. Each grabbed his Sam Browne belt, buckled it on and with revolvers drawn walked out of the restaurant. Next morning when recounting this incident at Army H.Q., they were reprimanded, since restaurants and other centres of entertainment in that area were 'out of bounds' to all officers of the British and Indian Army.

Anju did not know too many people in Bombay and before getting a job was reluctant to visit anyone. After he was commissioned and in his full uniform he visited his favourite cousin, Eudocina, now married to Franklin Noronha, and living at Ready Money Buildings, Clare Road, Byculla. She and her family were very proud of this handsome army officer cousin.

A House and Food, but No Money

A T Nachinola we now had the security of a house and basic food, but we had no ready money for day to day expenses.

Ivy promptly set about finding a job. She was informed that Manuel D'Cruz from Nachinola owned St Xavier's High School at Moira. She approached him for a teacher's job. When he read her certificates and heard of her teaching experience he was quick to offer her the job of head mistress. He had been unable to send up students for the matriculation examinations in Bombay without a properly qualified head mistress, and she just fulfilled this requirement. We immediately started school – Ivy at the high school building and Iza and me at the primary school building.

While staying at Nachinola, Ivy, Iza and I attended school at Moira from Mondays to Saturdays 09:00 to 16:00 with lunch break from 12:30 to 13:30. Thursday and Sunday were holidays. Ivy employed a maid, Marianne, to help Granny Leopoldina with the cooking. She would also bring our lunch to school. After reaching home around 16:30 and having tea, Iza and I would play in our compound or join Ivy for badminton at Mr. D'Cruz's house, where his three sisters were good players.

Later, as I made friends, I would join boys from our school for a game of football in front of Dattaram's *posro* (grocery store cum tavern). I wore shoes while playing football, but most of the boys played bare-foot. While attending school, most of the boys used *chappals* (open sandals). While playing football bare-foot, Ben Martyres kicked the ball and also kicked a stone, the skin on the top of the second toe of his right leg got cut and the skin peeled back to expose the bone. He had to go all the way to Dr Chico Athaide on the Moira Hill to get the skin pulled back and stitched in position. I think the wound was washed with *feni*, all the mud removed and then dressed with a bandage. Ben was forced to wear *chappals* till the wound healed. Fortunately this was in dry weather. Otherwise with muddy water from the road, the wound could have become infected, which would have been dangerous as there were no antibiotics at that time.

Ben, who must have been around 14 and was tall for his age, appeared very much bigger than the rest of us eight and nine year olds. He owned a bicycle and a special treat was to be given a ride on his bike. He could carry three of us – one perched on the handlebars with legs on the front mud-guard, one on the cross bar and the third standing behind him with feet on the extended rear axle. Later when I learnt to ride a bicycle, I would hire a bike from Dattaram at Re. 1 for a whole day. Owners of bicycles had to pay road tax to the Portuguese Government as evidenced by the engraved brass token fixed to the bike. Surprisingly at that time owners of motor cars paid no road tax.

During the rains there was a stream behind the Nachinola church which created quite a deep pool just behind Armand Nazareth's house. All of us school playmates would go there to play in the water but the pool was not broad or deep enough to swim.

From Nachinola, we would walk through Panarim across the *bandh* to Aldona – Ranoi and Quitula – to visit Agnes and Noellyn. Their house was built on a slope, the front entrance and sitting room about level with the road, then each room at a lower level, connected by steps till the lowest was the kitchen and bathroom alongside the well. The piggy toilet was further down the slope.

Noellyn, a toddler, was quite adept at climbing up and down from one end of the house to the other.

Along the way to Agnes' house, was the house in which Albert and Mary with Damas, Eugene and Dennis were living. Either on our way to Agnes or on our return we would stop over for a while. All our jaunts to and from Quitula had to be in daylight as there were no street lamps and trying to negotiate those pathways by torchlight was hazardous

At the end of the *bandh* at Panarim was a *manos* (sluice gate) and we would collect freshly caught prawns and fish on our way back to Nachinola. The prawns, which were delicious, were usually still alive when we got home. (Years later when I used to go home for holidays, this sluice gate controller's wife would somehow get to know that I had arrived. She would turn up the very next morning and tell Granny, "Your Grandson has arrived, so buy prawns for him.")

We all went to the fishing-beach village of Calangute for a week at the sea. Granny Leopoldina believed that one week's sea baths were essential to remain healthy throughout the year. We hired a fisherman's house for the week, but did our own cooking. For this we carried our own firewood, provisions and utensils, stacked on a *'matchbox'*[6].

At Calangute, the daily menu was freshly caught fish and prawns with some vegetables and, of course, rice with fish or prawn curry. Each morning and again early evening, all of us would walk down to the beach and soak in the sea water. Swimming suits and swimming trunks were not used; we used our normal clothes and Granny used a cotton sari. I remember one small accident when the sari of one of the ladies came unravelled and disappeared in the waves. There was no real swimming just playing in the shallows and being tumbled by the waves. Underfoot in the sand we could feel thousands of tiny shell fish *(mandoyo)*, which we collected in a basket. The water washed away the sand

---

[6]   The *gadee*, or 'matchbox' as it was affectionately called, was a colourful two-wheeled covered carriage drawn by two bulls on a yoke.

and left these tiny shell fish, cooked into a delicious soup each night.

Since Freddy (Antunis) was missing school, Grace sent him to us in Nachinola so that Ivy could teach him and he would not be behind his class when he went back to Calcutta. Freddy, who was older than both of us, was easily scared. In Nachinola at night he would virtually stick to either Iza or myself when we were carrying the *ponti*; he could not bear to remain in the dark. After getting into the large double bed with us he insisted that the *ponti* be kept lit. Granny Leopoldina objected to this waste of kerosene. Marianne was instructed to sleep on the floor in the same room so that Freddy would not be scared.

One Sunday morning, after a shower of rain, the slope in front of our house on the way to church was covered with little bright red spider like insects, which we called velvet *boochies* (I still do not know their biological name). We decided to collect them and take them home to have races. Bella and Leo were with us. Each collected a handful of these insects. Before entering church we decided that since Freddy was the only one wearing a coat, he could allocate one pocket for each of our collections.

During Mass these insects started crawling all over Freddy and down inside his clothes. He started to wriggle, and we, to giggle. When he tried to scratch himself where the insects were crawling, he squashed them, leaving pink stains on his clothes. By the time we got home, the four of us were bursting with laughter and Freddy was just waiting to throw off his clothes and get rid of all these insects. In spite of Freddy's scratching and squashing, there were quite a few of these insects left alive and we made them run races on the front cement benches of our house. Since that time, I have not seen these velvet *boochies*. Are they extinct, like so many other animals, birds and reptiles?

Commuting between Nachinola and Moira in 1942–43 was difficult, particularly during the monsoon. One had to walk back and forth as there was no public transport. During the rains we used *komphanas* (wooden sandals, foot-shaped pieces of wood with rubberised cotton straps) to go to and from school. We also used these sandals as boats for racing down the little streams along the way. With only an umbrella for protection we reached school wet and we were again thoroughly drenched when returning home. Ivy was very worried that we would get sick, in spite of Granny's prophylactic doses of *feni*.

Consequently, from June 1943 we hired a house in Moira very close to the school. Ivy, Iza, our maid Marianne, and I shifted there. Amy, who had taken up a job as teacher in the same school, joined us too. This house was on the main Mapuça–Moira–Nachinola–Aldona road. From the back of the house we could get to St Xavier's School, which was at the corner just opposite where our compound ended. The house was at the front end of the property and the rest was fairly wooded. We occupied one half of the house and the other half was occupied by the Lobos – Aloysius (nick-named Aloo) was in the same class with me and his elder brother, Patrick, who was in Iza's class. They had an older sister, Grace, and an elder brother, George, who were in senior classes.

The house consisted of a small front *verandah* with the usual cement seats, a sitting room, the bed room, with the dining room behind that and last the kitchen. Attached to the kitchen was the bathroom and finally the piggy toilet just outside the back door. As all the doors were in line you could see from the front *verandah* right through to the back. The well was at the rear of the house accessible from the Lobos' and our kitchens. The house had basic furniture, including a *morkhi* for heating bath water; dry leaves from the compound provided adequate fuel. There was a lean-to shed at the back for storing firewood and nets full of dry-leaves.

One complete set for twelve of beautiful, almost transparent, Japanese bone-china dinner cum tea set, with full set of cutlery from among Ivy and Anju's wedding presents had been brought by Granny Leopoldina to Nachinola on her return after their wedding. These we now took to Moira. *Koondlies* and *burkulos* (earthenware cooking vessels) were purchased from Mapuça.

Firewood was bought, chopped and stacked.

Opposite this house was the house of Laura D'Souza, one of Ivy's students, who had kindly allowed us to have our afternoon lunch during the 1942-43 period in her house. Marianne would bring the food from Nachinola, warm it up and serve us, and then take back the empty vessels and dishes. Probably it was through the recommendation of Laura's mother that we were able to hire Lobo's house.

Next to Laura's house there was another large house with only one old lady living in it. At night, however, we would hear the Rosary being recited in two voices – one naturally female and the second that sounded male. After quite a while we discovered that this old lady recited the Rosary in both voices, so that any one passing on the road would think that there was a man in the house. This was her security.

The first batch of St Xavier's matriculate students appeared for the examinations in April 1943. Thanks to Ivy's teaching a very large percentage of students had passed and some of them decided to celebrate. They wanted Ivy and Amy to join them for a movie at Mapuça. Because it would cost them too much to hire a taxi, Ivy declined their invitation. However, they went ahead with their celebrations, going to Mapuça on their own bicycles. After the film on the way back in the dark just before reaching the Moira bridge two of them rode off the road and dropped several feet into the field below. They were badly injured and were taken to Mapuça hospital.

In 1944, shortly after returning from Amy's wedding in Dohad (now part of Gujarat), Ivy contracted typhoid. She had very high fever, and the doctor prescribed alternative dips in icy cold water and hot water. Two galvanised iron bath tubs were obtained – in one hot water was filled from the *morkhi* and in the other well water into which ice had been placed. Ice had to be obtained all the way from the Bastora ice factory. Plus Ivy's hair was cut very short. Mrs. Lobo and Mariane would lift Ivy off the bed dip her in the hot water for a time then lift her out and dip her in the iced water for a time – alternatively – till the water in both tubs had come to about room temperature. Then she was dried and tucked into bed covered with heavy blankets. This was done twice a day for about five days, until finally Ivy started to sweat, the fever left her and she slept normally. On the day the fever left her, the entire crockery set, which had been on the table for so many months, suddenly fell down and crashed. No one had been near this table and this crash was a total mystery. Slowly Ivy recovered her strength. Dr. Chico Athaide, her cousin, who had been coming daily to treat her, now came over each evening to check on her and started teasing her about her new short hair style.

During Ivy's illness her entire Matriculation class came forward to help. One of the boys would cycle and bring the ice morning and evening all the way from Bastora, and the girls would come and sit with Ivy. Neighbours would come and stay with Ivy while Marianne got our food ready.

Because of Ivy's illness, Anju was able to get leave in February 1944, but as Goa was a Portuguese territory, he had to leave his uniforms in Bombay and come down in civilian clothes. He was with us for a fortnight and we made the most of his stay to go visiting relatives in various parts of Goa.

From the Nachinola house he collected Granny's five-year aged-in-the-well *caju feni*. Probably not realising how potent this *feni* was, and having to drink all alone, one night Anju imbibed too much. When dinner was ready, Ivy came to call Anju and found the front door wide open and Anju nowhere in sight. She thought Anju must have gone out for a stroll, but was surprised he would do so with the road so dark and without telling anyone. She called Marianne and each decided to walk in opposite directions along the road to look for Anju. Just as they were leaving, they heard a loud noise in the sitting room which sounded like a roar. Marianne was afraid and said, *"Vagh bhitor sorla!"* (a tiger has entered). Ivy with torch in hand and Marianne with a stick investigated and found Anju fast asleep and snoring on the floor.

A couple of mornings later, Anju had to leave. Ivy's students, the second batch from the school appearing for their Matriculation, showed their appreciation by presenting Anju a whole bunch of huge Moira bananas, the large sized fruit the village was then famous for. When loaded on to the rear seat of the taxi that was to take Anju to Collem, the weight was so great that the paving stone broke and we had quite a job getting the car out of the hole and pushed back on to the road.

Granny Leopoldina's Agro Industries

G RANNY (Leopoldina Isabel Sequeira e Souza, 1883-1975) had a sort of market garden in the *moiee* (plateau). To get to it, we had to go down hill through the jungle behind our house and then through the small narrow track that went towards Moira. This *moiee* was a fairly large levelled agricultural field with two wells and tamarind, coconut and *bin'na* (*kokam*, or *Garcinia indica*) trees. In this field Granny cultivated paddy during the monsoon and vegetables from September to May. On the upper portion of the *moiee*, which was a relatively steep hillside, there were mango and *caju* trees and a dense grove of bamboo.

Paddy cultivation is laborious work. Manure (clay from the creek bed mixed with dried cow-dung and fish manure) would be deposited in little heaps evenly spaced in the whole field. In the first rains towards the end of May, when the soil became soft, the ground was ploughed using two bulls and a wooden plough. The soil was thus thoroughly turned over so that the manure and roots of previous crops got mixed into the soil.

The field was then divided into large squares with earthen walls about six inches high (*bundhs*). During the monsoon rains these squares filled with water. Paddy seeds (stored in special straw bundles from the previous year's crop) was sprinkled evenly in two of these small plots. Then, two bulls dragged a plank behind them on which the ploughman stood. This ensured that all the seeds went into the soil and did not get washed away with the next rain or picked up by birds.

These two plots were carefully monitored to ensure that there always was standing water about three inches deep. If there was no rain for a couple of days, these squares were filled by drawing water from the well. Paddy seedlings sprouted in these plots and after about fourteen days they were transplanted into the other small plots in neat rows with about six inches between each seedling.

Transplantation was really back-breaking and was usually done by women labourers. Water depth in all plots was maintained at around three inches – gifted by the rain or drawn from wells. By mid-September the crop started to ripen, the green ears of paddy turning golden. This was a beautiful sight when a light breeze blew these golden ears.

Since the rains stop about this time, the fields dry and the ears of paddy fill. By September end or the first week of October, the crop was harvested, tied into sheaves and left to dry in the now dry fields.

Since our crop was relatively small, the grain is separated from the stalks (threshing) by being trodden underfoot by labourers. Iza and I helped. But at the end of a couple of hours, our legs up to our knees became red and itchy. In large fields, the paddy is threshed by bullocks going around in a circle over the sheaves of paddy.

The stalks are then lifted off the ground after thorough shaking and paddy grains mixed with chaff are left on the ground. These grains are then filled into *sup or supra* (baskets shaped like large dust pans). Each filled *sup* is held up to the full height of a man's outstretched hands and facing away from the wind he allows the grain to fall to the ground. Full grains of paddy fall almost vertically, while chaff and empty paddy husks are blown a little distance away – winnowing.

This cleaned paddy is then filled into sacks and taken home, where it is again dried in our *angan* (a small patch of beaten earth plastered with wet cow dung and allowed to dry) during the day time, and refilled into sacks at night. After about four or five days this dried paddy is stored in our *bahn*. The stalks of paddy (straw) were left to dry in the *moiee* and then either sold or built into a haystack. In later years when Granny kept buffaloes, the haystack would be erected behind our house easily accessible for the buffaloes to feed themselves.

After the paddy was harvested, the field would again be watered. The same organic manure mix was added and then completely ploughed up, destroying the small *bundhs* and ploughing into the soil the roots and stalks of the recent paddy crop. This field was then split into small sections separated by low earth walls (about three inches high) with water channels spreading through them. Granny grew a number of vegetables like red and green *baji, vosunde* (black eyed beans), chillies, onions, potatoes and sweet potatoes.

Granny, or a workman, would draw water from the well using the kerosene tin fixed with a long bamboo to the large heavy bamboo or timber lever with counter weight at the end. The person drawing water would hold the bamboo at the required height and put his full weight on it. This would pull the tin down to water level, where it would fill and then get automatically drawn up by the counter-weight. This tin was emptied into the stone trough, from where channels carried water to the various sections of the field. As each small section got its ration of water, the branch channel would be blocked with earth and water allowed to flow on to other sections of the field. We enjoyed helping Granny, watching the flow of water and then guiding water to other sections which required to be watered. This watering was carried out early in the morning and again in the evening. Granny had a small hut in the *moiee* in which she stored all the agricultural implements and the kerosene tins required for irrigating the field. This hut was 'locked' with a piece of string tying together the iron rings fixed to each half of the door.

Bamboos of the specified diameter (about 2") were cut from the grove. These were immersed in the well and left for quite some time to season. They were then taken out and dried. Unseasoned bamboos were reduced by insects to white dust within a short time of being cut, but not so bamboos that had been seasoned. The colour of the dry unseasoned bamboo was a light green, whereas seasoned bamboos acquired a golden-yellowish colour and gradually deepened with age to brown. These seasoned bamboos could be expected to give five to seven years in use.

About the time that we arrived, the *kokam* or *binda* trees were fruiting. The ripe fruit was a dark red colour, and when opened the flesh was deep pink with four seeds. This ripe *kokam* fruit was the basis of quite an industry. The skin, from which the pulp and seeds were scooped out, was dried to a brownish colour in our *angan* to become *binda-che solaa* (skin of the *binda*). However, to make them attractive for the market, these skins were then dipped in the juice from the pulp to acquire a deep red colour. *Binda-che solaa* is used in fish, particularly mackerel *(bangda)*, and prawn curries and other Goan dishes. *Binda-che solaa* has a definite anti-allergic property. Researchers have recently found in it many other medicinal properties, including anti-cholesterol ones.

The seeds are dried after being cleansed of pulp. They are pounded in a hole in the ground with a steel tipped five foot rod or bamboo of about two inch diameter and reduced to a coarse powder. This powder is then boiled in a *morkhi* (specially kept for this purpose) in the compound using dried leaves and firewood for around eight hours. When the *morkhi* cooled, there was an off-white cake on the surface, which was 'bindel' now referred to as *kokam* butter (or described as 'Goa butter' in the *Hobson-Jobson* dictionary of British times). This extract is further refined by boiling it in clean water, when only the pure *bindel* would float and all the seed powder would settle. *Bindel*, while still warm, is formed into small elliptical balls, which Granny used to sell. *Bindel* is used for frying some kinds of fish, but is primarily used to soften the skin of the soles and heels of those who use *chappals* or walk barefoot. It is now the active ingredient of Johnson & Johnson's 'Crack' ointment sold for this purpose. I am also told that *bindel* could be an ideal constituent of lipsticks and lip balms.

Granny used the *binda* pulp with sugar added to make *binda-che sirop* (*kokam* syrup) primarily for home consumption. This healthy coolant made a very refreshing drink in the heat of the day. Years later, when I was on holiday in May there was no *kokam* syrup at home. When I asked Granny whether she had not made any this year, she informed me that a doctor from the neighbouring village of Uccassim kept sending his patients to Granny for her *binda-che sirop* as it has medicinal value in helping reduce blood pressure of those suffering from hypertension. Today *kokam* syrup or *kokam amrut* is a popular product manufactured all along the west coast between Ratnagiri and Goa and commands good sales in Bombay and Goa. Another version of *binda* juice is unsweetened and is the base for *sol-kadi*, a sourish drink served as a digestive with most meals along our Konkan coast, particularly with sea foods.

The two tamarind trees in the *moiee* were the base of another industry. In April-May they would be loaded with fruit, brown curved tamarind. The ripe dry fruit would drop when the branches were shaken. These were collected and dried in the *angan*. They were then beaten with a sort of heavy wooden paddle to crack the skins which were then discarded together with the external thread-like veins. The brown mass was further dried. Then the laborious job of splitting each pod and removing the seed – done by women using the *addo* (a rounded upward curved knife mounted on a stool on which the woman sat astride. This finished product liberally covered with sea salt is formed into large oblong balls for sale.

In another field near the house, with very rocky soil, Granny cultivated *nachni* (the finger millets, a cereal widely grown in the arid areas of Asia and Africa). *Nachni* grown in our field, and for that matter all over Goa, is of a deep red colour, while *nachni* (also called *ragi)* grown on the Deccan plateau is whitish pink. Probably the Goan soil which is rich in iron ore is responsible for this dark red colour. All of us, kids and adults, were given *teezan* (*nachni* porridge with Goa jaggery) for breakfast specially during the months of November to February (our winter). *Nachni* gruel with salt, *vonn,* is given to a sick person as it is easy to digest and very strengthening.

(When Deepika was a toddler, I introduced her to *nachni* porridge, but to make it more attractive as compared to breakfast cereals like corn-flakes, I would add fresh milk, scraped fresh coconut, raisins, *caju* nuts and flavour it with nutmeg, cardamom and cinnamon. She enjoyed this porridge and now feeds it to her husband and to her baby since he was six months old and started taking solid food.) In coastal Maharashtra, to increase the nutritional value of *nachni*, people sprout the grain, dry it and then powder it. This powder is eaten as porridge or added in lesser quantities to milk or butter-milk as a health drink.

Turmeric (*haldi)* was grown in our own compound. August 1 is the day when Goans make *paatoyo* (ground rice paste, filled with scraped coconut mixed with jaggery coated in *haldi* leaves) which are steamed to make a wonderfully flavoured sweet. (My daughter got married in Goa on August 4, 2007 and the caterer, on his own, provided us with typical Goan food, in addition to the various fancy foods which formed the wedding buffet lunch. Among these were *paatoyo* of which I was fortunate to get the last one.) *Haldi* tubers are dug up around end-September, cleaned of earth and boiled. These are then dried thoroughly in direct sunlight in our *angan* for at least five days. Then these rhizomes are rubbed between sacking to remove the outside skin and what is left is *haldi* that we get in the market. Today most people only know *haldi* powder, very rarely do you see whole fresh or dried haldi for sale. Gujaratis incidentally make a pickle of fresh *haldi* tubers.

Amba haldi is a different type of turmeric which is not used as a spice, but as a medicine. I was told that the famous singer, Lata Mangeshkar, would chew on a small piece of *amba haldi* early each morning and this helped to keep her voice pure. *Amba haldi* ground into a paste with vinegar and *feni* is most beneficial for sprains, etc.

Granny also grew ginger in our compound. Fresh ginger is always used in food, but some dried ginger is used in medicines, particularly for coughs and colds. There is a large demand for fresh ginger from European countries, but because ginger rots when packed (pressure on the rhizomes) it has been very difficult to export fresh ginger.

In Rangoon, milk was always available, probably delivered by the delivery man direct to the kitchen early in the morning, but we had never known that a cow or buffalo or goat was the actual producer of milk. At Nachinola, Granny had two goats and she milked them in the morning and again in the afternoon. There was just enough milk for our coffee in the morning and tea in the afternoon. Plus there were their kids to play with, but we had to keep a wary eye for the mother goat, as she would charge and butt us if her kid bleated and she thought it was in danger. To prevent the kids having extra feeds, the goat's udders were covered with a cloth bag.

One of the female pigs (sow) had a litter of ten piglings – small and pink. Iza was most keen to play with one of them and set out to catch one. She managed to entice the sow and the piglings into the house and into the sitting room, where she had already closed the front door and the door leading to our bedroom. Immediately the family was in the sitting room she closed the passage door and then inched open the front door and the sow went out, but she closed the door immediately so all the piglings were locked into the sitting room. Then she tried to catch one, but these youngsters were very fast and though their hooves kept slipping on the tiled floor she could not catch one. While she was chasing them they were squealing at maximum volume, to which the sow responded with savage grunts and tried to re-enter through the main door. Then suddenly Iza got the fright of her life when the sow suddenly jumped up at one of the windows – her head and front legs were well above the window sill – and seeing her brood trapped inside let out a really savage grunt. Iza promptly ran out of the room through the passage calling for Granny to help. When Granny came and called, the sow quietened and when the front door was opened she took her brood off with her normal encouraging grunts. I am sure Granny must have given Iza quite a scolding and, probably more in fear of what the sow might have done, she never again tried to catch a pigling.

Granny Leopoldina kept some fowls. Eggs were collected every morning from the small hen house in the back portico. We were amazed to watch one of the hens sit on a dozen eggs and hatch out beautiful little fluffy yellow chicks. When the mother hen took her brood out into the compound someone had to keep watch as kites would swoop down to grab a chick. It was beautiful to see how immediately when she sensed a kite in the sky, the mother hen would cluck, calling her brood and they would all run and shelter under her wings, with sometimes one who was bolder peeping out through the top of her mother's wing. These fowls were of the local breed. In 1947 when Gerry shifted from Dandeli to Shivrajpur he brought Granny his flock of Rhode Island Reds – beautiful birds, much bigger that the local breed. The Rhode Island Red rooster was a huge fellow and was named Booty by Granny. When he walked through the house, his footsteps on the tiled floor of the sitting room sounded as though a full-grown man was walking in.

As recounted earlier, *caju feni* was another home industry, but the *feni* manufactured was only for home consumption. *Caju* fruit was collected from the hills, care being taken to separate the seeds and leave them on the ground for the owner to collect. Granny Leopoldina had a special sort of walking stick with a nail through the end. She would stick this nail into the *caju* fruit and thus pick it up remove the seed and then place the fruit in the basket which she carried. *Caju feni* has a very strong and distinct flavour and if one drinks it regularly, your whole body, particularly your urine, reeks of this odour. The Germans, marooned in Goa when their ships were sunk in Mormugoa harbour in 1941-1942, enjoyed *caju feni* but did not like the odour. They tried various methods to remove the odour, but the resultant product, though odourless, was not at all appealing to their taste. Now *caju feni* is available off the shelf in fancy bottles, but Anju swore that none of these came anywhere near Granny's matured-in-the-well product. He preferred *caju feni* to imported whiskeys like Johnny Walker Black Label and Chivas Regal, which I brought back from the duty free shop at Heathrow. I am told that *caju feni* is now being exported and has been given a sort of GI (Geographical Indication) – the name can be applied only to the product distilled in Goa.

Thanks to these agro-industries, Granny had by and large managed for herself from 1917 when Grandpa Sylvester had gone to France till 1945 when Grandad's insurance money reached her after his death. Anju and later Gerry had sent her money from time to time, but for her basic requirements she was largely self-reliant.

Later she organised quarrying of laterite stone from the solid rocks to the right and behind our house. This stone, being hard, was in demand for house building. One holiday Granny asked me to check her accounts of payments to the workmen who cut the stone and the cartmen or builders to whom she sold the cut stone. Basically there was a profit margin, but considering the rice, liquor and other household necessities she gave the workmen and their families who resided in our out-houses, I personally believe she was really doing social service. I had hoped that we could have used stone from our own quarries when building our house at Porvorim in 1970, but by then Granny was too old and the quarries were no longer in production.

In 1946 when we were on holiday in Goa, we found that

Granny Leopoldina had given up breeding goats and instead now kept a buffalo. This buffalo was bought by Granny in Belgaum and one of the men staying in the outhouse went with her and led the buffalo on foot all the way from Belgaum to Nachinola. The buffalo was pregnant when Granny bought her and she had calved just before we arrived. Iza and I had a new pet with whom to play.

The mother buffalo would be taken to the fields to graze after being milked in the morning and would be brought back around 16:00, when she would be bathed at the well and given plenty of water to drink. As soon as she entered the compound she would call to her calf and the young one would immediately respond and both Iza and I together could not hold her back. She was again milked at about 18:00 when she was fed with a mash of bran and oil cake. Then she would be tied up in her stall with plenty of hay to chew on.

Granny Leopoldina named this calf Mogra. Every afternoon, after she and all her animals had had their lunch, Granny would take her siesta in her bed (located in the dining room). All her pets, the dog, the cat and Mogra would come into the dining room and distribute themselves around her. The cock, a huge Rhode Island Red, called Booty, with his harem would perch on the head rail of Granny's bed. She would talk to them. As Mogra grew she found it more and more difficult to enter through the narrow back door. Finally she was too big to come through the door and she would stand in the back porch with her head in the doorway piteously calling to Granny. When she had grown quite big, she would go with her mother to graze in the fields. But as soon as she returned she would come to the bedroom window near the well, stick her head inside and call loudly. Granny would have to come and give her a snack, only then would she go to have her bath and drink water. When Anju came down for a holiday, he would take a *po-ee* (a circular bread made by a bakery from wheat bran) and feed Mogra when she called. Whenever, in later visits, Mogra heard Anju's voice, she would come to the window and call and refuse to move until she got her *po-ee*, and she would not budge if Anju offered her anything else. Granny grumbled that Anju was giving Mogra bad habits.

Now with a buffalo in the farm, Granny Leopoldina had milk in larger quantities, seven to ten litres per day, most of which she sold to customers in the village. Whenever there was excess milk, she would convert it into *case* (cottage cheese) by putting a drop of sour lime juice in the milk and stirring it while still warm. The curd would separate and she would place this curd in small wicker baskets each lined with fine muslin, so that each cheese was 4" in diameter and an inch thick. These baskets were then stacked one over the other and a weight placed over them. This would press out the whey and form the cheeses. These cheeses would then be placed in a brine solution and sold, if not consumed at home. Manufacture of cheese from milk is something the Portuguese thought us Goans, as well as other Indians in Bandel and Chittagong in eastern India. This type of cottage cheese is the base for all Bengali sweets, e.g. *sandesh, chum-chum, rassagoolas.* Whey is a refreshing drink if we were home – otherwise it went into the *dhon.*

Another by-product from milk was *ghee* (clarified butter). Granny would separate the cream – buffalo milk has between 7% to 11% fat – and churn it in a bottle with a number of fresh water rinses to wash out most of non-fat milk solids. Water from rinsing the milk fat was put into the *dhon* for dog, cat or pig food. She would heat this fresh butter with some added spices on a low fire with a ripe banana. All remaining non-fat milk solids adhered to the frying banana and clarified *ghee* was left. The fried banana with crisp browned milk solids adhering to it was delicious to eat and we would fight for it.

Surprisingly Granny never turned excess milk into *dahi* (yogurt or curd); in fact *dahi* was not eaten at that time by Christian Goans in Goa, who classified it as *Koknen che jevon* (food of the Hindus). There were no refrigerators then and in Goa's heat (even during 'winter') milk would curdle within at most four or five hours, hence conversion into cottage cheese and ghee had to be done twice a day. In north India, with more severe summers, fresh milk is consumed early morning and what is left is converted into *dahi* latest by 11:00 hours – *dahi* and *lassi* are served during the afternoon. Fresh milk is again drunk in the evening or night. This practice is gradually dying out since most people now have refrigerators and can store fresh milk. In spite of pasteurized milk being supplied to most Indian cities now, people still prefer to boil milk before use.

Another enterprise, not really for the market, was the felling and conversion of palms and other trees into useful products. When a tree stopped fruiting or it was not a fruit bearing tree, Granny would have it cut down and worked on. The trunk of a palm tree was split into two and each half hollowed out to form channels to be used to carry water from our wash basin to the plants in the garden. Trunks of solid trees were sawed into planks by hand with one man mounted on the top of the cutting trestle and the second pulling the large saw from below. Some of these trunks were required to be cut so that it could be dragged over the seeded paddy fields after ploughing and seeding. To shape this the men used an *adze*, a kind of axe with the blade at right angles to the handle. It looks very simple to use, and I tried and got the blade onto my leg just above my ankle, it took out a neat piece of flesh with little bleeding. I applied Dettol ointment and bandaged it with cotton wool but, as I did not wear socks to hide the bandage, Granny was quick to spot this and I got quite a scolding. From a mango tree that was cut down she made a tuck box for me to take up to school at Mount Abu (to save me from Customs Duty at the Bombay docks). I still keep this box, which is now my tool kit. Some of the main beams supporting our tiled roof are from our own trees. Minor branches were used as firewood, which were dried and stacked in sheltered areas, to ensure availability of dry firewood during the monsoon.

Green bamboos were the basis of another small industry. Wives and daughters of the men who worked in the quarries, sliced green bamboos into long strips, which were then woven into mats and various types of baskets and *supras* or *sups*. I marvelled at the intricate and numerous designs of baskets which these illiterate women could weave. However, with the introduction of cheap goods made mostly from recycled plastic, this basket weaving industry is being killed throughout Goa and in Maharashtra also.

On the Burma Front

A FTER recruitment and about ten days loafing around in Bombay, the Army finally organised the training for these young civilians who were now Viceroy's Commissioned Officers (VCOs). They were sent to Baroda for a month's basic training. This involved P.T., marching drill, handling of small arms and personnel management. And then off to Assam and the Burma Front to join the Fourteenth (XIV) Army also referred to as the 'Forgotten Army'.[7]

Anju, because of his previous experience in handling provisions, was deputed to the Canteen Stores Department (CSD). His superior officers were Major Bratley, who till recently had been manager of the Army & Navy Stores in Calcutta, and Major Clements. They were expected to build and equip warehouses for the various types of materials (mainly food, clothing and liquors) required by officers and soldiers at the front. They then had to

---

[7] The Fourteenth Army continues to remain a 'Forgotten Army' even today as far as India's contribution to World War II is concerned. The Burma Star Association, which honours and keeps track of Britishers who fought on the Burma Front, claims that they have no record of Burmans, Anglo-Burmans, Anglo-Indians and Indians, male and female (WAC(I)s and nurses), who also fought, many of whom died, on the Burma Front. Normally all the Indian Army Regiments as well as those from East and West Africa were commanded by Britishers. However one Indian, K.M. Cariappa, actually commanded a Regiment consisting of Indian troops with their British officers. India was also not invited to take part in the golden jubilee celebrations held in London in memory of V E and V J Days. This Burma Star Association also seems oblivious of the nineteen Victoria Crosses awarded to Indians and Gurkhas for their gallantry on the Burma Front.

set up the organisation for receiving, sorting and properly storing all goods and ensuring that the various units received their requirements in proper time and in good condition. This job was made all the more difficult since these units were all the time on the move, either going forward into Burma or falling back under Japanese onslaught. The CSD had to ensure that they were not feeding the enemy.

Each man at the front carried emergency dry rations on his person, which could keep him going for 48 hours. But fresh supplies had to reach them well in time. In addition to the problems of getting supplies to the various units, Anju had to keep in mind the different diets of each unit. Some were vegetarian, others would not eat beef and pork but eat other meat and fish, and still others would not eat pork but would eat all other kinds of meat or fish. Canned meat from Australia and New Zealand included corned (bully) beef[8], bacon and various types of sausages, but canned Indian food was then not available.

They had a couple of deaths of officers due to ptomaine poisoning – food poisoning caused by bacteria or bacterial products – because of eating bully beef straight out of the can. The can had probably been damaged in transit and the exposed meat had deteriorated in the heat. Thereafter, bully beef in 5 lbs. tins would be opened into large cooking vessels, onions, potatoes and spices added and the whole thoroughly stirred and cooked to ensure that all toxic germs were killed.

Diego had also been recruited into the British Indian Army and was posted to the victualling section. He was in charge of the actual cooking of food for the troops. This involved training Indian cooks to be posted to various base camps. Like Anju, he was posted 'somewhere on the Assam/Burma front'.

Base kitchens were set up where Indian and European food would be prepared. Units relieved at the front would come back to base to rest and recoup (R&R) and eat freshly prepared food.

---

8   'Bully' beef is tinned corned beef, an anglicized version of French *bouilli*, from *boeuf bouilli* (boiled beef).

Anju, with his basic cooking skills, got the Indian cooks (most of whom had no cooking experience whatsoever and were probably not of the 'right' caste) to turn out tasty and nutritious meals for the other ranks. He believed that these soldiers would definitely fight better if they were properly fed.

Anju told this story of a bet taken by two English officers in the Mess at Chittagong:

First Officer (F.O.): I can eat anything.

Second Officer (S.O.): Are you willing to take a bet of Rs.100 that you will eat anything I put before you?

F.O.: Sure, but it must be edible – if I refuse then you must eat it.

S.O.: You're on.

The Second Officer then went to the market in Chittagong and purchased a brand new aluminium conical chamber pot. This he got his batman to clean thoroughly. He then deep-fried three Oxford sausages (these are skinless beef sausages about one inch in diameter and three inches length) till they were an even brown colour.

These he placed in the chamber pot and poured a pint of beer complete with froth over them. This dish he served up to the First Officer, who took one look, almost brought up and refused to eat this meal.

The Second Officer calmly ate the sausages, drank the beer and claimed his Rs.100!

In the Officer's Mess there were English, Anglo-Burman, Anglo-Indian and Indian officers. Initially there was some opposition by the freshly arrived English officers to the fact that they were expected to eat 'Indian' food. Anju, who was in charge of the kitchen, decided to humour these English officers. The Mess would serve up English food for everyone on six days of the week,

but on the seventh, Sunday, an Indian meal would also be prepared for the Indian officers and any others who opted for this
meal. English food was usually 'bully' beef served up in different forms with little or no spices, with boiled potatoes and vegetables (out of cans). On Sundays the cooks prepared chicken
or mutton curry and rice, or *biryani* or some type of *korma* with
chapattis or *parathas* (spicing duly toned down for the palates
of the Englishmen). After some time, these same English officers
started demanding Indian food not only on Sundays but throughout the week. (In retrospect, maybe this move by Anju might
have started the trend which has resulted in *chicken tikka* becoming the traditional English dish in today's England even though
there is a move to patent this delicacy claiming that it is a U.K.
invention. More seriously, a 2009 news report said England was
to say "goodbye to bully beef" and that "the cornerstone of the
(British) Army for more than a century, is to be replaced by mush-
room pasta and halal dishes". *The Telegraph* also reported that "if
the trial is successful then a new ration system with 20 different
menus, plus six new ones for vegetarian, Halal, Sikh and Hindu
dietary requirements, will place corned beef hash firmly into the
history books and museums".)

At Chittagong they could get fresh chicken, eggs, fish, prawns,
mutton, beef and vegetables. But at forward bases they de-
pended on canned foods and condensed or powdered milk and
egg powder.

As the Army advanced from India into Burma, the CSD had to
move forward. They had a bad fright when suddenly the Japanese
broke through and almost surrounded their base camp. All men
at this base camp were non-combatants, cooks, batmen, water-
boys and the like. The officers were armed only with revolvers.
They were fortunate that there was an army unit behind them in
R&R (rest and recreation). This unit was ordered forward and the
immediate threat disappeared. They were bombed and strafed
by Japanese planes, but at this stage of the war the Japanese
had few planes and were operating from distant airports within

Burma and could not maintain pressure on the British Army. Anju's hearing was affected due to proximity of bomb explosions and artillery fire.

Many British Indian Army units were well within Burma. The Gurkhas, particularly, had earned themselves the reputation with the Japanese of being near invincible. Japanese snipers, in green jungle camouflage, tied themselves high up in trees and from there waited for British troops to advance and then picked out and aimed at the officers. When such snipers were located, the Gurkhas had little mercy and usually killed them with their *kukris*. They had no time nor desire to take prisoners. Japanese soldiers captured behind the advancing Gurkha troops were known to surrender pleading, "Save us from those guys with baggy pants." In a total of thirty Victoria Crosses awarded to troops in the Burma Campaign of 1942 to 1945, eleven were awarded to Britons, eleven to Punjabis (of pre-Partition Punjab) and eight to Gurkhas.

Transporting supplies to these forward units was becoming more and more difficult. Trucks could not be used because of a lack of proper roads and steep gradients, so mules were brought in. The CSD men had to go forward dragging these loaded mules through the jungle along narrow paths which were exceedingly steep. In the rains the going got even more difficult. The CSD had special extra strong rum, which they stocked only for the mules, who were given this when they developed a chill. Getting this stuff down the mule's throat was quite a feat. A tube was inserted into the mule's mouth, and the other end was attached to a funnel. This special rum was poured into the funnel and, hopefully, was expected to flow down the mule's throat. Often the mule got the better of the person trying to dose him by gripping the tube in his teeth and blowing up through it. The rum splashed all over that person who now smelt as though he had been on a binge.

Going on to Calcutta

NOW that Anju was posted at the Burma front, Ivy decided that we should go to Calcutta so that it would be convenient for Anju to come home even for a short leave. Immediately after the school year closed in April 1944, we packed up and left Goa by train for Calcutta.

As we were approaching Bombay, we experienced the same smell of death as when we had left Rangoon. This was because of the great Bombay Docks Explosion on April 14, 1944, when the SS *Fort Stikine*[9], loaded with bales of cotton, ammunition, explosives and gold bars, exploded. Many of the buildings along the railway line were in ruins and probably many dead bodies remained buried in these ruins. We read of great stories of honesty, when people returned two-kilogramme bars of gold blown into their houses or onto the roads.

(In 1951 Captain Victor Sampson invited us for a cruise around Bombay Harbour on his suction dredger. Noticing a strong mesh over the hold into which the sludge sucked up by the dredger was discharged, I asked him why this was necessary. He mentioned that this had been installed to ensure that gold bars sucked up from the bottom of the harbour were not lost. His

---

[9] *Fort Stikine* was a British Fort ship built in Canada in 1942. Leased from the US by the British Ministry of War Transport under the lend-lease scheme, *Fort Stikine* had only a short career, and was destroyed in an explosion at Bombay, in April 1944 that killed over 800 people and caused the loss of a further thirteen ships.

dredger had been responsible for finding a number of gold bars. Many gold bars had probably been sucked up and discharged at the dumping ground before that mesh was installed.)

Anju met us in Bombay and we travelled by a Military Special to Calcutta. Anju, now Captain, being the senior-most officer on the train, was made Officer-Commanding (O-C). We were allotted a four-berth first class compartment. Most of the passengers were British Other Ranks (BORs), but in an adjoining first class compartment there were four English lady nursing officers.

There were some British officers also in the other first class compartments. In first class compartments, as there was no air-conditioning at that time, a large block of ice in a tub was placed in each compartment, the steel shutters were closed and the overhead fans switched to maximum speed. The melting ice kept the compartment cool even though outside the temperature must have been over 100°F. Accommodation for BORs did not appear to be very much different from that described by Captain William Pennington, MC (Retd). His book *Pick up your Parrots and Monkeys – The Life of a Boy Soldier in India* during the 1930s makes references to the toilets as holes in the floor and bunk berths with little space to sit up.

We left fairly late at night. In the morning the train stopped at a major station. All the officers and the four of us had to go across to the refreshment room for breakfast. We stopped for lunch at another major station. Anju stayed with the train to ensure that the BORs were served a proper lunch; there had been some complaints about breakfast. Ivy, Iza and me crossed the lines (there was no foot over-bridge) and went to the refreshment room. Being about the last to arrive, we had to sit separately. Iza found herself next to one of the English ladies from the next compartment. We were faced with a battery of knives, forks and spoons, such a place setting as we had never experienced before. Iza did not know how to start until the English lady graciously showed her which implement to use. I just went ahead and used what I thought fit. Iza, as usual, was eating slowly, and before she finished one course the next was being served. Her plate was removed and a fresh plate given to her for the next course. Again she was eating slowly and her plate was removed and a fresh plate given for the third course. She was not even able to finish her dessert as we had to rush back to the train. While I had eaten my fill, Iza was left hungry even after being served a very substantial lunch.

Fortunately, when we got back to the train, some of the BORs, who had enjoyed their lunch, the preparation of which Anju had supervised and also partaken, were happy to give us their K-rations[10], which would normally have been all they had during the journey. These K-rations, double sealed in waxed paper, contained packets of hard chocolate, biscuits, chewing gum and other eatables, plus cigarettes, the last of which we gave back to the original owners. For dinner, Iza made sure she ate enough. We reached Howrah the next morning before lunch.

Anju reached us to Grace Antunis' place in Chandni Chowk, which is now long known as a busy and colourful market. We would stay there until the Army was able to acquire a flat for our use. With only three of us, the same small room was not as crowded as when nine of us had stayed here on arrival from Rangoon. Even though we were on the third floor, the noise level was far greater than what we had experienced in Goa. We had no furniture and used our trunks as tables and slept on the floor. Ivy bought some crockery and cutlery, a saucepan and kettle with a kerosene stove on which to heat the food and make our tea and coffee. We had to share the common bathroom and toilet.

A Chinese family was living on the ground floor of this building. They must have owned a restaurant as the women every morning would knead a large quantity of flour with eggs, roll out the dough and slice it into thin strips to make noodles. These were then dried on sticks in the small enclosed courtyard. One of

---

10 The K-ration was an individual daily combat food ration which was introduced during World War II, also in the US. It was originally intended as an individually packaged daily ration for issue to airborne troops, tank corps, motorcycle couriers, and other mobile forces for short durations.

the Chinese ladies wore special shoes and walked in an awkward way. I then noticed her very tiny feet. I learnt much later that this was because her feet had been bound as a little girl as per the earlier Chinese custom. There were a number of children, but we never got to know them because we started school immediately. None of these younger girls had their feet bound.

Anju introduced us to Edward Martyres from Nachinola, who ran a boarding house on Dharmatala Street. He agreed to send us lunch and dinner. The food was really very good and more than adequate for the three of us. In addition to supplying us with our lunch and dinner, Edward later ensured that we had good East Bengal cooks during the years we stayed in Calcutta. These cooks were Christians, with Portuguese family names like Gomes and Remedios. They all came from the Chittagong area and were descendants of people converted by the Portuguese some four centuries earlier. When we came to live in Bombay we discovered that these East Bengal (now Bangladesh) cooks were really top quality chefs, and many sophisticated Bombay hotels employed them to turn out first class non-vegetarian dishes, particularly sea-food.

Edward's elder brother, Benjamin, was a teacher in St Xavier's School and also owned and ran the Wyse Bakery and Confectionery at Moulvi Lane, with a retail shop in New Market. The delivery man from Wyse Bakery came around every morning with a box on wheels and gave us our requirement of bread. Milk came every morning in bottles from Keventers' Dairy, in payment for which we had to buy coupons in advance. Ivy and Anju met the accommodation officer at Fort William, who promised to inform her as soon as decent accommodation became available.

Anju then left us to return to his post at the Burma Front. Ivy next took us to get admission into school – me into St Xavier's at Park Street and Iza into Loreto Convent at Dharmatala, which was just around the corner. Since Calcutta schools followed the calendar year, we immediately started attending classes. Ivy later got appointed as a teacher at Loreto Convent, Sealdah, and Iza shifted from Loretta Dharmatala to Loreto Sealdah.

From Dharmatala there was no direct tram to Park Street, so I would travel by tram to Elliot Road and then walk that last block to St Xavier's. The tram fare was paid by buying coupons in advance, which were handed over to the conductor one on each trip. I soon made a number of new friends, including Joe Martyres, Benjamin Martyres' son.

About a month later, Agnes with Noellyn came from Goa and stayed with us. Noellyn (now two and a half years old) could speak Konkani fluently, but while she understood English she would not talk in English. In the late afternoons, the Firpo's ice-cream cart came around ringing a bell. Immediately we would request Ivy for money and run down to buy ice-cream sticks (popsicles). Ivy told us to buy one for Noellyn. She took one lick and pushed it away saying, *"Oon aha!"* (It is hot!) She had never experienced ice coldness in Goa and had no word to express herself. After allowing the ice cream to melt, she licked the plate dry and demanded, *"Anim zai"* (I want more).

With Agnes and Noellyn sharing this one small room, this accommodation became crowded. We temporarily shifted to part of someone else's house where we had two rooms, with bath and toilet and the use of the kitchen. Anju and Diego spent Christmas 1944 with us. I remember them arriving on Christmas Eve and leaving before the New Year. Diego volunteered to cook our Christmas lunch. He cooked a dish of meat with potatoes, but it got over cooked and turned into a 'mess'. I remember asking Diego whether this is the sort of food served to the soldiers and hence the name 'mess' for their dining room.

The military accommodation officer temporarily allotted us a flat on the first floor of a three-storied building further down Dharmatala Street.

While this flat was fairly large, it was dark as only direct afternoon sunlight entered the bedroom windows. We had one bedroom for the three of us and a separate bedroom for Agnes and Noellyn. From the bedrooms to the large sitting-dining room one had to come through corridors whose sides were open. Between these two corridors was a triangular space which extended from ground to top floor and was open to the sky. The kitchen was beyond the sitting-dining room. We used whatever furniture had been in this flat. We had a *jemadar* who would sweep and mop the whole house and clean the bathrooms. I think we employed one of the East Bengal cooks. Since the entrance to the flat was into the sitting room, one had quite some distance to cover from bedroom to the front door, and servants could leave without any one noticing them. It was in this house that the gold carriage clock, awarded to Anju by Sun Life Insurance Co. in 1934, kept on the sideboard in the dining room, disappeared.

I had a classmate, Gomes, an East Bengal Christian, who lived in this area. Both of us would walk through the Taratola (Taratala) area to school each morning and walk back in the evenings. With him I made more friends in the immediate neighbourhood and we used to play 'robbers and police' between the buildings. All the buildings in the area had boundary walls about head high. We would climb and run along them in and out of adjoining building compounds chasing each other.

In January 1945, thanks to Ivy's regular visits to Fort William to remind the accommodation officer of our need for a proper flat, we were allotted the entire first floor of a single storied bungalow in Taratola Lane (behind Wellesley Square, later renamed Haji Mohd. Mohsin Square). Entrance into the compound was through a large gateway, with high wooden doors, which were usually shut. On the ground floor, three Anglo-Indian families lived, two below our flat. The third family lived in the garage on the right as you entered, which had been converted into a residence. Our bedrooms therefore got the full benefit of the morning sunlight. Since we were waiting to go back as soon as Burma was re-occupied, we did not buy furniture, but hired what we required including a piano.

One day there was quite a commotion in the *bastee* in front of our house, and one of the children from there came to call Ivy for her assistance. A vulture circling above the area had got entangled in some kite string and unable to fly landed in their central courtyard.

There it found it could not take off (too short a runway) and kept walking around. One of the old ladies tried to shoo it off, and it pecked her arm, taking out a triangle of flesh, with surprisingly little flow of blood. Ivy entered the courtyard through the door of the man-of-the-house. She instructed him first to open the main door leading to the road and gradually directed the vulture out on to the road, from where it was able to take off. Then she immediately cauterized the wound to get rid of bacteria which must have come from the vulture's beak. She bandaged the lady's arm and sent her off to the hospital to have the wound properly treated. Thanks to Ivy's prompt action, the lady did not suffer any ill effects and the wound healed fairly soon. Thereafter for every *Id* they would send us a *balti* (bucket) full of *biriyani*. This *balti* of *biriyani* was too much for the three of us and even after sharing this with the three Anglo-Indian families in our bungalow there was too much to eat at one meal. We realised the full extent of the gratitude of this Muslim family during the pre-partition Hindu-Muslim riots in 1946-47.

Edward sent us a very good Bengali cook, Benedict Gomes, who turned out fantastic food. The dish I particularly liked was brain *masala*. His *parathas* made with whole wheat flour with multi layers in concentric circles were most delicious. While studying or playing on the terrace, the aroma of Benedict's food from our kitchen below only built up our appetites.

Benedict would serve us breakfast, usually Quaker oats, with coffee. He would make and give me sandwiches for my lunch at school. One day, because we awoke late or because the porridge was too hot, Iza and I left our porridge uneaten. That night we were served an appetising looking pudding. On tasting we discovered it was our morning's porridge, thickened and a little butter added. We did not dodge eating our porridge thereafter.

After breakfast, Benedict would go off to buy meat and vegetables and cook lunch. He took lunch for Ivy and Iza at their school, Loreto Sealdah. On his return he would prepare some snack for our tea. After serving us tea, he would give Ivy an account of his purchases of meat, vegetables and the like. Ivy would give him instructions for the next day's menu with money for provisions. He would then go off and start preparing dinner.

I normally walked to school. My friend, Gomes from Dharamtalla, would call out as he was passing our house and the two of us, joined by more friends along the way, would reach school in time for a game in the grounds before classes commenced. Ivy and Iza usually took a rickshaw to get to school.

Zig-zagging across the middle of the play ground at St Xavier's was a slit trench built up with bricks and cement and banked with earth – a bomb shelter in case of any Japanese bombing or strafing. We used to race across the top of this trench jumping from one side to the other while playing 'robbers and police'. One morning while playing I slipped and slid down the embankment on my stomach and scraped my knees thoroughly. I had to go to the infirmary where a Jesuit brother cleaned and dressed the wounds. I finally got to class an hour late and was surprised when my class teacher instructed me to go to the principal for permission for coming so late.

Now that we had a proper house, we accepted the offer from Tecla Menezes (Anju's God-mother) of a couple of pups, whom we named Nelson and Mitzi. They were black and white furry dogs. Iza would put Nelson, when he was a pup, on one of our roller skates and push him around the house. He seemed to enjoy this. Mitzi would stay clear of the skates.

Ivy once decided to make gooseberry jam. She had got our cook to put a *chula* in the open verandah and she cooked the fruit in a big *dekchi*. As she was going out, she instructed Iza and me to stir the mixture continuously so that the jam did not get burnt, but did not tell us when to stop. We kept stirring the mass until the whole *dekchi* was moving with the ladle. We took the *dekchi* off the stove and left it to cool. All through this operation Nelson was most interested. When we tried to take some to taste after it had cooled we discovered that it had become a sort of stick-jaw. Nelson begged for some. We gave him a nice big lump of this stick-jaw. It stuck to his pallet and he could not get it loose and started running round and round the house.

Once in a while Ivy would accompany the three of us, Iza, Noellyn and me, with the dogs. We would go to Eden Gardens (Calcutta's famous *maidan)* for a long walk. Ivy would treat us to Firpo's popsicles (ice cream on a stick), the dogs also got an ice-cream cup each. While passing through New Market we would stop at Wyse Bakery and buy some cakes or pastries. Other favourites were barley sugar and *amsaad* (caked layers of sun dried mango pulp).

The variety of fruit available in New Market was large and Ivy usually bought a good supply. In Calcutta we discovered *lytchees,* a fruit that we had never tasted in Burma or in Goa.

Although St Teresa's at Sealdah was our parish church, we often went for Sunday Mass to Sacred Heart Church, Dharmatala. We would meet a number of friends after Mass, including Balbino and his family, who had recently come to Calcutta from Goa. On the way home we would stop at Nizam's for a breakfast of *halva purees* (small *parathas* with *halwa* made from semolina. (When I went back to Calcutta in 1958 on work, I stayed at Great Eastern Hotel and went for Mass to Sacred Heart Church, Dharmatala. I decided to eat breakfast at Nizam's, but found a huge pile of garbage just in front of their entrance. In December 2009, I found Nizam's a very much cleaned up restaurant, but they had discontinued preparation of *halva purees.)*

Anju, posted at the Assam-Burma front, had his CSD Head Quarters in Calcutta. He was required to visit the HQ from time to time, and whenever he did so he was able to visit us and stay at least a couple of days, usually over weekends. On one such visit, he took all three of us to the canteen at the corner of Free School Street and Park Street. This had been set up for officers' families. I was amazed at the amount of food that was available

– particularly chocolates, like Cadbury's, Nestle's and Mars. Apparently there was no demand for these chocolates by officers at the front. Ivy bought such a large quantity that I was able to take a bar of chocolate with me every day to school to eat with my lunch. Chocolates were not easily available in the Calcutta market. (During this same period, as I discovered in 1978, friends of my age group in the U.K. could get at most one bar of chocolate per family per week.) Frozen beef and mutton from Australia and New Zealand were also available. Plus a huge variety of tinned products, mostly Australian, I specifically remember IXL jams.

The Guns Fall Silent

T HE War in Europe came to an end on V.E. Day, May 8, 1945. For all practical purposes the war in Burma ended on May 3, 1945, when Rangoon was re-occupied by a single RAF pilot, after the Japanese had fled. Unfortunately there is no record of the name of this RAF officer. Mopping up operations continued in Burma, Malaya, Siam (Thailand), Indonesia and Singapore for months thereafter.

The condition of British, Indian and Australian POWs in Japanese camps was so pitiable, many near death from starvation and disease, that even before the official Japanese surrender Admiral Mountbatten ordered all POWs released from the camps in which they were imprisoned and immediately hospitalised and treated.

Japan's final collapse came with the dropping of atomic bombs on Hiroshima on August 6, 1945, and on Nagasaki on August 9, 1945. Formal unconditional surrender of the Japanese Empire was accepted on September 2, 1945, by General Mac Arthur on the battleship *USS Missouri* anchored in Tokyo Bay. Senior representatives of all the allied forces – Australia, Britain, Canada, China, Netherlands, France, New Zealand and Russia – were present at this formal surrender. (Surprisingly, India which had contributed so much both in men and materials to the war effort was not represented. Also at the Golden Jubilee celebrations of VE Day in 1995, India was not officially invited nor were we accorded any gratitude for our contributions.)

The formal unconditional surrender of all Japanese forces – land, sea and air – in South East Asia was made to Admiral Lord Louis Mountbatten of Burma at Singapore on September 12, 1945.

During the war Anju never mentioned the location of their camps. After the war ended he told us of all the places they had been in, including Kohima, Cox's Bazar, Imphal, Chittagong, Comilla, Mymensingh. After reading Field Marshal Viscount Slim's book *Defeat Into Victory*, I now appreciate Anju's experiences.

A Return That Didn't Happen

After V E Day, Grandpa Sylvester Philip wrote to Anju that since civilian travel was now allowed, he had booked his passage by ship from Toronto to U.K. and onwards to Bombay, departing from Toronto on August 5, 1945. But on August 3, 1945, Anju received a telegram from Grandpa's solicitors in Montreal that Grandpa had died of a heart attack on August 1, 1945.

The solicitors asked for his instructions regarding execution of Grandpa's will, which followed the telegram announcing his death. As Anju was in the middle of the now critical phase of winding up operations on the Burma Front, he requested them to send all correspondence to Gerry in Dandeli and to take instructions from him. This they did and Gerry received Grandpa's money, including the settlement from his life insurance policy. As there were no banking transactions between India and Goa, Gerry had to take all this money to Granny in cash. (British Indian currency was accepted in Goa for normal commercial transactions, but one had to pay a premium and convert to *escudos*, the Portuguese currency, to pay Goa Government taxes and fees.)

From this money, Granny Leopoldina paid Bemvinda (and Salu) her dowry, which had not been settled at the time of her wedding in 1930. As per Portuguese Government procedure, Bemvinda and Salu signed a document at the *Regis Civil* (Civil Register) at Mapuça confirming receipt of this amount and that they had no further claim on Grandpa's and Granny's estate in Nachinola. One copy of this document was given to Granny Leopoldina and one copy to her daughter Bemvinda and husband Salu.

There was only one bank in Goa, *Banco Nacional Ultramarino,* the Portuguese Government bank, which had branches in Panjim, Margao, Vasco da Gama and Mapuça but did not offer banking facilities to ordinary people. Therefore Granny Leopoldina deposited the balance with Mhambro, the grocer who supplied all her requirements. He had his shops in Aldona and Mapuça. She had a little note book in which he would list the supplies made to her and their value and then show the balance in her account. I do not recall whether or not he paid her any interest on this money deposited with him. From what I remember of entries in this note book, Mhambro dealt very fairly with her and at no time did she complain that he was taking advantage of her trust in him.

(At that time the British Government was offering 200 acres of land in the prairie belt of Canada to officers who had served at the Burma front, together with a loan to help them build a house and purchase machinery to develop that 200 acre farm. I often wonder what the future would have been if Anju had accepted repatriation to Canada and established himself as a farmer there. More so since all Bemvinda's children and their families are now settled in Canada. Ivy's niece, Marie Pereira, and her family also emigrated from Karachi to Canada.)

Demob'ed from the Army

Diego was de-mobbed and left for Rangoon with Agnes and Noellyn on the first available ship in October 1945. For Christmas 1945, Anju was able to get 'long leave' – all of ten days. He arrived home on December 24 morning. We went together for Midnight Mass, but were up early on Christmas Day as Anju had promised to take us shopping for our Christmas presents. For me,

Ivy had made a replica of Anju's uniform (without the epaulets, of course), which I proudly wore that morning.

Col. Brately, Anju's O.-C., an Englishman, came over to our house for dinner as he was also on leave in Calcutta. That morning Anju personally went to the market and purchased king-sized prawns. He himself cooked them into a special chilli-fry, with lots of onions, garlic and, of course, red chillies. Iza and I could just about eat one prawn each, the dish was very pungent, but Col. Bratley enjoyed it. Between each mouthful he would take a large sip of whiskey and soda. He had gone red in the face and was sweating profusely, but continued with what he called the most delicious dish of prawns he had ever eaten.

Grandma Cheron, who was with Amy at Dohad, planned to join Diego in Rangoon. She now came to Calcutta, with Amy, Tim, Noel, Mayrose, John, Philip and Celine, to celebrate Christmas. This turned out to be a family re-union with Balbino and family also being in Calcutta. Virtually every day was a party, with birthdays and Christmas and New Year being celebrated.

During one afternoon, Ernest, clowning as usual, dressed up in one of Ivy's dresses, put on Ivy's hat and inserted two bowls to imitate breasts. We took a photograph of him in this outfit. Later we showed this photograph to his mother, Annie, and she kept looking at it and said "I know this lady, she is very familiar." She did not recognise her own son and was amazed when we told her.

We visited Alipore Zoo and Kidderpore Lakes as well as Victoria Memorial and Ochterlony Monument, now called Shaheed Minar. Eden Gardens (the *maidan*) was an every-evening walk. We also visited Bandel, which involved a train ride. At the botanical gardens we were able to climb up the 250 year old banyan tree, which is said to cover 10 acres, and walk fairly high off the ground along its spreading and interlinked branches.

Tim, Amy and Noel left for Dohad on January 2, 1946. John, Mayrose with Philip and Celine stayed on. Celine was just five months old and on February 8 sat up on her own for the first time. We were all around her clapping and laughing and did not notice that Grandma, who was diabetic, was not with us. When she did not come for lunch, Ivy discovered that she was in coma and sent for the doctor. He gave her some medicines, but she did not recover and died on February 9 morning. She was buried at the Lower Circular Road Cemetery, a beautifully laid out graveyard with plenty of shady trees and flowering and evergreen bushes. John, Mayrose, Philip and Celine returned to Ajmer and Mount Abu shortly thereafter.

Transfer to Poona

Now that World War II was finally over, the CSD depots at Chittagong and other places in North East India were being closed down. Anju was busy with winding up operations. A lot of stores had still to be sent into Burma, as units of the British Indian armies were still on duty in various places.

On June 7, 1945, the Secretary of State for India announced that the period of service in the Far East was to be reduced to three years and four months as far as repatriation was concerned, and that any man who had exceeded this was to be sent home at once. Many of the English officers, some of whom had been at the front since 1942, without a chance of going on home leave, were relieved and allowed to go back to England. Americans, and East and West African troops were repatriated. But CSD had still to cater to large numbers of BORs, particularly those wounded or sick with malaria and other diseases, who could not yet be sent home. There was, however, no longer that sense of urgency.

Finally in February 1946, Anju was relieved at Chittagong. As Captain, he was transferred as Officer Commanding to the newly set-up base at Lohegaon Airport, Poona. BORs, waiting for demobilisation, were being sent here to await ships to carry them home.

These men, waiting to go home, were in low spirits as ships to transport them were not readily available. All their food was provided free, but they had to pay for their drinks. They looked forward to their pint of beer each evening. But, after being stored for long in our hot climate, Anju noticed that many beer bottles would open with no fizz or froth. This caused a lot of grumbling. Anju got one of his *lascars* to squat just below the bar counter out of sight and shake each bottle of beer and then give it to the barman to open. The resulting fizz and froth was good and the BORs enjoyed their beer.

To cheer them up, Anju organised volley-ball, carom and table tennis tournaments and as prizes dispensed his stock of beer. He was keen to clear all stocks before the last BOR left, which would otherwise need to be destroyed.

Poona–Goa holiday

During our summer holidays in 1946 we went to Poona and stayed with the Pimenta family, as Mr. Pimenta was now Oriental's Poona Branch Manager. The family had rented a large double storied bungalow at Pool Gate at the end of Main Street.

Anju came here each evening after work, had dinner and stayed the night. Jimmy, Edigio and I would go with him back to his camp each morning, spend the day there, have lunch and return with him in his jeep around 16:00. I was required to do my holiday home-work during this period. In the evening all of us kids, including my future wife, Eslinda, who was only four years old, would go to play and fly kites at the Golibar Maidan (now occupied by the Defence Accounts Building).

The Lohegaon camp was huge, but by that time most of the BORs had been repatriated. Almost all the *bashas* (temporary shacks) were empty. It was like a ghost town. Anju's driver allowed me to drive the jeep in the camp area without letting Anju know. One evening when we got back to Mr. Pimenta's house, before all of us got out, the driver left the jeep to take Anju's brief case and papers into the house. He had left the jeep in gear. While I was getting out between the two front seats I must have accidentally kicked the gear lever and the jeep started to slide down the slope. I had the presence of mind to immediately haul on the hand brake. Anju thought I was trying to drive the jeep and I got a whack, since there would have been quite some trouble if the jeep had rolled down to the Pool Gate cross road and ploughed into people and vehicles.

Gerry, who was posted at Western India Plywoods, Dandeli, joined us in Poona. Ivy, Iza and I went with him to Dandeli, which was off a branch line from Londa. This factory was located in dense jungle. Large circular saws cut the tree trunks to the specified length. These logs of wood were then sort of shaved into thin sheets, which were then flattened. Three or more layers, laid at right angles to each other, were glued together to form plywood. The noise in the factory was considerable and one had to be very careful of moving logs.

Gerry had a small cottage to himself and a woman from the nearby village came and did his cooking and housekeeping. There were wild animals in this jungle and early each morning spotted deer would come grazing right up to his back door. In fact Gerry had been given a tiny spotted deer fawn, whose mother must have been killed by man or animal, which some loggers had found in the forest. Initially he fed her from a baby's feeding bottle. She was very tame and everyone's pet. He called her Chitra. Spotted deer are dainty and walk as though on tip toes. She would follow him every-where, even into the factory. So to protect her he put a bell around her neck, to caution the men working that she was near, and be careful. Finally, for her own safety, he had to tie her up at home when he went to the factory. She would cry pitifully when he left her and cry again as soon as she saw him coming home. Once home he would release her. At night she was kept indoors, but was released early morning.

Chitra discovered that the lady in the next bungalow sat on the floor at the door of her kitchen and made *chapattis* for her family's breakfast. She would roll out a *chapatti* on her left, bake it on the *chula* in front and put it into the plate which was to her right and slightly behind. Once, the lady called out to her husband to come and take the *chapattis*. When she turned to give him the plate there were no *chapattis*, and she saw Chitra walking away still chomping on the last of the *chapattis*, many of which she had already eaten. Although she laughingly complained to Gerry, she did not beat Chitra who was very much loved by her whole family. Thereafter, *chapattis* were specially made for Chitra.

When she was fully grown, Chitra tried to join a herd of spotted deer that came grazing just behind Gerry's bungalow. But, hearing the bell around her neck, these wild deer ran away and Chitra tried to follow them. After some time she returned obviously very tired. Gerry realised that he could not keep her as a pet and took off her bell. The next morning when the herd came to graze, she joined them and moved off. She would come back with the herd whenever they were grazing near the bungalows, but Gerry was careful not to try to call her as he would frighten off the herd and it was best for her to remain with her kind. Chitra's bell was kept at Nachinola house as a memento.

After spending a few days at Dandeli, we took the train to Londa and changed to the train for Goa. Gerry, who travelled back and forth quite frequently, knew most of the running staff on the Londa–Goa sector and we travelled like royalty. The first class compartment, in which we travelled, had an observation platform at the back and standing there we really enjoyed the scenery *en route* to Goa. We reached the Dudh Sagar waterfall in the afternoon and for our benefit the driver stopped and we were able to go down to refresh ourselves with the wonderfully cool water. We left the train at Collem and went on by bus to Mapuça.

Goa's brass-bound buses of those times were unique. These small buses, Chevrolet and Ford of pre-1939 vintage, were plated with sheets of brass, regularly polished so that they shone like gold. Though designed to carry maybe 16 passengers, with great persuasion the driver and his assistant would manage to squeeze in up to thirty or more people, not counting children, from whom no fare was collected.

Petrol was rationed and in short supply. The driver's assistant would be perched on the front mud guard with the side panel of the bonnet open and a bottle with petrol in his hand. This was because when climbing a hill, the little petrol in the tank could not be sucked up to the engine. So when climbing, the petrol suction tube was disconnected from the main tank and inserted into the hand-held bottle.

From Mapuça, we hired a taxi to take us directly home to Nachi-nola – and the taxi drove right up to our house through the widened driveway. We were fortunate to arrive in the middle of the mango season. Granny had plucked seasoned mangoes and placed them on hay spread on the floor of the second bedroom. In this room she placed one large basin filled with water and a second empty basin.

After breakfast, Gerry, Iza and I were told to go into that room, select ripe mangoes and eat them then and there, first washing the mangoes in the basin of water. The skins and seeds were to be placed in the second basin. After we had eaten our fill, in my case six mangoes each day, we washed our hands and face in the basin of water. This washing did not rid us of the stickiness of mango juice which seemed to be all over us, so Gerry and I had a bath at the well, which was most refreshing in the heat of day. All the mango skins and seeds were then given to the buffalo and pigs, who also enjoyed them.

Those ripe mangoes that we could not eat, Granny Leopold-ina would select and take into the kitchen, where she squeezed out the juice and pulp into a large copper vessel, added sugar and placed for slow cooking on the *chula* in which the fire had burnt down to embers. Each day she added pulp, juice and sugar into this utensil and stirred the whole mass. Gradually this thickened into *mangaad*. Granny packed it for us to take to Anju in Poona and for us to carry on to Calcutta. We were careful to ensure that the container would not burst in transit.

Jackfruits were also ripe and ready for eating. One variety of jackfruit produced soft, pulpy fruit, which was not liked as much as the firm variety. This jackfruit pulp, Granny would spread on large teak leaves and put them in the hot sun to dry. After about three days of drying, the pulp could be peeled off the leaves and stored in bottles to be eaten during the rest of the year.

There were other types of mangoes, which were not for ripening and eating. These were converted into pickle when green. These mangoes were first thoroughly washed and wiped with a cloth, then cut into quarters, kept in a large earthen pot and salt was added liberally. The next morning these pieces of mango were placed in the *angan* to dry, but not completely. After a couple of days these mango pieces were mixed with pickle *masala*. Vegetable oil – groundnut or *teel* (sesamum) oil – would be heated in a large vessel and, when boiling hot, poured over this mixture and thoroughly stirred. After the mixture had cooled it would be filled into already cleaned and dried ceramic jars with wide mouths with threaded covers and sealed for at least six months. Granny also made sweet chutney from green mango slices or grated green mango.

Green mangoes from either the eating or pickle variety, which dropped on their own, were not thrown away. Some we sliced and ate immediately as *korum* (a salad with salt and green chillies). Sliced fresh green mangoes were added to prawn and fish curries. Small green mangoes (without firm seeds) from one tree in the small field between our house and Dr Silveiro's were used for making *chepne aam* (salted mangoes) by placing these alternatively with layers of sea salt in a large jar with a heavy weight over them. After about a month the resultant wrinkled mango was an ideal pickle to eat with *kanjee*. (I tried without success to persuade some of the bars in Goa to use *chepne aam* as a replacement for olives, when imports of these were restricted after 1961.)

Other green mangoes, in which the seed had already formed, were cut into thin slices on an *addo* and put into an earthenware vessel with plenty of salt. After soaking for three or four days, these were dried to make *ambea-che sola,* or mango skins, which (like *binda-che sola*) was added to fish and prawn curries.

After about ten days we returned to Poona and again stayed with the Pimentas but only for one night. Early next morning Anju, Gerry and the three of us left by the Deccan Queen for Bombay. In Bombay we stayed for a couple of days with Gabriel and Theresa Sequeira (Fr Damas' relatives). With Allan Sequeira, I travelled by tram on a one anna transfer ticket from Colaba all the way to King's Circle. Allan also took me through a hole in the fence across the BB&CI railway line to the sea front, at Cuffe Parade.

Anju and Gerry saw us off on the 'One Up – Bombay–Howrah Mail via Nagpur' the following night. This time we were treated as ordinary first class passengers, no special status of the train O-C's family. We were back in Calcutta in time for school re-opening.

Back To Burma

A NJU completed his assignment of repatriating BORs (British Other Ranks) from the camp at Lohegaon Airport, Poona and was demobbed in December 1946. With the intention of returning to Burma and again working in his chosen field of life and general insurance, Anju had visited companies in Bombay who were planning to re-establish themselves in the insurance business in Burma. He was interviewed by Gresham Assurance Co. Ltd and appointed to start their insurance business in Burma.

Gresham had appointed William Jacks & Company as their business agents in Burma and Anju was instructed to take charge of the insurance business in Rangoon. He came to Calcutta and gave us the news of his appointment. After a short stay with us in Calcutta he left for Rangoon, arriving there on December 12, 1946. Ivy, Iza and I were to follow as soon as he had established himself in Rangoon.

When Anju returned to Burma, he together with his cousins, Arist, Alphonse, Isabelle and George, hired the upper floor of Diego's house, till they could find other suitable accommodation. Isabelle and George later shifted to a flat of their own.

Captain Victor Sampson, whose ship was in harbour, had visited Anju one night and, as it was too late to return to his ship, had slept over. Anju gave Victor a *baambi* (loose Shan pants tied around the waist with a knot in the cloth) to wear, a mat to sleep on and a pillow. It was too hot to wear a shirt or vest or for any covering. During the night, Victor's *baambi* came undone and he had kicked it off in his sleep. When the maid entered with the morning tea, she got a shock and dropped the tray with all the cups of hot tea.

William Jacks were also distributors for English language movies. While waiting for the necessary clearances to start the insurance business, Anju was asked to help in the movie business. This entailed giving previews of the films to the cinema owners and obtaining bookings from them for the various films. Payment for hire of the films was based on attendance. Some cinema owners tried to claim low attendance and thus pay less. Anju had to visit various cinema houses for all the shows (15:00, 18:00 and 21:00) and estimate the attendance. This was a thoroughly boring job as it meant watching the same film again and again and again. He therefore persuaded friends and acquaintances (including the Vaz boys, who were attending colleges in Rangoon) to attend different shows; he would refund them the ticket money plus a small amount for snacks. These guys would give him a report of attendance. This worked better, as the cinema ushers never knew who was coming to check attendance.

Britain decided to give Burma total Independence in January 1947. Immediately, Burmese was made the medium of instruction in all schools and colleges. It would now have been very difficult for Iza and me to study in Rangoon. Consequently, Ivy decided that we should enter boarding schools and she alone would join Anju in Rangoon. Since Mayrose was teaching music in Mount Abu in both the boys' and the girls' schools, she wrote to her about getting us admitted in those schools. Anju had been given special permission by the Burmese Government to remit money to Ivy for her and our maintenance.

When Anju went back to Rangoon in 1946, he met Bella's daughter, Marie, and her husband, Albert Pereira. Albert had been posted from Karachi to Rangoon by BOAC (British Overseas Airways Corporation, the British state-owned airline created in 1940, now British Airways).

Things in Burma deteriorated further with the assassination of Aung San and six of his ministers on July 19, 1947. Aung San was considered the Father of the Nation of modern-day Burma (Myanmar), and initially Communist and later Social Democratic politician, revolutionary, nationalist, founder of the Tatmadaw (Mynmar Armed Forces).

The grant of Independence on January 4, 1948 did not see any improvement in the political situation. In spite of unsettled conditions or possibly because of this insecurity, Anju's insurance business was in full swing before the end of 1947. His old friends, particularly Burmese and Shan, were keen to buy insurance policies from a well-known English company. He purchased a Morris 8–1938 model car, but had quite a job getting it operational, since during the war with no regular supply of petrol, the then owners had used all kinds of fuel. He had to get the engine completely stripped, cleaned and re-fitted.

Anju came on leave to India in June 1948 and with Mum visited me at Mount Abu. Ivy and Anju stayed in the guest room above the Mount Abu bus station, exactly opposite the gate to the Polo Grounds. For the days they were at Mount Abu, I was permitted to leave school immediately after classes were over and return just in time for classes in the morning, while being expected to complete my home-work. and study. Brother Looram, an American GI before joining the Irish Christian Brothers, got on really well with Anju, both of them having a lot in common and plenty of stories to exchange.

Iza had meanwhile joined the J J School of Art in Bombay and was staying at Villa Theresa Women's Hostel on Cumballa Hill. Because of the chaotic political situation in Burma, Anju dissuaded Ivy from returning with him. Anju, on his return, found the situation deteriorating further. Gradually the Burmese Government introduced various curbs on foreign business houses. Remittance of money out of Burma was restricted. As a consequence he could do very little insurance business. It was also no longer safe to move about because of insurgencies by various eth-nic groups in different parts of the country.

Indian papers in Bombay kept reporting the worsening conditions in Burma. This affected Iza so much that she wrote a letter to the General Manager of Gresham Assurance Co. in Bombay requesting him to transfer her father, Anju, back to India. Gresham meanwhile did decide to close down its insurance business in Burma. Anju was transferred to Bombay effective May 1949.

India gets Partitioned

On March 22, 1947, Lord Louis Mountbatten of Burma arrived in Delhi as Viceroy-Designate. He had been specially deputed by King George VI, Emperor of India, and the British Parliament with Attlee as Prime Minister, to finalize terms for grant of Independence to India.

His job was to prove far more difficult than anyone had expected. The Indian National Congress, which had been clamouring for Independence since 1922, could not make up their minds regarding how to deal with minorities, particularly the Muslims. Many of the numerous Princely States claimed direct allegiance to King George VI and did not want to be (sub)merged in the new democratic India. A further complication was those Princely states where the ruler was Muslim but most of his subjects were Hindu, or vice versa.

Even though their states was not contiguous to either East or West Pakistan, some of these rulers expressed their desire to merge with Pakistan. Pandit Jawaharlal Nehru and Mahatma Gandhi wanted India to remain whole and secular, while Mohammad Ali Jinnah wanted to split India, so that he could be Governor General of a Muslim country, Pakistan. He was suffering from terminal tuberculosis and knew that he had only a few months to live, so he wanted to go out in a blaze of glory. Sardar Vallabhai Patel was largely responsible for winning over the many Muslim *rajas* to join our Indian Republic.

With the possibility of some areas going to Pakistan (East or West) and other areas remaining in India, Hindus and Sikhs of the Punjab, in areas where they were in the majority, took up cudgels against their Muslim neighbours alongside whom they had lived for generations. In areas where Muslims dominated, Hindus and Sikhs were at the receiving end. In the Sealdah area of Calcutta, there were hundreds of Hindu refugees who had fled from East Bengal, now East Pakistan, and they continued to live in the shanties there up to 1970s. Thousands were murdered in their own homes and on the roads and railways, while fleeing from riot affected areas. No actual count has yet been arrived at as to how many people were killed during the riots which preceded and followed the partition of British India into the independent countries of India and Pakistan (East and West) on August 14/15, 1947.

There were incidents where brave Hindu and Sikh police and army officers were killed while protecting Muslim refugees whom they were escorting, and other incidents of brave Muslim officers killed while doing their duty of protecting Hindu or Sikh refugees. There are also incidents where Hindu policemen joined rioters in killing Muslim refugees and vice versa. We were told in Calcutta of one incident where two groups of policemen, one Hindu and the second Muslim, who were deployed to quell a riot between the communities, instead of shooting the rioters aimed at their own colleagues of the opposite religion. Finally British troops was called out and shot to kill both rioters and opposing police forces.

In Calcutta we were witness to riots which commenced from August 1946 and continued till well after August 15, 1947. At the early stages of these riots, shops were looted irrespective of who owned them – Hindu or Muslim or others. You saw people carrying sewing machines, bicycles, bales of cloth and various household items running through the streets. After law and order was temporarily restored, the police carried out house to house searches and arrested those people in whose homes looted goods were found. As a result, overnight there were piles of sewing machines and other items lying on garbage heaps.

We were living among *bastees* (slums inhabited by the poor) populated by Muslims. During this period, Muslim men all around us would remain awake and alert all through the night shouting *"Lā ilāha illā allah – Allahu Akbar"* (...there is no god but Allāh..., God is the greatest) from roof-top to roof-top, since there were mobs of Hindus going around setting fire to Muslim homes and killing those who tried to escape from the infernos. With these continued cries interspersed with sporadic gun fire, we could not sleep or if we did fall into a fitful sleep, we woke with a start.

Later *goondahs* were imported into Calcutta by both sides to actually carry out the killings and looting. One of the East Bengal Christians from the adjoining *bastee*, was wearing a white *longi* and not the checked *longi* worn by Muslims. Mistaking his white *longi* for a *dhoti* (usually worn by Hindus) a group of these *goondahs* attacked him and in spite of the fact that the Muslims from our area recognized him and shouted at these hooligans to stop attacking him, these *goondahs*, filled with blood lust, killed him using the wooden shafts of rickshaws which are tipped with iron. This incident took place even while we watched helplessly from our terrace. After killing him they opened his shirt and discovered a cross around his neck. His body lay where they had thrown it for three days since neither the Hindus nor the Muslims would remove his body.

Goondahs came to set fire to the house in which we were living because it was Hindu-owned. The Muslim family from the *bastee* opposite, where Ivy had helped an old lady, came and stood in front of our gate and prevented them from setting our house on fire. We were virtually imprisoned in our own house, not daring to leave in case the *goondahs* returned to set fire to our house. Ivy was a tower of strength not only to the two of us but also to the Anglo-Indian families living downstairs and our Christian East Bengal cook, Benedict, and his assistant,

Solomon. Benedict subsequently managed to get away, but there was no safe way of sending the young East Bengal Christian boy, Solomon, back to Chittagong. So Solomon, dressed in my shirt and shorts, stayed with us and was given the job of looking after the dogs.

When curfew was relaxed for a few hours each day, we would take the dogs for a quick walk, but garbage and dead bodies were everywhere even in Wellesley Square. Finally, in May, Ivy was able to get through to Fort William and beg for and obtain an army vehicle to take us, the dogs and our luggage to Howrah Station. From there we traveled to Delhi. Military protection was provided on the train. We were not permitted to leave the Delhi station, but just changed trains to the one that was to take us to Dohad that same night.

Ivy had booked our heavy luggage through to Dohad, where Amy lived. All of us went to Dohad where Solomon, the dogs and the heavy luggage remained while Ivy with the two of us and our clothes went on to Abu Road and then on to Mount Abu.

Mayrose with Philip and Celine and her mother-in-law, *Mai*, were at their home overlooking Nakkhi Lake. They had no news of John, who was on tour with his boss, the Inspector General of Police, Rajputana. Mount Abu was peaceful though; there had been no rioting.

We were immediately admitted as boarders, Iza in the Convent of Mary of the Angels and I in St Mary's High School (SMHS). Both of us started school on June 1, 1947, as these boarding schools held classes continuously from March to December with holidays from December to March.

Ivy went back to Dohad and arranged to store our luggage in the quarters of one of Tim's colleagues, who was a bachelor and whose quarters were almost totally bare. She went back to Calcutta, returned the hired furniture, packed the furniture which we needed and sold the rest for little or nothing. She returned the house to the Controller of Accommodation, Fort William, and returned to Dohad.

Anju had confirmed that the situation in Rangoon was not at all peaceful and that Ivy should not join him there. On returning to Dohad she was lucky to get a teaching post in St Joseph's School, Dohad.

The Inspector General of Police, Rajputana, an Englishman, together with Hindu and Muslim policemen who remained loyal to him, had guarded a transit camp filled with Muslim women and children at Jaisalmer. Their men folk had crossed the unmarked border, across a few miles of desert, into the new country of Pakistan. This small police force under the English IGP had quite a job saving these women and children from blood thirsty Hindu mobs until they could be escorted safely into Pakistan. When John returned to Mount Abu in August he gave us eye witness accounts of the harrowing scenes during that time.

From John's house, which was just below the Residency in Mount Abu, we saw our Indian tri-colour hoisted over the Residency at sunrise on August 15, 1947. We were all invited to a *burra khana*, served Indian style in *thalis* on the floor, at Rajputana Club that afternoon. All along the roads in Mount Abu even as far as our school (two miles from Mount Abu town) there were employees of the Maharaja of Sirohi distributing sweetmeats to all passers by. Boarders from our school took full advantage of this by going from one road to another so as to get extra helpings of these sweetmeats.

Protection of Muslim refugees by the English Inspector General of Police, Rajputana, was not appreciated by the newly appointed Indian government officials. As an Englishman the IGP had the option to stay on or go back to UK. After this experience he opted for the latter. John felt his future prospects were not likely to be good if he continued in this same job, so he resigned from government service and went to Bombay to look for a job. This was not an easy decision for someone with a family of wife, two children plus one more on the way, his aged mother and older unmarried sister. His resignation also meant giving up the house overlooking Nakkhi Lake. Fortunately Lawrence School, where Mayrose also taught music, had an empty staff quarter into which she could shift the family for the remaining three months of that academic year.

On December 7, 1947, all three schools closed for the holidays and Mayrose, *Mai*, Philip, Celine, Iza and I left for Dohad via Ajmer, where *Mai* left us to stay with her daughter, Mrs. Lina Pinto.

Trains at that time were excessively crowded and there was no security for passengers in any class. Thanks to John's previous association with the police, we were accommodated with our luggage in a third class compartment in which a group of policemen were traveling. We had to make do with just two lower and two upper bunks with our trunks and suitcases placed between the lower bunks to give us additional sleeping space.

On the route our train suddenly halted after crossing a high bridge over an almost dry river. A herd of cows, grazing along the railway line had stampeded, and some animals had run ahead of the train on to the bridge, from which they fell to the river bed. *Sadhus* travelling on the train pulled the emergency chain and insisted that they go down to the river bed to administer first aid to these fallen animals. Our train was delayed at this spot for well nigh two hours because of this. I do not think they were able to do very much for those animals, but their attitude was so incongruous, when human beings all over India were being killed without compunction.

We reached Dohad without any untoward incidents. We took over Tim's colleague's quarters and he shifted in with another bachelor colleague. While there had been Hindu-Muslim riots in Dohad city and the neighbouring cities of Ratlam and Godhra, there was peace within Dohad BB&CI Railway Colony.

There was an open ground between Tim's quarters and the shopping complex. This was a natural playground where we learned to cycle on hired bikes. Philip (4), Noel (3) and Celine (2) would walk across this open ground to Mr. Coelho's bakery for snacks. First-in-line Noel asked for one rupee's worth of biscuits, and Philip and Celine behind him put out their hands and were each given the same quantity of biscuits, but Noel only had one rupee. When Mr. Coelho asked for payment from the other two, all three promptly ran home clutching their biscuits. Mr. Coelho did not lose out as he got paid by Amy later, but these three scamps learnt the value of money that day.

In spite of communal strife all around, life in the Dohad Railway Colony that holiday was full of fun. Midnight Mass with a Christmas party was held that evening at the school hall. More parties, including a fancy dress party and an evening of sports, were conducted at the railway *gymkhana.*

An interesting fact in Dohad was 'pay-day sweets'. Every pay-day, the fifth of each month, a line of handcarts with a variety of sweet meats would form just outside the main gate of the Dohad Railway Workshop. Workers, flush with funds, would buy sweet meats to take home as they left the workshop.

Also standing at the gate awaiting the men coming out with their pay-packets were the Pathan money-lenders. Before proceeding home, the loanees had to pay these Pathans the instalment that was due, mostly interest. The original capital borrowed hardly got repaid and thus these loanees were indebted to the Pathans almost for life, at least for the rest of their working lives. If a loanee defaulted, he could end us with a severe beating or a broken arm, leg or head. Pathans showed no mercy to defaulters.

One Sunday, the three sisters, Ivy, Amy and Mayrose, decided to give us a Burmese meal. We were all roped in to help. I grated green papayas, Iza and Celine peeled roasted *chana* and peanuts, Noel and Philip pounded dried prawns, *chana* and peanuts. Solomon cut and deep-fried garlic and onions. He also finely cut *cothmir* and onion leeks. These ingredients were served up each in a separate bowl. Drumstick leaves and flowers were collected, to be boiled with dry prawns to make *hingyo* (soup). As there was no *ngapi* we had to add salt to taste. Each of us was given a cup of *hingyo.* Then we were served portions of the grated green papaya and had to add a little of each of the other ingredients and a teaspoon full of the oil in which garlic and onions had been fried. There was a small bowl of powdered roasted red chillies, for those who liked it hot. All these were thoroughly mixed by each with his or her own fingers and we enjoyed the *lettho* licking our fingers with gusto. Here too we missed *ngapi*. Tim, a thorough Goan, took one look at what we were eating and decided that this was a meal fit only for cows. He demanded and got his normal curry and rice, which in fact was the main meal, *hingyo* and *lettho* being mere appetizers.

Solomon had by them developed into a fine cook and his *parathas* were comparable with what Benedict would prepare. Running with the dogs he had fallen and broken his right hand, which was put into plaster. Thereafter, he would knead the flour with his left hand and I learned to roll out the *parathas*, which he would then fry. When the situation in Bengal settled to some extent Solomon was able to go back to Chittagong. After he left, Mum could not look after Nelson and Mitzi and they joined the Jesuits at Baroda.

The railway had built a central bath house in the middle of this open area. Once in a while the local tribals, *Bhils,* men and women, would come to this bath-house to have a communal bath. All of them would go in and scrub each other with bricks and sand, no soap, and then wear new clothes, discarding the old clothes which were frayed with constant use. It was believed, rightly or otherwise, that they never changed clothes between their half-yearly baths.

The men got back from the workshop around 16:30 and all of us would then play various games before dinner. On moon-lit nights, there was time for games after dinner also. One of these games was *gilli-danda*. On February 20, 1948, a Friday, they brought back from the workshop beautifully shaped balanced *gillis* and a purpose-designed *danda* cut from hard wood used in building railway carriages. We immediately decided to play *gilli-danda* to try out their products in anticipation of a tournament planned for this coming week end. The very first hit sent the *gilli* soaring high and fast and in my attempt to catch it, the *gilli* bounced off the edge of my palm and hit me in my right eye. That was the end of the game, and no one has spoken of *gilli-danda* since.

I was rushed to the railway hospital, where the doctor was probably more nervous that I was, and Ivy had to steady his hand when he examined my eye. I remember him pouring hot water into my eye, which was more painful than the injury itself. By morning he declared that there was nothing he could do, so Ivy decided to take me to Bombay for treatment, in spite of the fact that there was rioting in Godhra and the city was aflame. That night on the train, with the steel shutters down, you could see the glow of the fires and feel the heat inside the train.

At the Bombay Central Railway Station we were met by Gabriel (Sequeira) and taken direct to J.J. Hospital, where Tim's nephew, Leslie, was a medical student. Although it was Sunday, he had managed to persuade Dr. S.N. Cooper, the famous eye surgeon, to come to the hospital to inspect my eye and give instructions on the course of treatment.

His diagnosis was that an immediate cataract had formed and only after it was removed could he check if there was any damage to the eye. The cataract was removed the next morning and I was required to go to his private clinic each afternoon for the whole of the next week for dressings. He daily injected penicillin in oil just under the skin of my forearm. It raised a small bump and gradually, as the antibiotic was absorbed, the bump flattened. After a week the wound dressing was removed but I had to wear shielded dark glasses to protect this eye from dust. Unfortunately nothing could be done to give back sight to my right eye. At the end of one week he permitted me to go back to Dohad but I had to report back within a fortnight for a check-up. These fortnightly checks continued till end May, after which I was permitted to return to school. During my treatment and for the fortnightly check-ups Ivy and I stayed with Gabriel and Theresa, who were not directly related, but who deserved the title of Uncle and Aunt much more than direct relatives of whom there were quite a few in Bombay.

As a consequence of the excitement caused by my eye accident, Mayrose went into labour and delivered Frances on February 22, well ahead of her expected date of delivery.

While staying in Dohad, Mayrose had put out feelers for teaching jobs with the BB&CI railway. She was able to secure an appointment as a primary school teacher at the railway school at Ratlam (in the Malwa region of what would become Madhya Pradesh) effective June 1948. This entitled her to living quarters.

Meanwhile John had secured a job with Air India. Unfortunately the company was forced to reduce staff and, being one of the latest to join, he was retrenched. Through the good offices of his boss in Air India, he immediately got a job with BES&T and remained with them till retirement. Initially John stayed as a boarder with a Goan family at Kurla on the third floor. All the residents on that floor used a common toilet, where the waste went straight down a pipe to the bucket at ground floor level, which was periodically collected and disposed of by the *jemadar*. In spite of being on the third floor, rats and worms were able to climb up the inside of this almost vertical pipe.

For about two years John had to live separated from his family. His boss at BES&T who knew the general manager of the GIP (Great Indian Peninsular) Railway was able to influence him to get Mayrose transferred from BB&CI (Bombay, Baroda and Central India) Railway to GIP railway and appointed to their school at Kalyan, which had quarters attached, so that John could once again live at home with his family. He commuted daily from Kalyan to VT to his job at BEST (originally the Bombay Electric Supply & Tramways), Colaba. A later transfer to the GIP railway school at Lower Parel resulted in Mayrose being allotted quarters at Sion which they occupied till she retired and then shifted to their own flat at Everard Colony, Sion.

In spite of all the hardships John and Mayrose went through, there was always laughter in their house. They even adopted a little motherless girl, a neighbour in Goa who had a tough family situation. This little girl grew up as a sister of their children and was educated up to secondary school. A friend of the boys, a wonderful young man, surprised Mayrose with the request that he wanted to marry this young girl, after knowing her background. She made him a wonderful wife and mother of his three children who loved and respected her. Unfortunately cancer cut short her life.

While in Bombay for treatment of my eye and knowing that Anju would be returning to India sooner or later Ivy felt that admission to schools in Bombay might be better than continuing at Mount Abu. Accordingly we visited St. Xavier's, Dhobi Talao, but they had no boarding. Next on the list was St Mary's, Mazagaon, which had boarding only for 'Whites'. Finally, we went to St Stanislaus, Bandra. We had almost decided on this school as Iza could be admitted to St Joseph's Convent across the road. Ivy asked to be shown around the school and was quite impressed with the clean dormitory with steel cots, each with its own mosquito net. Surprisingly, the principal, a Jesuit Catholic priest, told us that this dormitory was for first class boarders. I would be in the dormitory for second class boarders who slept on bed rolls which were unrolled on the floor each night and rolled up every morning. I then asked the priest who the 'first class boarders' were: "Are they white-skinned?" I refused admission to this school. We then discovered that St Joseph's Convent also had first class and second class boarders, based on the colour of their skin.

I decided to go back to St Mary's, Mount Abu where the Irish Christian Brothers treated all of us – White, Brown or Black – equally. I rejoined school on June 1, 1948. Iza got admission to the J.J. School of Art, as mentioned earlier, and stayed at the Villa Theresa Women's Hostel, Peddar Road. Ivy stayed with Amy at Dohad, where she continued teaching at St Joseph's School till Anju returned from Burma.

On my return to SMHS the Sisters at 'Hospi' were instructed to apply penicillin eye ointment to my right eye every morning and every evening. I was not permitted to play games – football, hockey and cricket. I was permitted to take part in athletics, but I was only selected for the club drill and march past. When we again started playing football in October, I pleaded with Bro. Bennet, our sports master, to allow me to take part. Unfortunately during the very first game, I tried to head the ball, misjudged and the ball hit me in my right eye. I then realised I had lost my ability to judge distances, as I was seeing with only one eye. But it also meant "no more football".

Possibly as a reaction to the penicillin injections, I started getting very painful blind boils all over my body. These only stopped after I went home for the holidays in December and have never recurred.

Originally I was scheduled to spend this holiday in Dohad, but at the last moment Mum decided she would meet me in Bombay and both of us proceed to Goa. My trunk with clothes and books had already been consigned to Dohad, so we had to stay five days at the Bombay Central railway retiring room until my trunk, redirected from Dohad, reached Grant Road. At the Bombay Central retiring room I soaked in the bath tub and was dismayed at the amount of dirt that was deposited on the sides. After two additional soaping the water was clean.

After waiting five days for my trunk, we went by steamer to Goa where we enjoyed the Christmas tree and Bom Jesu feast. Mum arranged for a tailor to come to our Nachinola house and stitch virtually a whole new set of clothes for me as I had outgrown all those I currently had. Then she returned to resume work at her school in Dohad and I stayed on till March 5, 1949.

I came back to Bombay by steamer and brought with me plenty of tuck (some to be shared with Iza) viz. Trebor sweets, Nestlé chocolates, and other home-made sweets. These I could not pack with my clothes and books, so I carried them separately in a basket. On arrival at Bombay on March 6, 1949, I was surprised when the very considerate Customs Officer insisted I pay customs duty on these goods, even though he reduced it to the minimum. He advised me to carry my tuck in future in a trunk or suitcase.

Back in Bombay

On return to Bombay in May 1949, Anju reported to Gresham Assurance and was appointed inspector of agencies. His job consisted of appointing and training insurance agents and helping them to secure business. Other inspectors of agencies included Parsi, Gujarati, Muslim and South Indian gentlemen. Each had an impressive individual desk in one large office on the third floor of Gresham House at the corner of Sir Pherozeshah Mehta Road and Mint Road.

He met as many friends as he could immediately remember and started work. As to be expected, Anju's initial contacts were Goans and Anglo-Indians whom he had known earlier.

On arrival Anju stayed at Rocha's Boarding House at Crawford Market. Captain Victor Sampson, a friend from his Rangoon days, was now Dredger Master of the Bombay Port Trust. Victor's brother, Bernard, and his wife, were staying in a large ground floor flat at Star Chambers, Motlibai Street, Byculla and offered Anju one bedroom as a paying guest. Anju was happy to accept this accommodation until he could rent a house for all of us.

Anju experienced the Bombay cyclone and torrential rains of November 1949. Iza, a hostelite at Villa Theresa, had spent that weekend with Anju, and was with him when the flat was flooded. She used her tee-square to keep measuring the water level inside Anju's room, which reached 15 inches, just below Anju's bed. If the water level rose any higher they would have had to raise Anju's bed. They had moved everything else onto the desk and on top of the wardrobe.

I came down from Mount Abu with the Bombay batch of boys on December 8. As the train slowly moved forward the name 'Bombay Central' became visible one letter at a time and all of us craned our necks to read the letters and confirm that we were home. Anju met me at Bombay Central and I was happy to introduce him to a number of my friends and their parents. We went to Motlibai Street, which was virtually around the corner.

There were traces of the recent cyclone everywhere. The entire flat had a musty smell as the walls were still damp. Trunks of large uprooted trees partly obstructed roads. When we cruised around Bombay harbour in Capt Victor Sampson's suction dredger, there were ships lying on their sides in the harbour.

Ivy came from Dohad and all four of us spent Christmas together. Anju had reason for celebrating since he had achieved far more business than the target set for him by Gresham.

After celebrating Ivy and Anju's wedding anniversary on December 28, I went to Goa to be in time for Bom Jesu Feast at Nachinola on January 1, 1950. Ivy returned to Dohad to finish the academic year. She had already submitted her resignation to take effect from February end.

Around Motlibai Street, a number of SMHS boys resided. Anju had met their parents at Bombay Central while waiting for the Bombay batch to arrive. These parents together with their sons and daughters had organized a picnic to Elephanta Caves, to which they had invited the Brothers, who after Christmas and New Year at Mount Abu, enjoyed a month's holiday at Palmgrove Hotel, Juhu. Anju enjoyed himself at this picnic and made a number of new friends. He became particularly friendly with Bro. George Bennett, whom he initially took to be husband of one of the young ladies and father of one of the boys.

I returned end-February to the Motlibai Street flat. This time all the tuck I brought back from Goa was in my new wooden tuck box which ensured that I paid no Customs Duty.

Anju had been house hunting and discussed with us the various flats he had seen and the two he had short listed. One was a large flat on Queen's Road near Churchgate Station, which involved payment of *pugree* or *pagdi* (cash premium) of Rs. 2,500 and monthly rent of Rs. 200. The other was a paying guest accommodation on first floor of a single storey bungalow at Bandra next to St Anne's Church, fully furnished with two bedrooms (one large and the other smaller) with full length front verandah, sitting room, dining room and kitchen for our use at monthly rent of Rs. 200. An important condition was that we had to prepare all meals for the landlady, who occupied the third and largest master bedroom. There was a large attic with an ornate staircase leading to it, but we were not given access to this.

Iza immediately opted for the flat at Churchgate; it was closer to town and the the latest movies. Ivy and I felt that we may not be able to sleep with the noise of local trains through the night. Anju felt to be in town would be convenient for work, but also felt the Churchgate flat would be too noisy.

We went ahead and shifted to Bandra on March 1, 1950. In hindsight all of us regretted this decision, as each flat in that building on Queen's Road near Churchgate was later sold to the respective tenant for Rs. 10,000 as the building was declared 'evacuee property' since the landlord had migrated to Pakistan in the aftermath of Partition.

I had only seven days in which to explore the surroundings, but we loved the open country-side with St Anne's Church just about 100 metres from our house. Since the church was on a hill, Anju claimed that he would be able to participate at Mass from the front verandah.

We had left my trunk with my school clothes and books and my tuck box (filled with goodies from Goa, out of which I grudgingly gave Iza some) at Mr. Sampson's house, from where we handed it to the Brothers on March 6 to be booked with the luggage of all the other boys to Abu Road. With change of trains at Ahmedabad, this ensured that our luggage reached Abu Road on the same day or ahead of us. On March 7 evening, Ivy, Anju and Iza came to see me off at Bombay Central station.

It was great fun meeting all our school friends again. While many of the Mums and sisters were crying at our departure, we boys were happy. One problem of getting three months' holiday was that it did not coincide with the holidays of friends in Bombay. They only had a fortnight's holiday at Christmas, and boys in Bombay schools also had their final exams in April. So, while in Bombay, most of us had to fall back on SMHS friends for company after the locals went back to school in January.

Anju had to commute from Bandra to his office every day. He would take the BEST bus from Perry Road terminus to Bandra Railway Station, then the Harbour Branch train of the GIP Railway to Victoria Terminus (VT), from where it was a short walk to his office. He could alternatively take the BEST bus, but that went through Ballard Estate and one wasted time waiting for the bus. He soon had a fixed time table and thus had a regular group of traveling companions on the bus to Bandra Station and on the train to VT. It was fun to watch as one or other of these travelling companions tried to pay the bus fares of his friends; it must have been just two *annas* each.

Iza also commuted to J J School of Art, which was almost opposite VT. She had a number of college mates, boys and girls, living in Bandra, who travelled as a group. As both of them had first class season tickets, only Ivy and I had to buy tickets whenever we went into Bombay to meet friends or attend any function.

Later when I attended St Xavier's College from June 1952, I also traveled on a first class season ticket (at student's concession) on what had now become the Central Railway – Harbour Branch. (GIP and BB&CI Railways had been nationalized on November 5, 1951 and converted into Central Railway and Western Railway respectively.)

First class compartments on the Harbour Branch were fitted with luxuriously upholstered bench seats, each meant for three but which usually seated four without discomfort, with plenty of leg room and elbow space. There were overhead racks for briefcases or hand luggage. Unlike long distance trains there were no toilets attached to the compartments of these local trains.

Since I returned from college in the afternoons, the train was almost empty and I could relax. I usually napped until the smell of the Bandra slaughter house woke me up in time to detrain. I remember I overslept only once and had to come back from the Khar station, fortunately without being caught by a ticket collector, or TTC.

Getting back home at night was sometimes a problem. The last BEST bus from Bandra Station to Perry Road left at 22:00 hours, so if we missed this bus we had either to walk home or take a taxi. There were probably only five taxis available at Bandra station in those times; so you could not be sure of hiring one. The last train from Churchgate for Borivali left at midnight and the next train was at 05:00. When attending any house party, particularly those at Uncle Gabriel's house, one had to constantly watch the clock and leave well in time to board at least the last train from Churchgate. We could not attend the last (21:30) show at any of the cinema houses in town. Fortunately, Christmas, New Year and Easter dances at Catholic Gymkhana continued till early morning and we could take the first or later train back to Bandra.

On March 21, 1952, the Senior Cambridge results were published in the *Times of India*. I found that all eighteen of our class had passed. Bro. Morrow sent my detailed results in a few days. I had done very well and had earned a scholarship from the Association of Anglo-Indian Schools. I could not, however, avail of this scholarship as it was intended for Anglo-Indian children and one had to prove that one or other of your parents or grand-parents was born and was registered in Great Britain. Our family prides itself of being thorough-bred Goans, without any foreign blood in our veins.

I had decided to join St Xavier's College and as soon as my detailed Senior Cambridge results were with me, I went to college, was assured of admission and told to come back in June after the SSC results had been declared.

Just about this time, Gerry, who had set up his own diesel engine repair workshop in Secunderabad, came to Bombay to buy a car. With time heavy on my hands in Bombay, I persuaded Gerry to allow me to drive down with him to Secunderabad. He readily agreed and we left early one morning, drove to Poona and stepped in at the Pimentas to wash and freshen up. Mrs. Pimenta insisted that we have lunch with them. Then we drove down to Sholapur – the road was not macadamised, but of beaten earth. Passing trucks raised huge dust clouds and there were not too many cars on the road. When it grew dark, you could see approaching trucks from quite some distance by the glow their head lights created. Many of these trucks had chains of coloured lights all around the driver's cabin, so they looked like moving Christmas trees. By around 10 p.m. we stopped at a roadside *dhabha*, had dinner and then both of us squeezed on to one *charpoy* and slept for a while. We were up around 5 a.m. and, after a quick wash and some tea, were on our way. We overtook a truck, which Gerry recognised as belonging to one of his clients and whose engine he had recently overhauled. He waved to the driver and pulled up a little ahead. The driver stopped but was afraid that he had been pulled up for some offence by RTO officials. He had difficulty recognising Gerry, we were covered in red dust, and dishevelled. As roads in those days had no road signs, he gave us detailed instructions on how to reach Secunderabad without loss of time.

Although he owned a car, Gerry still preferred to use his motor cycle with sidecar for going to and from his work shop. Initially, I went with him in the morning, stayed the whole day with him, eating lunch sent by Molly and going home with him in the evening.

After about a week, he encouraged me to go back home by bus for lunch and then go sightseeing in the afternoons. I would take the green double-decker buses to visit various areas of Secunderabad and Hyderabad. I remember going to the Hyderabad end of the Hussain Sagar bund road and seeing a film in which the theme song was 'City side-walks dressed in holiday style'; the snow scenes were quite a contrast to the weather outside. I visited a handicrafts exhibition, where for the first time I saw Bidriware, black metal with silver inlaid designs. This is metal handicraft from Bidar in today's Karnataka, which was developed in the 14th century C.E. during the rule of the Bahamani Sultans.

Gerry entrusted me with my first purchase job. He urgently needed a fly-wheel for an old imported diesel engine that had come to him for repair, and gave me the address of a dealer in Bombay from whom this flywheel was said to be available. I met this dealer and he quoted a price much above what Gerry had estimated. So I decided to visit a few other dealers thereabouts and was lucky to get the same flywheel at a price lower than Gerry's estimate. Taking the dealer at his word and without phys- ically checking the flywheel, I purchased it and had it wrapped in gunny for transportation. I paid the dealer cash and immediately took it with me to VT and boarded the train for Secunderabad. When Gerry opened the parcel, he was dismayed to find that this flywheel, though unused, was very rusty, being old stock. He had to polish it before he could fit it to the engine being repaired. I learnt that not only the price but a detailed check of specifica- tions and visual inspection was essential when purchasing any goods. You cannot trust dealers.

After an enjoyable stay of about two months I returned to Bombay, well in time to join St Xavier's College.

I stayed for about two months with Gerry and Molly and got back in time for admission to St. Xavier's College. I started college on June 20, 1952. After an introductory talk by Fr. Melchior M. Balaguer, the Spanish Jesuit principal, we were permitted to roam around the college. All rooms were kept open to students. I was most impressed by the botany and zoology museum. There were beautiful stuffed specimens of various Indian animals, some of which I had never heard of before, let alone seen.

In the first year science that year there were three divisions, each with 75 students, in alphabetical order. In our Division III there were 21 boys with the surname D'Souza. Eugene (Ginger) Reghilini, from SMHS, Allan Saldanha, Uncle Gabriel's son, and Carl Soares, Jovian's son, were my classmates.

Since Anju, Iza and I traveled from Bandra to Bombay every day, I proposed to Anju that we buy a car and get it registered as a taxi. I would drive all three of us to town in the morning, attend lectures, ply it in the afternoons, when I did not have science practicals, and then pick up Anju and Iza and drive back to Bandra in the evening. (One of our college mates, a Parsi, owned a taxi, which he plied after going home from college. His family also owned another car, which he drove when the family or friends went out. His friends, particularly his girl friends, did not know that he also drove a taxi.) Anju would not hear of his son being a 'taxi driver', so this proposal was dropped. Although Anju had owned a car in Burma from 1922 to 1942 and again when he went back in 1946, he did not invest in a car while in Bombay. We had to rely on local trains and BEST buses.

Ivy took up teaching music at home and a number of local boys and girls would come for lessons and, if they had no piano at home, to practice. One of these young ladies was Joan. One evening when Ivy had gone out and I was busy at my studies, Joan came to practice. Ivy had asked me to ensure that she practiced for the requisite half hour. Joan was playing a waltz, and would breeze through at top speed those sections which she knew well and then stumble along on those sections with which she was not sure. After listening to her four or five times, I finally went to her and told her to imagine her mum and dad dancing to the music she was playing – and I mimed how they would have to dance at top speed when she played fast and then stop in mid-step while she found the next note. Joan laughed and the message went home. (Years later, I stepped into First National City Bank – as Citibank was then called – at the Junction of P M and D N Roads, and got the benefit of a very charming smile from the young receptionist, who looked somewhat familiar. She reminded me that she was Joan and I pretended to dance to her music. She laughed so loudly that her colleagues at other counters all looked around. She must have had some explaining to do.)

Immediately I joined St Xavier's, Iza insisted I join the Catholic Students' Union (CSU). She would like to attend CSU parties and dances and the JJ College of Arts did not have their own CSU. Her best friend, Melanie Rodrigues, whose brother had died in an accident a couple of years earlier, had no escort and, though a member of the Sophia CSU, could not attend their functions. In anticipation of these parties and dances, Iza took pains to teach me to dance. Melanie's car would drop us at Bandra Station and come back at around 23:00 to pick us up, so we did not have to rush home in time for the last BEST bus.

Most CSU dances were held at the first floor hall of Green's Hotel (where the modern extension of Taj Mahal Hotel now stands). I was instructed by Ivy that I must partner my sister for the first and last dances. For other dances or games, both of us could find our own partners. During that first year I was not interested in dancing nor had I made friends with girls – most of these being from Sophia College. So I would carry a novel with me and between the first and last dances find a corner where I could comfortably read my novel.

Later, as I made friends, and Melanie's younger sister, Ingrid, joined college, I learnt to dance and enjoy myself at these parties and dances. After Melanie got married, I had the pleasure of escorting Ingrid to the CSU parties and dances. I particularly loved to dance the waltz, which was Melanie's favourite and became Ingrid's favourite also. Unfortunately, the waltz seems to have lost favour now and rarely at weddings or public dances do I get a chance to dance it, though I cannot dance a series of fast waltzes as I earlier could. It is also difficult to find young partners who can dance the waltz; those of my age usually have some problem or other and cannot dance.

With Anju's increasing circle of business and family friends, throughout the year all four of us attended birthday parties and weddings. We attended dances during the Easter and Christmas seasons.

Bandra is the East Indian bastion, while Santa Cruz is the Goan base. On Christmas night the big dance was at Bandra Gymkhana, which most of the boys and girls from Santa Cruz attended. By the end of the dance, liquor being freely available, everyone was in a joyous mood, and someone or other would say something to rile the East Indians and this would result in the Goan boys literally being chased home to Santa Cruz. On New Year's night the big dance was at the Willingdon Catholic Gymkhana, Santa Cruz. The story would be repeated in reverse with the East Indian boys being chased home to Bandra. Care was always taken to ensure that the young ladies from both areas were safely reached home. Bringing in the New Year was celebrated by everyone at the Catholic Gymkhana at Charni Road, which was so crowded that one could hardly dance, but everyone was interested in meeting and wishing friends rather than dancing.

Iza would celebrate her birthday with a big party in spite of it being in the middle of the monsoon. I was never too keen on celebrating my birthday with a big party, but thanks to Iza, there would normally be quite a gathering. Ivy and Anju had low profile birthdays, usually with close friends and relatives calling.

The Bandra Feast (September 8 or the Sunday immediately thereafter) however, was celebrated in style with friends from other parts of Bombay calling after their visit to Our Lady of the Mount on the feast day and through the week. Ivy would have cooked a large quantity of *sorpotel* or *vindaloo,* which would be served to visitors with some salad and bread or rice. This quantity would normally suffice for the whole week. We joined youngsters and children to visit Bandra Fair – with its merry-go-round, giant wheel, whist drives, dodgem cars, etc. There was usually a dance at the Bandra Gym on the Bandra Feast evening. We were careful not to visit the Bandra Fair on Thursday as that was the day when the mill workers had a holiday and the fair was more than normally crowded and girls got their bottoms pinched. On the Sunday following the Bandra Feast, we were sure that there would be no further visitors and Ivy would make pepper water and rice to be eaten with pickle to give our own tummies a rest. And surprise: more friends would turn up to share this spartan diet.

For special friends Anju would offer his precious whiskey. These were the years when Bombay had 'Prohibition'. He had a permit against which he was permitted to purchase two bottles of whiskey per month. We began to notice that there were a few of his 'friends' who only visited us to get Anju's precious whiskey, and they would stay on till Anju's bottle was empty. On one or two occasions the 'friend' was sick, since he was not a regular drinker. So Iza decided to take control action. When one of these 'bottle friends' came over, she poured enough whiskey into an empty bottle, adequate for at most two drinks – one for Anju and the other for the 'friend', and hid the full bottle. Anju, who had not been taken into confidence earlier, was most annoyed, but Ivy twigged on and said "Don't you remember that so and so had come over and you drank most of the whiskey that night?" Subsequently when the 'friend' had gone, Iza explained to him why she had taken this course of action. This became standard practice for such 'bottle friends'.

Every year our St Anne's Parish organized a Christmas Tree, in the afternoon. There were sports for the kids followed by distribution of prizes and gifts by Santa Claus. This was followed by a dance where we youngsters enjoyed ourselves. It was held at the Kooka Gymkhana on St Cyril's Road. I had been on duty for the sports and was hot and dusty by the time Santa Claus put in his appearance to distribute the sports prizes and Christmas gifts. I borrowed a cycle from my class-mate who lived just next to Kooka Gym, went home, had a shower and changed. Ivy gave me dinner which included the usual salad containing raw onions. Keeping to my instructions, I got back in time to have the first dance with my sister, who got most annoyed that I had eaten onions at dinner. After this dance I asked the gentleman who was manning the snack bar for some peppermint sweets. At the snack bar there were a policewoman and a policeman seated. They got very interested in me – prohibition had recently been imposed – by their definition someone wanting peppermint sweets must have been drinking. So they checked my breath and got a good whiff of onions.

One year our parish church, St Anne's, had a gala fete at the D'Monte Park to collect funds for the repairs and maintenance of the church. All of us college students had volunteered to help. I was put in charge at the entrance, to collect the gate money. I was only able to enjoy a ride on the giant wheel after 21:00, by which time there would be few new entrants. The East Indian ladies from our parish took turns to cook and sell some of their delicious food and sweets at the fete. As a consequence I did not have dinner at home that whole week.

This was my first experience of the adulation that youngsters had for a singer . There was a guy who did a good impersonation of Elvis Presley and our young ladies were going ga-ga while he sang.

Anju had joined the St Vincent de Paul Society, which used to help poor families in the parish. To raise funds for Christmas hampers for these families, the SVP decided to go caroling. Anju was elected Santa Claus. He was dressed in a long red robe trimmed with fresh white cotton from a pack of surgical cotton. From the same pack of surgical cotton they fabricated a lovely beard and moustache. He also stuffed a pillow above the rope sash gathering his robe around his middle so that he acquired a nice rolly-polly image. All the carolers, including Santa Claus, carried Chinese paper lanterns with burning candles inside. They dressed Anju at our church and then came past Mrs. D'Sylva's house and on to Rajan. While turning into the little lane in front of the shops at the corner, Anju tripped. In trying to right himself, he caused the candle to fall over, light the paper lantern and then flames shot up the cotton trimming of his robe to his beard. He tried to pull off the robe and concentrated the flame onto his face. Fortunately in pulling up the robe the flames got extinguished, but his face was badly burnt. Someone came running down the road and informed us of Anju's accident. I charged there and was instructed to call Dr. Eustace D'Souza, who lived up the road, and to tell him that they had applied Tanofax (a purple) ointment to

Anju's face where it was burnt. I raced off on my bicycle and informed Dr Eustace of the accident and requested him to come immediately. When asked about first aid given, I told him that they had applied Tampax to Anju's face. Somehow he kept a straight face and came with me on my bike and attended to Anju. (I met Dr Eustace recently and he recognized me because of this incident.) Anju spent Christmas at home – no visits, his face was not bandaged – ointment was applied more or less continuously till the burns had healed. Thereafter Anju would liberally apply coconut oil to his face and sit on the terrace facing the sun. Miraculously, Anju's burns healed and left no scars. In spite of this incident, Anju volunteered to be Santa Claus at later functions both in Bombay and in Goa – but without Chinese paper lanterns with lit candles in them.

City 'bumpkins'

Friends, who lived in south Bombay, particularly the Sequeiras and the Manricks loved to visit us. Since Gabriel and Theresa could only leave after their petrol pump closed at 20:00, the Sequeira family usually arrived for our birthday parties after 22:00 hours, when most other guests were leaving. Then they would chat and have fun and when they finally left the younger ones, Ghislein and Kevin were asleep.

These two would be placed on the platform behind the driver's seat in Gabriel's two-seater and the others would get into the fold-away back seat. All the kids would be fast asleep long before they reached home. On one return journey, Gabriel himself fell asleep and the car banged into a sign post. After this, Ivy and Anju decided that the kids could come across a day or two earlier, specially if it was a week end, stay with us and go back with their parents after the birthday. This for the kids was a far more enjoyable arrangement.

While at our place they could go to the beach, have a dip in the sea and enjoy feeding the fowls. On one occasion they discovered a hen brooding over a clutch of eggs in our pantry. They were most interested. They knew eggs, they knew chicken but they did not know that hens laid eggs and that these, when hatched, brought forth chickens. They were real 'city bumpkins'. They sat in the pantry in front of the broody hen, waiting for the eggs to hatch. When their parents came to take them back, they refused to go because they wanted to see the chicks. They finally agreed to go when Ivy promised to tell them when the chicks were hatched and to invite them again to see the chicks.

Elvira and Francis Mandricks, with Malcolm, Evelynn, Enid and Fred, had spent the day with us. After playing in the compound the whole day, we all went to the beach at Carter Road in the evening. The kids could not resist the temptation and though they had no change of clothes, they waded into the sea in their underclothes. Then, they dressed without any underwear. After an impromptu dinner they all got into a taxi for home carrying their wet clothes. Francis instructed the driver to take them to Strand Cinema, Colaba. Barely a few minutes after starting off they were all fast asleep. When they reached Strand Cinema, the driver woke them up. They were really most grateful to reach their destination safe and willingly paid him his fare plus a large tip.

The Slow Ship to Goa

W E all went to Goa for the Exposition of St Francis Xavier's body in December 1953–January 1954. On December 21, Anju, Ivy, Iza, Max Miranda (our landlord) and I with our cook left home around 07:00 to be in time for boarding the ship for Goa at *Bhaucha Dhakka* (Ferry Wharf).

Bemvinda with Bella, Alex, Allan, Ronnie, Rudy and baby Collette with their servant boy came directly from their home to the docks. To make sure they left home well in time, Frank Lobo, who was at our house *en route* from Aden to Bangalore, went to Bemvinda's house early in the morning and found everything in disorder and no one ready. He shouted, got the boys to dress without any further delay, while Bemvinda and Bela attended to the packing and getting breakfast and dry lunch. I am sure if Frank had not been there Bemvinda and her family would have missed the boat.

We were well in time and got ample space on the upper deck to spread our bedding. Our cook and Bemvinda's servant boy found space for themselves on the lower deck. The ship moved out from the jetty on schedule at 10:00. Ivy and Bemvinda had provided a packed lunch, of cutlets, boiled eggs, bread and butter.

The ship provided water for drinking. A much better attraction for the men was *feni*, of which the caterers' staff clandestinely kept an adequate stock of. Unknown to us, our cook had

1

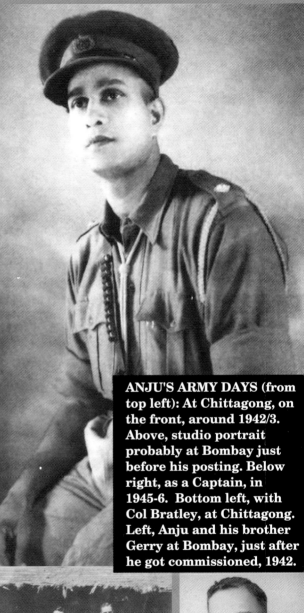

ANJU'S ARMY DAYS (from top left): At Chittagong, on the front, around 1942/3. Above, studio portrait probably at Bombay just before his posting. Below right, as a Captain, in 1945-6. Bottom left, with Col Bratley, at Chittagong. Left, Anju and his brother Gerry at Bombay, just after he got commissioned, 1942.

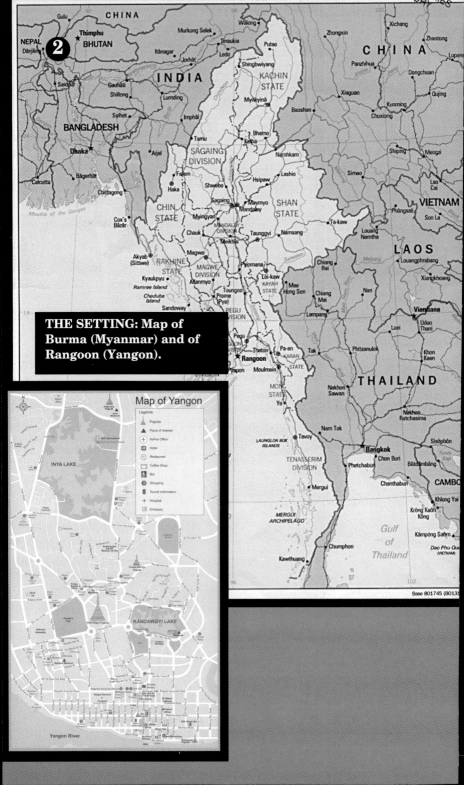

THE SETTING: Map of
Burma (Myanmar) and of
Rangoon (Yangon).

③

N BURMA AND GOA: Above, the Shwedagon (Golden) Pagoda, in Rangoon/Yangon. Below, the family home at Nachinola. Burma photos and maps courtesy of the Wikipedia.

2007 b 16

IN THE FAMILY: Aunty Flory (Ivy's eldest sister) married Jose Marie Xavier Menezes. He was over 6'5" tall and proportionally broad, while she was just about 4' tall.

WOMEN ACHIEVERS THEN: The author's mother Ivy poses for her graduation day photo. Above, the Cheron (the author's mother's) family, showing Ivy as a young girl, third from left.

6

FROM A FATHER'S FAMILY ALBUM: Top, grandad SP, just before he passed away in Canada, circa 1945. Above, a younger grandad (SP) with granny Leopoldina and Anju, as a young boy in Calcutta, around 1914. Right, a *photo* of grandad's letter, during World War I, addressed to dad. Original letters were sometimes not sent in wartime to avoid chances of smuggling across coded messages hidden in them.

ALL IN THE FAMILY: Above, the author's parents with Iza and the author. In Calcutta, in 1946. Below, around December 1954, from left U. Gerry, Granny, Aunty Amvinda and the author's father Anju visiting during the Goa Exposition.

STRICTLY, TIME OFF: Family pi[cture?]
at Kokine Lake. Formerly known [as?]
the Royal Lake, it is now called th[e]
Great Royal Lake (Kandawgyi La[ke]

The Vaz family house at Taunggyi, Burma, around 1936. Seen above, the author's parents, aunt and sister Iza, with the author.

Frank and Iza, the author's sister, marry at St Anne's, Bandra, in 1957. Above is a photo at the church, and below, the reception at MacRonells, Bandra.

Above, the author's wedding at Poona in 1965 at St. Anne's.
Below, Anju's cousin, George D'Souza, weds Isabel, at Rangoon in 1940.

12

THE VAZ CLAN: Portrait of a large and enterprising Goan family in 1958 at Taunggyi, Burma. Seated at the centre is Louis Jose Vaz, the patriarch, and his wife. Standing in the back row are his nephew Jose Cordeiro (later *sarpanch* of Saligao), and six Vaz brothers -- (from left) Sonny aka Tony, Alex, Peter, Alexander, Robert and Frank. At extreme right is Patrick, Alexander's son. Some of their families are also seen.

14

Above, in Thanlyin (formerly Syriam), a historic, Portuguese-built church. In 1599, the city fell to local Rakhine forces led by the Portuguese mercenary Filipe de Brito e Nicote, who was made city governor. Brito declared independence from his nominal Rakhine masters in 1603, defeated the invading Rakhine navy in 1604 and 1605, and successfully established Portuguese rule over Syriam (then called Sirião) under the Portuguese viceroy of Goa.

FAMILY & MORE: Top, the Pimenta (author's wife's) fa[...] Above right, the author wit[h] mother and sister.

BACK IN BURMA: Anju, centre with dark tie, with friends in Burma, after the War. From left: Albert Pereira, Mrs Bhacho, to his left Marie Pereira and Mr. Bhacho, who was with dad in the army. Lady in front unidentified.
At right, the author's dad with his Morris 8, in Burma, in 1946.

Mum's brother Diego de Souza and his family, in Burma after World War II, circa 1948.

17

SETTING DOWN ROOTS IN PORVORIM: The author's father lays the foundation stone for one of the first homes in the fledgling Defence Colony at Alto Porvorim, Goa. Below left, the author's Dad and (right) the author's parents, with pets Patch and Chicko II, respectively.

18

THE FAMILY GROWS: A young Deepika (the author's daughter) around 1972 in Bombay, seated atop the family Fiat 1100 car, BMF 7109, a 1962-model in those vehicle-scarce days. Below, Deepika takes to wheels of her own with help from her mum, Hazel.

19

FAMILY OCCASIONS: The author's mum and dad (at right) with their god-daughter Sr. Rozaria, of the Convent of Jesus and Mary, Colaba. Below, Sr Mary Adelia, the author's sister-in-law, on the occasion of a landmark jubilee.
Also seen are Jennifer, Lourdes (the author's sisters-in-law) and Hazel (right, second row).

Above: Anju's sister, Bemv: (third from l: with her fam: -- (from left) daughter Collette, husband Sal and, to her l: son Ronnie. Left, Michell and Jason Nogueira, th author's cousin's, children in / Porvorim around the 1 1990s.

BUSINESS MATTERS: Top: Anju's LIC office at Laxmi Building, Fort, Bombay. Centre, the inauguration of the author's factory at New Bombay (Navi Mumbai) in 1988. Among others seen: Anju, Uncle John, Lloyd Vaz. Below, the same occasion - Hazel (back to camera), Sr Mary Adelia, Lira Pimenta, Sr Rozaria, Sr Celine, other sisters-in-law of the author.

SPREADING FAMILY TIES: Above, in Toronto, Canada, the author's maternal cousin Marie Pereira and her family. Top, the family with Joseph Cordeiro, the first Cardinal of Pakistan (second from left).

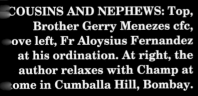

COUSINS AND NEPHEWS: Top, Brother Gerry Menezes cfc, above left, Fr Aloysius Fernandez at his ordination. At right, the author relaxes with Champ at home in Cumballa Hill, Bombay.

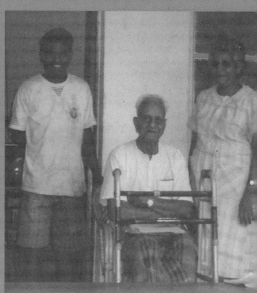

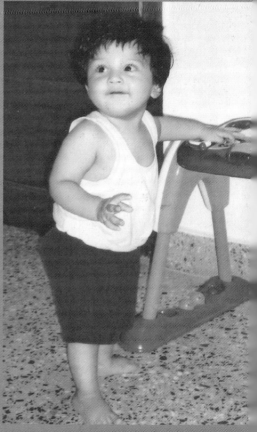

imbibed 'some' *feni*. Bemvinda's servant boy managed to get him to sleep without creating too much trouble and did not tell us.

For dinner we ordered from the ship's caterer some fish, curry and rice. I watched as these caterers kept catching fish as the boat sailed. Consequently the fish was fresh and tasty. We youngsters enjoyed ourselves playing cards and other games on the emergency rafts stacked at the rear of the ship. When it got dark, we continued sitting on these rafts enjoying the sight of the beautiful star-laden sky and lights along the distant shore, along which we were running parallel. As this was a specially chartered voyage for pilgrims to the Exposition, our ship did not stop at the usual mid-way points of Murud-Janjira, Malvan, Devgadh-Baria and Ratnagiri. Early next morning we were at the mouth of the Mandovi river and docked at Panjim at about 07:00.

Sodder & Co., the organizers, had arranged buses to meet us and take us direct to Bom Jesu Basilica at Old Goa. Our luggage was safely stacked for retrieval after our return from Old Goa. At Old Goa we were immediately conducted to Bom Jesu Basilica to view the remains of St Francis Xavier – his uncorrupt body had just been sealed into a glass case. We paid our respects and then participated at Mass. We had brunch at one of the numerous food stalls in the church compound and were ready to return to Panjim by 13:00.

We retrieved our luggage and waited to load it into the *pathmari,* the sailing crafts which would take us direct to Aldona. (The normal motor launch was out of action and hence this *pathmari.*) Sitting on the jetty waiting for the luggage to be loaded, we suddenly heard shouts and saw our cook in the hands of the local police. He had obviously added to his intake of *feni* in Old Goa and was now in a belligerent mood. When the constables had asked him where he was going, he cursed them. They immediately caught him and said in Konkani that they were taking him direct to *Kalaboosh* (the local jail). Anju had to intervene and pleaded on his behalf that the cook had been away from Goa for so long that he was celebrating and requested the constables not to arrest him. They finally agreed provided he did not create any more noise. Just then the *pathmari* came alongside. We loaded the luggage and got him into the *pathmari* lying on top of our bed rolls, where he promptly fell asleep. Leaving Bevinda's servant boy to look after him, we did a quick tour of Panjim, as the boat was scheduled to leave only at 17:00 hours. Among other goodies, Anju bought one *garrafão* (a demijohn, or large bottle with short neck often with a small handle at the neck, sometimes encased in wickerwork) of Portuguese port wine.

The voyage upriver to Aldona was very pleasant. We stopped at the riverside villages of Britona, Ecoxim, and Pomburpa, where passengers got off the *pathmari* into little canoes by the light of small kerosene lanterns. It was a hazardous operation to look at, but these intrepid travellers would do this every morning and night when going to and returning from work in Panjim. Even during the rains, while holding umbrellas over their heads and standing and perilously balancing in the canoe.

From Aldona we got taxis to take us and our luggage to Nachinola. Our arrival so late in the evening put Granny in turmoil. Anju had not informed her of our trip, which meant she had the tasks of cooking dinner, heating bath water and getting bedding organized all at very short notice. The younger kids were very tired and cranky, so Anju opened the *garafou* of Portuguese port wine and gave each of us a wine glass full after our baths. Then dinner was served and without further ado all of us were fast asleep on mats spread across the sitting room.

We boys spent the whole of December 23 investigating the Nachinola house and the compound, checking if any fruit was available. At around 16:00 two cars drove up our driveway, and out stepped Gerry and Molly with Sylvester and baby Lea together with two of Gerry's friends. They had driven from Secunderabad. Their appearance was unexpected but very welcome. Granny Leopoldina now had a full house – eleven adults, five youngsters and two babies. This was the first and last time that Granny had her whole extended family with her.

Granny took charge of the kitchen with our cook, Bemvinda's servant boy, Granny's own maid and the ladies from the out houses. They were all supposedly getting our food cooked, but there was more confusion and noise than effective cooking. Ivy took charge of ensuring that everyone got fed. Bemvinda and Molly were left free to look after their respective babies, both about nine months old. Ivy had to ensure that the children and ladies were served meals well in time so that the men could get their lunch or dinner before they had too much *feni* inside them.

Anju organized the drinks. Granny Leopoldina promptly got one *burnee* of *feni* pulled up from the well. This matured *feni* was filled into bottles for consumption by very appreciative connoisseurs.

One afternoon in their enthusiasm Anju and Gerry called a fisher woman and bought all the *bangdas* (mackerel) in her basket, probably at Re. 1 for a hundred mackerels. With the heavy demands already on the kitchen, Granny refused to take on the job of cleaning and cooking this large quantity of *bangda*. So Anju and Gerry decided to do the job themselves. They cleaned the fish in the compound, near the well, salted them, wrapped them in threes in plantain leaves and built a fire of dry leaves around all these bundles. Then, having washed their hands, they got down to the serious business of drinking mature *feni*. They left us youngsters to watch over the fire. We were called for our lunch and promptly left the fire to look after itself.

After the ladies finished their lunch, the men were called for lunch too. They remembered the *bangda,* for which they now had worked up a really good appetite. Their fire had gone out quite a while earlier. The *bangdas* had cooled and – obviously well done – had already been finished by the dog and cat, who could hardly move after their giant meal.

All of us, except Granny Leopoldina, Bemvinda and Molly with the two babies, went for Christmas Midnight Mass and got back around 02:00 to hot coffee and Christmas cake, *neories, kulkuls, dose, doldol* and other Christmas sweets.   We slept late, while the ladies went off for Christmas morning Mass. We were awakened (we youngsters were all sleeping on a mat stretched across the sitting room) when guests, including our neighbours Antu Bothelo and Zuafart D'Souza, started dropping in to wish us for Christmas. Of course every guest had to be given some of this fine mature *feni*, but I noticed that our neighbours who lived in Goa did not appreciate this *feni*, but asked for imported whiskey, which Anju and Gerry had thoughtfully bought. By stay-at-home Goan standard, *feni* was for every day, but imported whiskey should be served to guests at festivals.

There was no specific breakfast, but all of us feasted on Christmas sweets and were ready for lunch at 13:00. Lunch was really special – *sanaa, vorre ani maas – with sorpotel, vindaloo* and *pullao*. Every one was given a tot of port wine – small doses for the little fellows and glasses full for Iza, Bella, and the ladies. After this heavy meal all of us found some place to sleep on the cement benches of the verandah, in the deck chairs, and on mats on the verandah floor.

December 27 was Gerry and Molly's wedding anniversary and the next day was Ivy and Anju's – both events were suitably celebrated. On December 29, Gerry and the Secunderabad gang went off to Old Goa to pay their respects to St Francis Xavier. This was their first experience of driving a car onto and off a ferry to cross the Mandovi river and they considered it quite an achievement when they got back safe and sound.

Around 19:00 on December 31, Gerry decided that they must go to the New Year's Eve dance in Saligao. So off they went in the two cars, the men folk with Iza and Bella. They had an enjoyable time at the Saligao dance, meeting lots of friends and relatives. While returning around 02:00 they saw that the dance at the Moira Club was still going on. So they stopped to join in the fun. They met a number of friends, when suddenly Gerry spotted George Nazareth (he used to be in charge of the lighthouse at the entrance to the Rangoon River, Burma) in *baambis* and a singlet standing on the play ground outside the club. Gerry jumped through the window (the club is at ground level) and went and embraced this old friend and pulled him to the window to join them in a drink. George would not enter the club in his casual dress. This quite upset some of the younger element, who wanted to have Gerry thrown out of the hall. But Anju and Gerry had too many friends among the club members for them to prevail. They finally reached home around 06:00 when some of us were just getting up. Iza and Bella really had a good time at Saligao and Moira.

January 1 is the *Bom Jesu* Feast – the Nachinola Church Feast – and all of us youngsters went for the feast Mass at 11:00. Granny Leopoldina, Bemvinda, Molly and Ivy had gone for the early morning Mass. Alex, Allan, Ronnie and Rudy were given some money to spend at the fair, which is set up in the form of stalls around the church. Each spent his pocket money on feast sweets as per his desire and had eaten most of these before getting home. Immediately on getting home they were instructed to get into their home clothes and not to spoil their good clothes. There was quite a mix up in their clothes – all khaki short-sleeved shirts and shorts. The first to change, Rudi, had worn the first set that came to hand and the next to dress did the same, but when Alex came to change he found that he was left with clothes much too small for him. Then he ran around catching his brothers and, much to the amazement of all of us, looking at the inner side of the waist band of their shorts to ascertain who was wearing his shorts. When he located his own shorts he demanded that the wearer immediately take off and give him his shorts. This led to quite a squabble. The intake of all the feast day sweets had not dampened their appetite and they were promptly at the table when lunch was served.

Early on January 3, Gerry, Molly with Sylvester and Lea and their friends left for the long drive back to Secunderabad.

Port wine from the *garafous* does not keep and once opened all the wine has to be consumed within a few days. As we were to leave on the Jan 5, Anju instructed me to see that all the wine was consumed by Jan 4 night. Each of the youngsters were given two full wine glasses at dinner on Jan 3 and again on Jan 4. Iza and Bella were also given double their normal quota, but on Jan 4 when there was still quite some wine left, I kept refilling their glasses without their knowledge. This naturally loosened their tongues and they started telling each other and every one at the table about their various boyfriends and other interesting news. When they finished dinner there was only one bottle of wine left for the ladies to share.

The Bombay gang left by boat on January 5. Taxis had been called at 05:00 and we were on our way by 06:00 all the way through to Panjim to get to the docks before 10:00. We had an uneventful return trip.

Our enjoyable holiday was somewhat spoiled by some bad news when we got home. Michael, the Dachshund, came to our house just after we had left for Goa and found the doors locked. He went off sulking. Apparently he was bitten by a snake in the fields behind our house and died there. Only when he did not return to the church that night did anyone start looking for him. The next morning they found him dead in the fields.

Granny naturally felt very lonely after this invasion and, after a few months, loneliness got the better of her sound judgment and she got a telegram sent to Anju stating that she was not well and requesting him to come down immediately. Since college holidays had started, Anju and I took the last ship of the season from Bombay to Goa and on reaching Nachinola found Granny perfectly well. Anju was justifiably angry, but when Granny explained her loneliness he was mollified. She lavished her whole attention on the two of us and we really enjoyed very good food and plenty of fruit.

Chicko, not a brother, but...

That June Anju's friend, Bertie Fernandes, gave us a pup. It was a cross between his male Dachshund and Noshir's female Spaniel.

He had the colouring and short coat of his father and the height of his mother. We named him Chicko.

It became my responsibility to look after him, wash and bathe him once a week, remove ticks and take him for a run each evening. I used to buy old golf balls from the shop just in front of Metro Cinema and with this the two of us would go to the golf links at the end of Carter Road. Both he and I would run after the ball and I thus had an excuse for running to compensate for no regular games. He was totally my pet and was most upset when I went off to SMHS (St Mary's High School) to teach in 1956. Later, when I was with JWT and was getting ready to go on tour, he would get into my suitcase to prevent me from packing.

Ivy, Anju, Iza and I had gone up to Mount Mary's for the First Saturday devotion. I on my cycle, as small taxis at that time carried only three passengers. After service Ivy, Anju and Iza decided to visit friends in St Sebastian's Colony. I had to get back to my studies. As I was leaving, Anju said "Chicko has been left alone in the house, make sure you take him for a walk". A classmate overheard Anju's instructions and said, "I did not know you have a younger brother?" I explained that Chicko was our dog. He had a younger brother named Chico.

Quite often on Sundays and holidays, with a group of friends we would walk across at low tide from Danda to Juhu-Tara and onwards to Juhu beach proper for a dip in the sea and playing on the beach. When I dug in the sand, Chicko would promptly join me and dig most vigorously searching for some hidden bone. I encouraged him. Then, for fun, while we were all sitting around on the beach playing word building, dumb charades, etc, I would go behind one of our new guests, usually a young lady, and start digging. Chicko would promptly take over and keep digging, while I crossed over to the other side of the circle. Suddenly the sand behind the young lady would crumble and she would be precipitated into the hole with her legs up in the air much to her embarrassment. (Those were the days when girls wore skirts, unlike now when young ladies think nothing of wearing the briefest of skirts or 'ABCD' jeans to show the world the brand of panties they are wearing.)

Chicko would promptly run away. Looking for the culprit, she would first suspect me, but I was standing opposite her and it was impossible for me to have done the digging. This trick was repeated several times and more so when I was at JWT and we had picnics at the JWT shack on Juhu beach.

Goan sweets, for Christmas

College closed for Christmas holidays on December 22 or 23. But much before college closed our services were in demand for making Christmas sweets – *dol-dol, chonneache dose,* Christmas cakes, etc.

Goan Christmas sweets are the most labour-intensive sweets that have been devised, most probably by a mother-in-law who had to keep a number of daughters-in-law busy. Our maid would grind the rice and *channa dal* and extract coconut milk in advance. As soon as we got home the *chula* would be lit in the backyard and each of us – Ivy, Iza and I – would take turns at stirring the dough. In doing so, we kept trying not to get burnt by the hot dough that bubbled out of the huge tinned brass vessel no matter how long the ladle.

As the water evaporated, the mass became tougher to stir requiring a second person to hold on to the vessel. Usually at this precise moment, Anju, if he had got home earlier and had been roped in to stir the sweet, would discover some client that he must visit immediately as he would like to include his case before Gresham closed their books on Christmas-eve. He would arrive back in time to help spread the sweets in dishes and to taste and comment on the prepared sweet with no explanation as to whether or not he had closed that case.

Our dog, Chicko, was most interested in this sweet making and would come and sit close to the *chula*. This way, as the mass bubbled, some of the dough would land on his fur. We would get burnt, but his fur prevented the heat getting to his skin and after the stuff cooled he would lick it off and smack his lips. His share was the scrapings from the vessel after the mass of sweet was taken out and placed in plates to cool.

After completing her diploma in commercial art at the J J School of Art, Iza took up a job as a commercial artist with National Advertising. She would tell us about the various advertisements she was working on. This subject was something totally new to all of us, and made me aware of advertising agency work. Little did I know that I would soon be part of the advertising business.

One day on my way home, I was cycling down Kantwadi Road fairly fast when at the junction with Perry Road, a car coming fast down Pali Hill Road nearly hit me. I swerved, skidded and landed standing but my front wheel was hit by the side of the car and was bent slightly. On her way home that evening, Iza heard of this and reported to Ivy that I had been knocked down by a car and was unconscious for a while. She had learned advertising!

Brahmin... and RC

Major Finnimore, Commandant of the Western Railway's Watch and Ward Brigade (they were earlier called the 'Watch & Rob Brigade'), was a very good Christian. One Sunday morning he came striding down the road to our house waving that morning's *Times of India.*

Ivy came quickly to meet him thinking that there was some emergency. He pointed to the classified 'matrimonials' column and asked Ivy what was the meaning of the various advertisements which specified 'Bride/Groom wanted for Goan R. C. Brahmin bachelor/spinster from good family, etc ....' There were also advertisements for non-Brahmin R.C. brides and grooms. He wanted to know how R.C.s (Roman Catholics) could be Brahmins or non-Brahmins.

Ivy had quite a problem explaining that this caste classification was a carry forward from the fact that our ancestors were Hindus. He left quite puzzled that Goan Christians still followed the Hindu caste system.

Years later I raised this same question with the Redemptorist Fathers who gave us a Lenten Mission at Sacred Heart Church, Santa Cruz. While this European priest could not explain or justify the fact that Goan Christians still believed in Hindu castes, he advised me, to avoid conflict within the family, not to think of getting married to a non-Brahmin girl.

As late as the end of the last (20th) century, you could come across matrimonial advertisements in newspapers, including the Bombay R.C. Diocesan official weekly *The Examiner*, for Christian brides or grooms which specified the caste required. Fortunately, this practice is disappearing, but in Goa some 'Brahmin' Christians still consider themselves superior to their 'non-Brahmin' Christian neighbours.

Insurance, after nationalisation

In 1956, the Government of India nationalized all insurance companies – both life and general. Anju's new office was on the fifth floor of Laxmi Building, which was far less impressive than his office at Gresham House. This office was crowded and dark with artificial lighting permanently on. Initially his officers were the same as at Gresham, but this soon changed as the new management set-up of the government-run Life Insurance Corporation of India (LIC) became effective.

Anju still continued as inspector of agencies, and basically his work remained the same. But he had lost the USP of a foreign insurance company backed by reserves in Pounds Sterling. He sold his clients 'special' benefits, but these were the same benefits that all other LIC agents offered.

Anju scored over other agents in that he studied his client, took down his history, particularly his health and family background, emphasising the benefits to those dependent on his client, who would suffer on his death or disability. Anju then typed up a proposal showing the costs and benefits of the insurance policy, which from his knowledge and experience would be in the best long term interest of his client. Anju faced competition from unscrupulous agents, who sold policies on the basis of what percentage of their commission would be returned in cash once the policy was issued.

In addition, in the event of death of any of his clients, Anju would visit the widow and bereaved family and offer his help to get the policy claim settled with the minimum delay. In many cases this resulted in the family entrusting all their other insurance business to Anju. In one or two cases I know, this happened even in preference to another agent who was a close relative of the family.

Of course he made sure that he remembered the birthdays and wedding anniversaries of his clients, calling on them if they lived in Bombay or sending them a greeting card if they were outstation. Anju taught me the value of keeping a diary. At the start of a new year, one of the first things he did was to go through his old diary, enter birthdays, anniversaries and other events and copy addresses and telephone numbers into the new diary.

A wedding in the family

During the years I was at college, I met Iza's friends – but I could not remember one from the other and inevitably called one by the name of one of the others. Iza would be furious and would complain to Ivy. Obviously among these young men she had not found one whom she considered good enough to be her husband.

Finally, she decided in favour of Frank Vaz, the youngest son of Mrs. and Mr. Vaz from Taunggyi, Burma, who had been Anju's very good friends since 1922. As he needed to resume work in Burma within a short time, the wedding was arranged promptly. The engagement on December 28, 1956, and wedding was scheduled for February 2, 1957.

With the limited time available, Iza had to work at top speed to get her trousseau ready. Plus she wanted to have favours for her guests which would be as original as those at Ivy and Anju's wedding. Since February 2 was Candlemas day, at which candles, for use by members of the congregation in their homes, are blessed, she decided to use small birthday candles as her wedding favours. She recruited all her girl friends from the JJ School of Art to come over to our house where they tied two candles of different colours with a silk ribbon bow and attached a safety pin at the rear. It was painstaking work. I tried it and ended up breaking candles and got chased away.

St. Anne's, our parish church, was a beautiful setting for the wedding with its split circular staircase. Iza made Anju rehearse how he was to march up to the church and up the aisle to give her away. (Normally when Anju and Iza went anywhere he would be way ahead and she would literally be running after him.) She had not long before seen the movie *Father of the Bride* and tried to ensure that the mistakes made there would not occur at her wedding.

My job was that of prompter, to ensure that Frank and Iza responded correctly at various parts of the nuptial Mass. They did have a rehearsal the previous evening. Like Ivy and Anju, she decided to have three bridesmaids and three bestmen, but took pains to ensure that when the photographs were taken the dresses of the bride's maids would be properly displayed. She got Anand, a colleague from the JJ School of Art, who was now a commercial photographer, to take all the photographs after being thoroughly briefed.

Anju and Iza, with the bridesmaids, bestmen and flower girls walked in procession from our house to the church, with almost the whole village following them and crackers being burst along the way. Frank with his mother and father, his sister Queenie, and brother Alex, and their Bombay relatives met the bridal procession at the entrance to the church. Fr. Theophilus Lobo, our parish priest, greeted both groups and led the procession into church. At the altar, Anju officially gave Iza away to Frank. Iza and Frank exchanged vows of marriage and then Mass commenced. In spite of the previous evening's rehearsal, I was required to prompt them at various stages of the Mass.

After Mass photographs were taken on the staircase of the church and then the bridal couple walked, as per East Indian custom, in procession under a red umbrella (Iza used a red Burmese umbrella) held over their heads to Leo Rodrigues' house. They came back to our house when lunch was ready. As our house was crowded with our own close relatives and the Vaz family, Iza and Frank, after lunch, went back to Mr. Rodrigues' house to rest for the afternoon.

The wedding reception was held on MacRonells' Roof Garden from 19:30 onwards. All of us went ahead and Iza, Frank and the bridesmaids came in the car hired for the day. They entered the hall to the strains of the Wedding March through the archway of joined hands formed by all those guests and family members who had already arrived.

The bridal couple went to the centre of the hall and cut the wedding cake while the band played 'Congratulations'. The MC (master of ceremonies) led them to their throne. Fr. Tarcy Mascarenhas raised the toast to the bride and groom. Frank replied to the toast and kept it short. Otherwise too, Frank was a man of few words; his conversation would usually be about his agricultural projects and progress at various sites.

MacRonells' served a scrumptious dinner – buffet style – including a roasted pigling. Many guests, mostly Anju's office friends, left early after the toast as they would not partake of non-vegetarian food. However, they had been counted and would be included in MacRonells' bill. Max, our landlord, got the kids off the dance floor by sending them to the upper terrace and ensuring that plenty of snacks were sent up to them. He organized games for them up there. The dance floor was free for all those who felt like dancing and most of us danced to the lovely live music provided by the band. When dinner was served, Max organised the kids to come down first and get their plates filled and then sent them back up to eat their dinner.

While the elders danced and chatted and slowly went for their food, the kids were already having ice cream – not a single serving but as much as they could eat. Fortunately, the mamas were busy and could not stop them having second and third helpings. There was more than enough ice cream as dessert for the elders. I think there were about five hundred guests, children included. After most of the guests had left, family members stayed back for photographs.

Finally just before midnight, Iza and Frank left for Grand Hotel, Ballard Estate, where they would spend their first night. The hired car broke down near Shivaji Park and Iza and Frank completed the trip by taxi.

The next couple of days were hectic. Frank had to get a visa for Iza to travel to Burma, and pack all their things including the wedding presents. We were advised that as per RBI rules, Iza should carry a detailed list, in triplicate, of the jewellery and wedding gifts she would be taking with her and get it signed by the Indian Customs at Calcutta on departure and by the Burma Customs on arrival at Rangoon. I sat down to type this list using Anju's Underwood portable typewriter.

I was typing with two fingers, when Ivy's cousin, Felix Athaide, noticed me and suggested I learn to type with four fingers and thumb of each hand as this skill would always be useful. I followed his advice immediately after the wedding. (This list proved very useful when Iza, who had retained her Indian passport, returned to India in 1966 when non-Burmans were being replaced by Burmans in every job and Frank and his brothers were rendered jobless. She could bring back all her jewellery and most of her household items. The Burmese Government did not object to her bringing her five kids to India, although they had been 'acquired' in Burma.)

Iza and Frank left for Burma within a week of their wedding.

Mrs. and Mr. Vaz with Queenie and Alex stayed back. Lourdes and Jennifer Pimenta from Poona had come down for Iza's wedding. They stayed a couple of days after the wedding. On the Sunday following Iza's wedding, Jennifer, then about eight years old, went for Mass with girls of her own age from our neighbourhood. After Mass she came out from the side door and took the road directly opposite and kept walking and suddenly discovered she had lost her way.

She asked someone the way back to the church but was directed to St Andrew's church, which she found totally different. When all of us reached home there was no sign of Jennifer. We checked with the neighbours and the girls confirmed that she had gone to church with them but did not return with them. I got onto my cycle and went off to investigate, while Anju decided to get the police involved. I cycled up our road and then through Kantwadi to Chimbai and just near St Andrew's Church I saw a group of people surrounding a young girl in a white frock. I went closer and found Jennifer, and brought her back on my cycle.

Queenie's wedding had been arranged to John Vas of Loutolim and was celebrated soon thereafter. John was employed in East Africa, so Queenie went from one old British colony to another thousands of miles apart. As both Queenie and John were not local people, they had a small wedding for the few relatives present in Bombay. Mr. Vaz then returned to Burma.

Alex had suffered from polio as a child. He needed special orthopaedic braces and a body belt which were not available in Burma. He took this opportunity to get himself fitted with the special braces and other equipment he required.

After all these events, Mrs. Vaz found that she was unable to eat her meals as there seemed to be a blockage somewhere. Our family doctor advised that she have a series of X-rays of her food passage using a barium meal. Ivy, in her far from fluent Konkani, tried to explain the procedure. What Mrs.Vaz understood was that the doctors wanted a picture of her insides and to her way of thinking this would involve cutting her open.

The appointment was fixed for early the next morning and she was asked to eat her night meal twelve hours earlier, before 19:30. Mrs. Vaz went to bed early and woke at 05:30 and, with the fear of what was to come, fainted. When she revived, she said she would prefer to suffer, but did not want to be cut open. Then Anju explained in his fluent Konkani what an X-ray was, and why it involved no cutting. With this explanation she agreed to go ahead. The X-rays found no blockage, it was the stress of the last couple of months that had caused her problem. Once she relaxed she was okay. She lived on to over 90 years and died a natural death in Goa.

Scouting out for work

All through these hectic months, I had continued to scan each day's *Times of India* and apply for each and every likely job. With my background of mathematics and statistics, I was selected for district development work by the Government of Bombay. All the selected candidates attended a three-week orientation course and, after successful completion, I was offered the post as assistant to the Development Commissioner of the Dangs District. This is a tribal area more or less totally forested. I was quite happy and looked forward to this posting. However, the government required that I sign a five year bond not to leave this service. On consulting senior family members and friends, I was advised against signing such a bond. Regretfully I had to turn down this job offer.

While sitting in Anju's office on the fifth floor of Laxmi Building and discussing with him all the vacancies against which I had un-successfully applied, one of Anju's agents told me that his friend, Ruy Menezes, working with the prominent advertising agency J Walter Thompson on the sixth floor had mentioned that they were looking for staff for their Market Research Division, which had just been started. I walked up with him and met Ruy, who turned out to be the husband of an old family friend, Vera

D'Souza of Jubbalpore.

Ruy promptly took me across to Mr. Borkar, head of the Marketing Research Division. He interviewed me and with my background of B.Sc. Mathematics with Statistics, decided I was quite a suitable candidate for this job. The only extra requirement was that I should know to type. Fortunately, having learnt to play the piano, I had picked up touch typing with Felix's encouragement, within just one month. When I typed out a copy of a page from some book quite fast and with no mistakes, Mr. Borkar was satisfied and offered me the job. This was, of course, subject to final interview by Mr. E.J. Fielden, Managing Director of JWT.

The next morning Mr. Borkar took me to meet Mr. Fielden, an Englishman. Mr. Borkar kept addressing Mr. Fielden as 'Sir', while I addressed him as 'Mr. Fielden'. Mr. Fielden approved Mr. Borkar's choice and confirmed that I may be appointed right away. After the interview Mr. Borkar said that in future I should address Mr. Fielden as 'Sir', to which I could not agree. I told him I would give Mr. Fielden all the respect that was his due, but I definitely would not call him 'Sir'. In my six years of service with JWT, I had no reason to regret this decision.

Anju and I now had our offices in the same building and Ivy could send one tiffin carrier with both our lunches through the *dabbawalla* – persons from Bombay involved in the unique enterprise of delivering home-cooked food to offices. I would go up to Anju's office and join him for lunch. If he was out, there was always one of his colleagues ready to join me to ensure that the tiffin carrier did not go back full of food.

One admission Anju did make was that Gresham charged a higher premia for their insurance policies. He had taken out a life insurance policy for me immediately after I joined college. In view of a certificate signed by Dr S.N. Cooper that loss of vision in my right eye was not a handicap to my normal life, Gresham had charged their standard premium with no surcharge. In 1957, after I started work, Anju suggested I take a new policy for a larger sum assured from the Life Insurance Corporation of India. Based on the fact that Gresham had charged no extra premium, LIC granted me the standard rate. Later that year I surrendered the Gresham policy and bought myself a National Ekco radio, manufactured in India in collaboration with Ekco of U.K., with the money from this policy.

Tribute to silver

December 28, 1957 was the silver jubilee of Ivy and Anju's wedding. Iza, while in Bombay, had been planning to celebrate this event in style. Now from Burma she was constantly writing with suggestions of how Ivy and Anju should celebrate this event. Finally Ivy and Anju decided to celebrate their silver jubilee by bringing the statue of Our Lady of Fatima to our house and observing the day as one of prayer and thanksgiving.

The whole village led by Fr Theophilus Lobo came in procession on December 28 morning, installed the statue on the beautifully decorated altar Ivy had built in our sitting room and offered prayers in thanksgiving for all the favours that Jesus and the Virgin Mary had granted our family in the last 25 years.

Ivy served cake and soft drinks to all who attended. Ivy's sisters, Clare, Amy, and Mayrose, with their families were present and they stayed on for lunch. In the evening friends from other parts of Bombay came over to congratulate Ivy and Anju and to join them in offering thanks to God. Family members stayed overnight with prayers being offered at regular hourly intervals. In the morning the statue was taken in procession back to the Church.

Iza had informed us that she was expecting her baby in early March. Ivy applied for and obtained her passport and then obtained a visa to visit Burma valid for a stay of three months. March is pretty cold in Taunggyi, so Ivy had to get warm clothes for herself as also a full set of warm clothes for the new arrival. Ivy went to Calcutta by train and then by plane to Rangoon.

From Rangoon she flew up to Mandalay where Frank met her and they traveled in his jeep to Taunggyi. Iza was well looked after by Mrs. Vaz and other members of the Vaz clan. Baby Glen arrived on March 4, 1958. Ivy managed to get her visa extended and stayed on till September, after celebrating Iza's birthday on August 31.

Shifting and spoons

Anju and I managed for ourselves at Sherly, Bandra, with the two young Marathi-speaking sisters, Gauri and Susheela, whom Ivy had trained to do the housework.

In June, Anju's friends, Gerard and Archie D'Sa of Nachinola, informed Anju that the ground floor of their cottage, Flora Building, was being vacated by Peter Dunbar, who had just retired from Esso to settling in Goa. They offered this accommodation to Anju at a monthly rent of Rs. 75, which he readily accepted.

One Sunday morning in June, Anju and I loaded our furniture and everything else on to a truck and shifted to Flora Building, Central Avenue, Santa Cruz. Our dog Chicko and I traveled in the truck with the luggage. Our two Marathi maids traveled in the driver's cabin. I had to shout out to stop when our full cutlery canteen fell off the truck, scattering spoons, forks and knives across the road, all of which we retrieved. But the beautiful cutlery case was a total loss. Except for this small casualty our possessions reached safely. Our two maids had agreed to stay till Ivy returned. Chicko was most at home in the new compound.

A fortnight after we shifted in, Mrs. Pimenta came in from Poona to meet her son John who was due from Chicago, USA. We met John at the airport and they stayed a couple of days at our place before proceeding to Poona and then to Goa. During this visit he met Lira and they were married before the Civil Registrar as per Portuguese law. John brought Lira with him to Bombay, when he flew back to Chicago. Lira joined him after a couple of months and their marriage in church was on April 19, 1959 in Chicago. John's sister, Lourdes, was able to come from Montreal to be present at their wedding.

Goa Blockaded

I N June 1960, I took leave and went to Secunderabad to travel with Granny Leopoldina to Goa. From Secunderabad we came to Poona to take the train to Goa. Since there was no detailed information over how to proceed to Goa as the Indian Government had now blockaded Goa and left only the southern border open for travellers, I left Granny at Pune station and went across to the Pimentas to get this information. Mrs. Pimenta insisted I have an early lunch and gave me a cake to share with Granny that afternoon.

Our train left Pune that evening and we arrived by early morning at Belgaum. Leaving Granny in the train, I got off the train and crossed to the bus terminus just outside the Belgaum station to check if there were buses that would take us to Goa. Granny panicked and got off the train with our luggage. By the time I got back, the train was just about ready to pull out. We were left with no alternative but to take the bus from Belgaum to Karwar.

Leaving Belgaum around 09:00 we travelled all day to Karwar and then crossed the ferry to Sadashivgadh. We arrived around 19:00 hours and were allotted a couple of beds in the dormitory style lodge. After a bath and dinner of rice and fish curry (very similar to what we would have had in Goa) we went to sleep. A couple of hours later I woke to find my silhouette on the bed outlined by bed bugs, which were literally feasting on my blood. I promptly left the bed and went out to the Goa style porch and sat there for a while. I could not force myself to sleep on that bed. Finally I walked across the road to the church, stretched out on one of the benches in the portico and slept the rest of the night there, awakening when the church bell was rung for Mass.

After an early breakfast of bread and tea, we boarded the bus for the Indian border post of Majali. We arrived there around 09:00 to find that there was already quite a queue of persons waiting to cross the border. Granny's travel papers were in order and they permitted her to cross over at around 11:00.

I had a cyclostyled Indian Citizen's ID, countersigned by the Honorary Portuguese Consul in Calcutta (Dominic Pereira). This was not acceptable since this document, obtained a year earlier, had since been replaced by a printed form of ID. I was asked to wait, while the Indian Border Police referred my case over radio to their headquarters in Bombay.

Detained along with me was a Hindu gentleman, who worked in the Bombay Customs, and whose village in Bombay State is just across a small rivulet from his wife's village in north Goa. He had to cover a distance of over two hundred miles to meet his wife who actually lived not even one mile from his home.

We hung around this border outpost until evening, checking with the radio officer every hour if he had received any message from Bombay. Except for pretty bad tea there was no refreshments available. The cake Mrs. Pimenta had given me for the journey was our lunch.

At 17:00 we were ordered to leave the outpost. I decided to head for Bombay, as I could not bring myself to stay another night at Sadashivgadh and return the next morning. My new friend persuaded me not to go back and suggested that we stay the night at his grand-aunt's home at Majali village, close to the border. We were cordially welcomed by his grand-aunt. We visited another of his friends in the village, an ex-Customs officer, who had recently retired from his post in Bombay. I was surprised when he requested this gentleman if we could have dinner with him as I had assumed that his grand-aunt would give us dinner, as there were no restaurants in the village. I was too tired to question him.

We went back and had our baths at the well and freshened up. After my bath I sat on the wooden bench in his grand-aunt's verandah and dozed off, while he went into the house and was chatting with her. Quite some time later he returned and surprisingly conducted me around, rather than through, the house to the kitchen where his grand-aunt fed us dinner. He explained that the front room was her *puja* room and that was why he had brought me around the house.

The food she served us was hot and delicious, although very simple vegetarian food. Maybe my hunger was the best sauce. I noticed that I was served food on a porcelain plate with a ceramic cup for water, whereas he had a brass *thali* with a brass *vati* for water. After eating my fill I returned to the well and washed my hands. My friend said he would join me later. I asked him about his Customs officer friend and whether we should not inform him that we had already had dinner. He confirmed that a message had already been sent.

I again waited on the wooden bench in the portico. My friend joined me quite some time later, and when I asked him the reason for this delay, he told me that he was required by his grand-aunt to take my plate and cup out of the house and leave it near the well. The servants would wash these the next morning, and then take fresh cow dung and spread this over the space of the kitchen floor where I had sat to eat. Obviously, Indian hospitality had prevailed over caste prejudices. His grand-aunt was an orthodox Brahman whereas I was a Christian who ate non-vegetarian food, including beef and pork.

We slept on the wooden benches in her portico and rose refreshed early. After a quick breakfast with his Custom's friend, we were back at the border outpost. No news had been received overnight, so we hung around that whole day and were forced to leave when the border closed at 17:00. No clearance had been received for us to be permitted to cross the border into Goa.

This time I refused to stay another night and left for Sadashivgadh and then on to Karwar, *en route* to Bombay, where I was welcomed back at work after only one week of my one month's sanctioned leave. Some months later I met this friend in Bombay and he informed me that sanction for both of us to cross into Goa was received that third day.

The next year, in May 1961, armed with the official printed Indian Government ID, I again presented myself at the Majali border post. At the Indian side of the Majali border, I met Olga and Anthony Athaide, both born in Burma, and we got chatting while our papers were processed. Theirs came through quite fast while I had to wait quite some time. When I finally crossed over at around 11:00 I found them waiting outside the Portuguese Customs office, so I sat down on the kerb alongside and continued our chat.

Suddenly, a Goan police constable or *cabo* was standing in front of me waving my Indian ID. He had been calling my name with the Portuguese pronunciation – to which I had not responded. He gave me my ID and told me I was free to go. When I asked him what about my friends – they had Goan IDs – he told me that as they were Goans they would have to wait till all those ahead of them were cleared. Finally, just at around 13:00 their papers came through and we were free to leave. As the next bus was not due out for some time, we decided to have some lunch.

The primitive restaurant had tinned foods, but I doubted they would have fresh meat or fish. Olga however decided to order a slice of fish fried in batter and we ordered a tin of corned beef and bread. Olga's food looked and smelt delicious and we were regretting our choice until she bit into the first mouthful. The face she made was adequate proof that she had not selected wisely. It was a slice of salt fish, dipped in water and then fried in some sort of batter. Fortunately the one can of corned beef and the bread served up was adequate for all three of us.

Our bus left around 14:00 and the next stop was Canacona where we halted for fifteen minutes. Tony and I promptly got down and bought two bottles of cold beer. While returning to the bus we were hiding the bottles, until we realised that we were no longer in 'Prohibition Bombay'. I enjoyed my first taste of cold beer. We reached Margao where we were able to get some snacks to go with our next bottle of beer. Olga shared Tony's beer. We reached Panjim around 18:00 and then crossed over to Betim by ferry and took a bus for Mapuça. They were from Sangolda and invited me to stop over that night as they were going to a dance at Saligao. The rest of their family was already at Sangolda. As I had not informed Granny of my arrival, I decided to stay over.

After a bath at their well and a substantial dinner, we all went to Saligao for the dance. Goa in May is hot and humid, plus with all the Petromax lamps the hall was really hot, so cooling fluids were essential. Surprisingly, a bottle of beer was available for 12 *annas*, but a sickly yellow lemonade cost Re.1, so we persuaded the girls to drink beer instead of lemonade. We must have got back to Sangolda around 06:00. After a couple of hours sleep I left for Nachinola around 09:00.

Granny Leopoldina was overjoyed to see me. She told me that after she left me at Majali, she waited on the Goan side till late evening and then travelled home. As a consequence she got a chill and was very ill for some days after getting back.

I enjoyed my holiday, with Granny taking pains to cook all the foods I liked. I would hire a cycle every morning, ride to Mapuça (or Mapusa), get the newspapers and enjoy a glass of cold beer before coming home for lunch. I had carried with me the permitted allowance of Rs. 100 plus an extra Rs. 400. In addition Granny helped me to draw my *zonn* (a form of earnings shared among members of the village community) of about Rs. 300. Fancy imported goods were plentiful but with this limited cash I only bought a Parker Jotter ballpoint pen plus refill. Our next door neighbour, Dr Silverio D'Souza, advised me to purchase a car – he had an Austen 6 for which he had paid just Rs. 6,000. He probably had a inkling that India would soon 'liberate' Goa, when having a car in Goa would be fantastic. Fiat cars in Bombay at that time cost around Rs.12,000.

After about two weeks, Molly with Sylvester, Lea, Michael, Joseph, Goiya and Baby Gemma arrived. Molly really had her hands full as Granny had not been able to get a servant to help her with the children. I helped with drawing water for the kids' baths, but washing of their clothes was a real problem, in addition to the fact that clothes did not dry fast in the rains. They left after ten days. I left a few days later.

Playing... and praying (for a job)

Iza with Glen and Noella came for a holiday in 1961 while her husband, Frank, was deputed for a training course at Kew Gardens, UK. She traveled on a direct flight operated by CSA (Czechoslovak Airlines) from Rangoon. But on arrival there was very heavy rain at Santa Cruz airport and the plane had to circle a couple of times before finally landing. They had to deploy a parachute from each wing to halt the plane on the runway. Iza was then expecting her third baby, Leon, who was born on November 8, 1961 at Silverene Hospital (now Holy Family Hospital), Bandra.

Glen would be dressed in his shirt, shorts, socks and shoes with minimal fuss. Possibly because of this and also because he missed Frank, he would get into lots of mischief and get scolded by everyone. Our cousin, Celine (Nogueira), spent a day with us and made a lot of fuss of Glenn and he became most well behaved. Thereafter, on arrival from management college between 21:30 and 22:00, I would mentally relax by playing with him and with Chicko. As baby Leon grew he also joined in the fun and the four of us would chase each other round and round inside the house, two on two legs and the other two on all four, till the three of them were tired and only then would go to sleep. I could then get down to my books and projects.

While working on my projects or studying various text books, I would work on them at my table which was next to my bed and fall asleep sometimes with the light left on. Mum would come and switch it off. I would get up as usual, get dressed and rush off to work leaving my books interleaved one with the other to keep my position in each book. One day, out of the goodness of her heart, Iza decided to clean up my desk. She put all my books in order on the shelf and dusted my table thoroughly. I came back and threw a fit since I would now have to search the various books for my specific reference pages.

Chicko proved most protective of Iza's kids. Miss Eula D'Cunha had purchased the property on which our house stood and the kids from her Rose Manor Garden School would play around our house. Glenn, Iza's four year old son, was riding his tricycle in the compound in front of our house, when one of the school boys, much bigger than him, grabbed the bike from him. Chicko promptly went for him, but did not bite him. He went off crying and the school or his parents informed the police that there was a "dangerous dog" at Flora Building. The police inspector who came to investigate was talking to us at our front door and telling us to keep our 'savage' dog in check. When he looked down and saw Chicko. "Is this the dog?" he asked. When we answered in the affirmative, he decided to hear our side of the story and then called the school boy, who confessed about snatching Glenn's tricycle. No action was taken by the police. I think he warned the school not to file such frivolous and untrue complaints.

In April 1963, I decided to switch over from one side of the advertising table to the other side. I joined Calico Chemicals at Chembur, in charge of advertising and public relations. I did only a short spell of six months with them and discovered that even after the basic plan and the budget had been approved by the directors, my immediate bosses would not allow me to go ahead and achieve the approved planned programme, without first referring every individual proposal back to the directors. Thus, in the bargain, missing some very fine opportunities for developing Calico's image as a manufacturer of PVC plastics (in addition to its original image of a textile manufacturer). This was totally frustrating. I resigned and was jobless from October 1, 1963. This prompted Noella, Iza's second child, in her night prayers to add: "Jesus, please find Uncle Loysius a good dob".

Frank completed his studies at Kew Gardens in September 1963 and returned to Rangoon by ship. Frank (Lobo) met him when his ship touched Aden (today part of Yemen), which incidentally was another centre of Goan migration. Iza with Glenn, Noella and Leon left Bombay by plane to reach Rangoon at about the same time as Frank's ship. All of them returned to Taunggyi where Frank now had his headquarters.

Home to Goa

Anju retired from the LIC on November 10, 1963, the day he completed 60 years. The divisional manager invited Anju for a farewell meeting and was surprised to find that Anju at 60 years looked much younger than *he* did; he had just completed 50 years. Anju believed that when selling insurance it was essential to give his clients confidence and looking old would definitely reduce this level of confidence. Anju continued working as an insurance agent – direct, without any inspector – until he was 90 years old.

Anju and I went down to Goa after he retired, as he was keen to settle in Goa. Living in Santa Cruz, Bombay, with the continuous noise of children of Rose Manor Garden School could by no stretch of the imagination be considered a peaceful retirement.

Anju also requested Gerry to come down to Goa at the same time, so that he could evaluate the possible opportunities of setting up a branch in Goa. I obtained a number of letters of introduction to potential employers in Goa and decided to investigate the opportunities available to me, so that I could also be based in Goa.

Making Nachinola liveable

Our first priority was to make our Nachinola house convenient for Ivy and Anju to live in, with running water and flushing toilet (with septic tank). Good quality deep-well diesel or petrol pumps and imported high grade galvanized iron pipes were available much cheaper than in Bombay. An overhead tank would have to be installed. The septic tank could be installed in the old quarry behind the house, quite some distance from our well. Modern sanitary-ware was available. A modern bath and toilet could easily be built in the room that was used as a godown.

The kitchen could be modified with tiled floor and work counters. The major cost item was the roof. Granny Leopoldina had not had the roof tiles removed, cleaned and old broken tiles replaced where necessary for quite some years and we expected that many of the beams and rafters might have been attacked by white ants and would need to be replaced. Over the kitchen and the store room, the roof tiles would be changed to Mangalore tiles.

Gerry was most knowledgeable in respect of these modifications and repairs. A rough estimate of costs was Rs. 20,000 for the roof alone and another Rs. 20,000 for all the other work. Electricity had not yet reached Nachinola by then. Running a small generator for our own use would be too difficult for Ivy and Anju to manage and so we would have to make do with kerosene lamps. Besides Petromax and Alladin lamps in the sitting and dining rooms.

Gerry then went off to investigate the potential for a diesel workshop, his specialty was machining and re-calibrating diesel fuel pumps. In Goa up to Liberation, if the fuel pump did not operate correctly, it had been the practice to discard and buy and install a complete new fuel pump with all accessories. There had been no demand for repairs. Now imported fuel pumps with Customs duty had become very costly and were not readily available. Goa iron and manganese open cast mines were totally dependent on tipper-trucks, earth moving equipment, air compressors – all of which were powered by diesel engines. His expertise would be in great demand. Gerry decided to shift to Goa and locate his diesel engineering workshop at Sanvordem, in the midst of the mining heartland in interior Goa.

With Gerry deciding to shift to Goa, the question of whether Anju or he should take over the Nachinola house had to be decided. It would be far more comfortable for Molly and their six children (the seventh, Carl, was born after they shifted to Goa) to stay in Nachinola, while Gerry stayed and worked in Sanvordem and came home on weekends. To this suggestion Gerry addressed me, saying: "I can not take over your birth right" – since Anju was the elder brother – and I replied, "You cannot take my birth right but I gladly give it to you." However, by the time we parted in Goa and Anju and I returned to Bombay, no decision had been taken as to which brother would live in this house and look after Granny.

Gerry returned to Secunderabad, promptly shut down Espee Diesel Engineers, loaded all his machinery in railway wagons (Secunderabad and Goa were both on the same metre gauge railway) and dispatched the wagons to Sanvordem Railway Station.

His new workshop, G. D'Souza & Sons, started functioning from December 1963 in the front rooms of a hired house. Anju was worried that Gerry had closed down his running business in Secunderabad and decided to start anew in Sanvordem, where he was totally unknown, but Gerry was confident. Further, the delicate work of machining valves and nozzles and calibrating diesel fuel pumps was his personal skill. He could not have operated simultaneously in both Secunderabad and Sanvordem.

Back at Work... in Goa

I had letters of introduction from various friends in Bombay to the major industrialists in Goa, viz. Chowgules, Cosme Matias Menezes (CMM), Dempos, Nazienzo Fernandes, Salgaocars, Dr. Jack Sequeira and Talaulicars. All these had licences granted by the Government of India to set up various industries.

I was confident that my marketing research and advertising experience coupled with my management training would definitely be an asset to any of these new industrial units. I visited each in turn, without any prior appointment, showing the particular letter of introduction as the ticket to enter. I was received very cordially by every one, in most cases by the senior most member of the family who was the CEO. All were impressed that my reason for looking for a job in Goa was to help in Goa's development.

V M Salgaocar and Pascoal Menezes of CMM each made me a job offer, but that of the Salgaocars was far more interesting. I took a small reduction in salary as compared to what I had been earning in Bombay. This job entailed staying in the port town of Vasco da Gama, as it would be impossible to commute from Nachinola every day.

I accepted Salgaocar's job offer and agreed to join from Saturday, December 14, 1963. This was initially to work in charge of sales of all the products for which they were the selling agents for Goa and within a year at most when the new industries were set up, to take charge of marketing their products.

Anju and I were back in Bombay by December 6. I immediately packed and came to Mormugao by ship, reaching Vasco on Friday, December 13, 1963. Initially I stayed in a room at the Hotel Rebelo, just next to the Vasco Da Gama railway station. It was not really a room but just a partitioned cubicle with a bed fitted with a mosquito net and a small writing table with chair, and a common bath and toilet for the whole floor. This was not too uncomfortable as the hotel had only a few guests.

I was pleasantly surprised to find Leslie Britto from Bandra residing at this hotel. While I had not known Leslie personally, his sisters, Lorna and Loretta, were at Sophia College when I was at St Xavier's and we had met at various CSU and other functions. Leslie had just joined Salgaocars in charge of its transportation department.

Reporting... to Vasco

I reported for work at the Salgaocars the next morning, Saturday, December 14, 1963 and was introduced to my immediate boss, Constance Mascarenhas. He was the head of the Engineering Department which controlled sales of all engineering products, sold directly from Vasco and through their retail outlets at Mapuça, Panjim, Margao and Ponda.

They had a wide range of products, properly labeled with bincards giving date and cost of purchase and religiously updated manually to tally with the stock in hand. These were mostly spares for imported machinery and equipment used in their own mines and by the clients who had bought these imported items from them.

These spares were listed by the 'Part N°.' designated by the original manufacturer. Even bolts and nuts, which appeared identical to me, were kept separate as per the manufacturer's "Part N°". I subsequently discovered that there was some reason for keeping these identical looking products separate as some were designed to last more or less permanently, while others were designed to fracture if overloaded.

We had huge stocks of wearable parts of mechanized shovels, which to my way of thinking could be repaired instead of being thrown away and replaced. There were large stocks of imported GI pipes of various sizes, which were not being sold, as "they might be needed in our own mines". Original cost of all these products, imported duty free during the Portuguese regime, was ridiculously low when compared with prices of similar products in India.

My first impression was that we were largely over-stocked. Wear and tear of machines operating in the mines ensured that their life was very limited, whereas stocks of spares were adequate for maybe ten to twelve years. Besides, given the changed political situation in Goa, there was no question of new equipment and machinery of those manufacturers being imported hereafter.

Saturday being a half-day, I went to Nachinola to tell Granny that I was now working in Goa. Gerry had also come home that weekend. He had discovered that though most of the trucks and other heavy diesel engines were operated from Sanvordem and mines in adjoining areas, no decision regarding their maintenance or repair was taken at the offices in the mines. Everything was referred to the respective head offices at Vasco or Margao or Panjim.

He was planning to come to Salgaocars in the course of the next week. We left Nachinola together on Sunday afternoon to return to our respective places of work. We agreed to meet at Nachinola on the first and third weekend of every month.

On my first day at work I did not get a chance to meet most of my office colleagues. But by the time I walked into the office on Monday, I was surprised that all my colleagues knew my family history – my village, my grandparents, etc. Manuel D'Cruz, in whose school Ivy had taught and where Iza and I had studied in 1942-44, was now working with Salgaocars and greeted me very loudly when he passed our department.

I subsequently met two of Ivy's pupils, Peter D'Souza and Wilfred Pereira, who were working also with the Salgaocars. Jose Pereira, nephew of Fr Theophilus Lobo, our parish priest at St Anne's Bandra, worked in the civil engineering department.

Coloured typewriters and explosives

I spent the next week trying to analyze the stocks in hand and to work out some procedure for recovering the large amount of capital invested in them. I discovered a consignment of 32 Remington typewriters, painted in a variety of colours – totally different from the standard grey of most office typewriters.

When I asked the reason for these coloured typewriters, I was told that they had been ordered because one of the potential customers had expressed a need for different coloured typewriters to match the décor of his offices. On the basis of this 'expression of interest', these typewriters had been specially ordered from Remington, Calcutta. When they arrived, the customer showed no interest in taking delivery or paying for them. Other customers who wanted a typewriter would not agree to take any of these brightly coloured typewriters. To me these were proverbial 'coloured elephants'.

Among other products were explosives and detonators manufactured by Indian Detonators Limited and Cissy Pvt Limited, who had in the previous year appointed Salgaocars as their sole selling agents for Goa. These explosives were stored in a special godown at Kalay, remote from the main road and any residential area. These goods arrived in special 'explosives' trucks with police escorts and were delivered direct to the explosives godown at Kalay. Salgaocar's man in charge of this explosive godown would send confirmation of arrival of these explosives trucks through any of the trucks from our mines which went there to collect their requirements of explosives.

During the course of the one year that this agreement had already been in force only one truck load had been purchased and used only by Salgaocar mines. No explosives had been sold to any other parties.

By Wednesday I gave my boss my opinion of what I could do to sell some of the stocks, and was told to draft a letter which would be sent to all potential customers with details of products and prices. Against orders received, the respective goods would be dispatched to the showroom or store nearest to the customer, from where he could take delivery.

All sales were on credit, payments would be subsequently collected. On further enquiry with the accounts department I discovered that many of these customers already owed Salgaocars substantial amounts for extended periods.

I spent the next week studying sales records and listing potential customers. This involved drafting our circular listing prices of the various products available from ready stock and which we were interested in selling. We also listed explosives, fuses and detonators which would be available against order. These cyclostyled circulars were mailed to the head offices of existing and potential customers. I had to sit at my desk and wait for replies.

In the meantime, on my way home that Saturday through Panjim and Mapuça, I visited the showrooms and introduced myself to each of the managers. I gave them copies of the circular and list of customers in their area to whom these circulars had been sent. I requested them to contact any of the persons they knew in these organizations and assess their reaction and get an idea of their requirements. These managers were keen to follow up on these circulars as they would get credit for goods sold through their respective showroom.

During the next week we had replies from some of the customers. As follow-up, I tried to telephone the parties concerned and faced a problem. Telephones in Goa were then antique – even a person whom I could see in the building across the road could not hear nor understand me over the telephone. I might have done better to shout across to him. Calls to Vasco and Mormugao were local calls, which could be dialed by our telephone operator; calls to Panjim, Margao, Mapuça and Ponda were trunk calls that had to go through one or more exchanges. In addition, my personal brand of Konkani was something the entire office sat back to listen.

I enjoyed Christmas and New Year at Nachinola, but on both days I had to rush back in the afternoon so as to be on time for work on December 26 and on January 2. Later I discovered that during the fair weather there was a launch at 08:00 from Dona Paula to Mormugao and a connecting bus which got me to Vasco to be in office by 09:00. By this route I could leave Nachinola by 06:30 on a Monday morning instead of leaving on Sunday afternoon.

At the end of one month, i.e. by mid-January, I felt that I had not generated sales enough to meet my own salary leave alone the salary of other staff in our department. I drew this to Mr. Mascarenhas' attention and requested that I be permitted to personally visit these potential customers, but his reply was in the negative.

Blood(y) questions

One morning in February my name was called by the director's personal peon; he did not know me. On identifying myself, he informed me that I was needed immediately by the director, R.M. Salgaocar. Mr. Salgaocar's first question (this was my first meeting with him) was why I donated blood. I replied that I did this to help someone who was seriously ill or had to have a major operation.

He then told me that he had received a call from the Blood Bank in Panjim asking especially for me as they urgently needed my blood. He placed a car at my disposal with instructions to the driver to take me to the Blood Bank and bring me back and cautioned him that he had to be very careful as I was giving my blood.

On reaching the Blood Bank, Dr. Barbosa, who was in charge, greeted me almost like royalty and informed me that they had requested St George's Blood Bank in Bombay for one pint (300 ml.) of Group B Rh-negative blood. In turn, Bombay had replied that their donor was in Goa and they could draw the blood direct. (B Rh-negative blood is very rare and at that time there were only five registered donors with this blood group in Bombay. We would be called upon to donate blood only when it was urgently required. Blood of our group was not stored.)

After donating the blood, I got up to return to Vasco, but Dr. Barbosa insisted I rest for at least an hour, have some biscuits and coffee and only then permitted me to return. I reached office just as everyone was leaving for lunch and was treated as though I had done something fantastic. In fact, I had donated blood many times in Bombay and to me it was a routine procedure. (One outcome of this blood donation was a proposal for marriage, which I could not avail of.)

Sanvordem was convenient to visit from Vasco as there was a train every afternoon and I could return that same evening. One Saturday, I visited Gerry and was dismayed at the amount of dust in his workshop and his residence. However, his business was improving by leaps and bounds as word spread from truck driver to truck driver that he was basically giving their diesel pumps a new lease of life and there was no need to throw away the old one and buy a new one at the current high prices. However, he had not yet broken through to the large companies who had fleets of vehicles, earth moving equipment and compressors. When this happened he would have assured large scale business.

On another Sunday I hired a car and visited Consua in Mormugao taluka, which was Mrs. Pimenta's ancestral home where we had spent a few days in 1942. Her brother Jose, while greeting me cordially, regretted that as I had given him no warning, they could not prepare some special dishes for me. I assured him that prawn curry and rice, which was more or less their standard everyday meal, was for me the best meal.

He mentioned that he knew V.M. Salgaocar personally and would be happy to put in a word with him for my advancement. I assured him that this would not be necessary. A few months later, he had reason to visit Mr. Salgaocar, and on arrival he called me to the entrance lobby and, while handing me a cake his wife had made, again suggested that he speak to VMS about me. I felt most embarrassed and assured him that this was not required and might do me harm.

A tip from Dr. Loyola Furtado

A few Sundays later, at Anju's request, I visited Dr. Loyola Furtado, who had been with Anju at the Burma Front, at his home in Chinchinim. His was a huge house almost on the main road, with no compound wall or gate, built about four feet off the ground with a grand entrance stairway and broad verandah across the front of the house.

I walked up to the main door, which was open as were all the French windows in the large hall which faced me. As there was no doorbell I called out and it was quite some time before someone from inside heard me and came to the front door. They were surprised that I had not entered directly. Dr Furtado was very happy to meet me and hear about Anju, whom he had not met for over twenty years. I promised that when Anju next visited Goa, I would make sure we came and visited him. I dodged out of his lunch invitation on the pretext that I had promised to be back in Vasco for lunch.

Visiting Dr Loyola Furtado at his house in Chinchinim had a very beneficial outcome. Dr. Furtado had been elected to the first Goa Assembly as member of United Goan Party. Later, on one of my visits to Panjim, I bumped into him and he told me about the recent decision by the Goa Government to allot a large plot of land on Alto Porvorim for a housing colony for officers of the Indian Armed Forces – both serving and retired. He advised me to get Anju to immediately apply for membership. I obtained the details from the Naval Base in Vasco and Anju filled in the necessary details and I paid the application fee of Rs. 250.

In due course, Anju was allotted Plot No. 75 in Defence Colony, Alto Porvorim. We had to pay Rs. 6,250 towards the price of the land.

Vasco in the Sixties

A FTER work each day, Leslie and I found ourselves with nothing to do. We had no home and Hotel Rebelo had no lounge or indoor games. Most other bachelors spent their evenings at the bars, which neither of us was keen to do. Leslie's sister, Lorna, married to Joe D'Souza, ships' surveyor, lived in Vasco. She introduced us around and I found that Anju's cousin, Iris Noronha, now Mrs. Cajetan Lobo, lived in Vasco.

Iris and Cajetan stayed in a bungalow of which one bedroom was unoccupied. They invited me to stay with them, but I insisted that they fix a fee for boarding and lodging. Having agreed a price I was happy to shift in and enjoy home food and the company of their three children, Rohini, Raju and Avi. Raju is my godson.

They had a maid, Mickey, who did the cooking and looked after the kids. Iris helped Cajetan in his office and reached home long after the kids came back from school. I would get back after work by 17:00. Mickey would give me tea and a snack. After a shower I would read or play with the kids.

Being close to the Dabolim airport, Bombay's newspapers reached us the same evening, but books were hard to obtain and there was no public library. Cajetan was an active member of the Lions Club of Vasco da Gama and consequently had quite a social life. Gradually they got me involved in some of their activities and thus life in Vasco became interesting.

Being an early riser I had plenty of time before getting to work at 09:00 so I started going for a walk each morning and attending Mass at St Andrew's Church. I discovered that the pews and kneelers were always very dusty and my shirt and trousers would get red mud stains on knees and elbows. I met the parish priest to complain about this and was informed that the church had no funds to employ more than the one man who was bell-ringer, grave digger and cleaner of the church. Being at the junction of the main road, dust would settle almost immediately after he had swept and dusted.

Leslie and I decided to organize games for the youngsters in the church compound. Initially, the parish priest was somewhat reluctant, but when I explained that these youngsters could then be organized to help in cleaning the church and also with the Sunday collection at Mass, he was happy to give us permission to go ahead. We purchased a football and started kicking it back and forth between the two of us. Before that first evening was out, four boys joined us. The next day there were more and by the end of the week we were able to organize teams to play regular matches. Once these boys were playing regularly it was a matter of just suggesting that they help in keeping the church clean and go around with open collection plates at each of the Sunday masses. Our parish priest was overjoyed with the way the collection money mounted – real money and not buttons and the like.

Finding buyers for the typewriters

I had a lucky break in early March. The Government of Goa's General Administrative Department issued a tender for 60 typewriters to be delivered on or before March 31, the closing of the financial year. We immediately quoted the best price that we could offer and confirmed that we had 40 typewriters (32 'coloured elephants' plus eight standard units) in ready stock and would get the balance as soon as it was possible for Remington to send them from Calcutta.

We received the confirmed order on March 24 – Tuesday of the

Holy Week – which did not leave us much time as Friday and Saturday were holidays. The typewriter mechanics worked on these 40 machines. They needed to be cleaned, oiled and checked and kept them ready for delivery on Easter Monday, March 30.

When I reached the office that morning, while the typewriters were ready, there was no transport available to carry them to Panjim. Finally a small Simca[11] van was given to me. We managed somehow to fit 40 typewriters into this van in three layers, with the fortieth placed on the passenger seat next to the driver and I sat on top of it.

We left Vasco at about 12:00 noon and reached Panjim just after 13:00. The government lunch hour was from 13:30 to 14:30. On arrival at the Secretariat, I could find no one to help me unload these typewriters. My driver declared that this was not his job. I picked up one and walked to the first floor office of the Secretary of the General Administration Department, A.M. D'Souza, and placed it on his desk. Then I produced the delivery challan and told him that the other 39 were in the car outside the side entrance and, since there was no one else available, I would bring up the rest one by one to his office.

He promptly corralled a number of peons and got them to pick up and deliver the machines to the offices for which they were meant. He requested me to deliver some of these machines to other government offices in Panjim. The balance 20 were delivered about a fortnight later.

Meanwhile, my regular visits on Saturday afternoons to the showrooms in Panjim and Mapuça began to yield results. The personnel there were following up with existing and potential customers and goods were starting to move on a limited scale.

I had yet to meet the staff at Margao and Ponda. Correspondence with these two showrooms was sent through trucks or jeeps going to and coming from the mines. Margao also sent reports through some of the staff who lived in there and commuted

---

[11] Named after the French automaker, Société Industrielle de Mécanique et Carrosserie Automobile, Mechanical and Automotive Body Manufacturing Company.

by train. This whole policy of selling through correspondence and through show rooms was very frustrating, particularly since I knew customers were just waiting for these products.

Barge Workers See Red

O UT of the blue suddenly there was firing by the police on striking barge workers, who had formed a trade union assisted by the Communists and demanded better wages and working conditions. The main reason for dissatisfaction was the new rule to be enforced shortly that all barge 'drivers' must pass the Mercantile Marine Department's (MMD) tests of proficiency.

These barge drivers were virtually illiterate (just able to sign their own names, having passed out of the primary schools run by various churches), but from hands-on experience they well knew the Rivers Mandovi and Zuari and the Kumbarjua Canal connecting these two rivers with their turns and twists and moving sand banks.

The Indian National Trades Union Congress (sponsored by the Congress Party) tried to break the strike by bringing in barge operators from Kerala. This resulted in riots at Mormugao Port, which necessitated the firing by the police. Mine and barge workers' unions were supported by the Communist Party, while the port and dock workers' union of Mormugao was supported by the Congress Party.

With the formation of trade unions in the mines and among dock and barge workers, office workers also decided to form their own labour union. They approached Cajetan Lobo, who as a Congress worker had been very active in the *satyagraha* movement which finally led to the Liberation of Goa from the Portuguese. Since I was staying in Cajetan's house, I was fully informed of these below the surface currents.

We strongly advised these workers not to join either the Communist or the Congress Party, but to form their own independent labour union. They explained their ignorance of all matters relating to forming a labour union and then using it to bargain with their employers. (Most of the office workers of Salgaocars and Chowgules were paid salaries as low as Rs. 200 to Rs. 300 per month, which might have been somewhat adequate during the Portuguese regime when imported food stuffs and clothes were very cheap. But since Liberation prices had risen substantially and everyone was feeling the pinch.)

We explained to these office workers that they really held the key to the operations of these companies who were dependent on mining and exporting iron and manganese ore. I volunteered to help them and got them a full set of the relevant government acts and rules (labour law and the handling of industrial disputes had been part of my management training).

Staff members from Chowgules and Salgaocars got together and formally applied for registration as an Office Workers Labour Union. I did most of the typing on my portable typewriter. Once the labour union was registered with the Labour Commissioner at Panjim, the union drew up a charter of demands and presented it to the managements at Salgaocars and Chowgules.

All hell broke loose. R M Salgaocar took it upon himself to find out who was behind the union. Although my name was not mentioned anywhere, nor had I joined the union, his spies, who obviously stalked the committee members, soon found out that they were coming to me for advice. The company took the stand that I was not a 'worker' as defined by the Industrial Disputes Act and as such could not be protected under this Act.

The union took up this issue with the Labour Commissioner. I was summoned before him together with committee members of the union. A L (Sonny) Correa, personnel manager of the Salgaocars, represented the company. I argued my own case and proved to the Labour Commissioner's satisfaction that, since I was not authorised to sign any letters nor did I have any subordinates, I was definitely not a 'manager' and he gave his decision that I was a 'worker' and advised me to join as a member of the union.

Thus in the eyes of Salgaocar's management I had become a trouble maker.

One of our most reliable sources of information of management thinking, planning and actions, were the car drivers (all were members of our office workers union). These traveled with the senior executives and directors who discussed all such matters without realising that the drivers could understand every word and report to the union.

Probably as a sort of punishment or to keep me out of circulation, I was instructed to proceed to the Bagalkot Cement Works, Bagalkot, to organize the dispatch of four wagon loads of cement allotted to our company, which was urgently needed for work in the mines so that all construction could be completed before the onset of the monsoon. My scheduled departure was May 27, 1964, and that same day news reached us that Prime Minister Pandit Jawaharlal Nehru had died. All offices declared May 27-28 as holidays. In spite of this, I proceeded with my trip and on arrival at Bagalkot (after quite a tedious journey) was able to arrange for empty wagons, have them loaded and then dispatched to Vasco. Having seen that the four wagons were dispatched on Friday, May 30, I sent off a telegram to Salgaocars, Vasco, giving dispatch details.

From Bagalkot I took the evening train to Pune and was there early Saturday morning. Hazel had completed her training at the JJ Hospital, Bombay and was home in Pune. We spent the weekend together and I left for Vasco on Sunday night to reach office early by 09:00 Monday. Thereafter, for quite a few weekends, I would take the afternoon bus from Vasco to Belgaum and then the train to Pune, reaching early Sunday morning, spend the day with Hazel and return by the evening train to resume work on Monday.

Molly and the kids joined Gerry at Sanvordem only after the school year ended in April 1964. The family lived in the rear portion of the house in which he had his workshop. With heavily loaded trucks and earth moving machinery constantly on the move on non-macadamized roads, the quantum of dust was beyond imagination.

During the dry weather, dust, though everywhere, could be wiped off. But once the monsoons started, the area was a quagmire. Rain acquired a red tinge and everything – books, clothes and food – was completely covered with this dark red coating which could not be wiped or washed off and left permanent stains behind.

There was a parish school at Sanvordem and all the kids readily got admission. They did well at school as the standard of this school was well below that of the schools they had attended in Secunderabad.

Nachinola on our mind

Anju came down in early June and spent one weekend with me at Vasco. On Sunday we visited Gerry and Molly. Fortunately, or rather unfortunately, it rained very heavily while we were at Sanvordem and the road in front of Gerry's house was almost a river of mud. Being a Sunday there was little truck movement, but we could well imagine the mess with the large number of trucks moving on this road.

Anju again requested Gerry to send Molly and the kids to live at Nachinola, but he would not make a firm commitment, preferring to wait out a full year and then decide. He still felt that Anju, as the elder brother, should take over the Nachinola house.

Of Explosives and Mines

O N the explosives front there was no progress. Another truck load was ordered and delivered for consumption in Salgaocar's own mines. In two years that this sole selling agency was in force, only two truck loads of explosives had been ordered and sold, whereas Indian Explosives Ltd. the only other competitor, had sold a truck load almost every month.

In spite of my brush with the management over the formation of the labour union, Salgaocars sanctioned me leave of one month in December 1964 to enable me to attend the Marian Congress in Bombay.

Hazel was a member of the choir that sang at the various services held at the Oval Maidan in Bombay and stayed with her cousin, Thelma Coelho, at Byculla. In spite of the hectic programme of events, we managed to spend quite some time together including Christmas and New Year dances at Catholic Gymkhana. She returned to Pune on January 2, where she was now working at Sassoon Hospital and I was back at work in Vasco on January 3, 1965. For that trip, I flew down, the Indian Airlines fare was only Rs. 90 with the round trip costing Rs. 170.

In the first week of April 1965, senior executives of Indian Detonators Ltd., Mr. Abraham and Mr. Khatoj, visited Goa. Since I was supposedly in charge of sales of explosives, I was required to accompany them on a survey of users in various parts of Goa and to our explosives godown at Kalay, incidentally my first visit there.

Mr Abraham had first-hand, in-depth mining experience both opencast and underground. Being with him was an education in various aspects of mining that were practiced in Goa as compared with what happened in the rest of India. Using time-delay detonators on a rock face, he explained that there would be no spread of debris and the size of ore could be controlled to some extent. Fines commanded lesser price than fair sized particles of iron ore.

With them I visited all the mining areas of Goa and was surprised at the cordiality of our welcome by every mining office and the personnel who were actually planning and extracting iron and manganese ore. I had managed to keep my manager and our two directors informed on our activities during these ten days.

On April 13 and 14, these gentlemen had a conference with the directors and senior executives of Salgaocars, where they obviously pulled up the company for its very poor sales, when the sales potential was huge. On April 14 afternoon (Wednesday), I was called into the meeting and was asked by R.M. Salgaocar if I agreed with the opinion of these IDL executives and whether I could achieve substantially higher sales.

When I confirmed that I considered this very possible, provided I could regularly visit the mines and not just write to their head offices, RMS immediately instructed that I be provided with a car each Thursday (commencing the very next day) to visit the mines and report back on Friday morning the outcome of my visit. (That Thursday was Maunday Thursday and I suspect RMS felt that I would use this as an excuse not to go to the mines that day.)

More as a measure of goodwill rather than in anticipation of good sales, Salgaocars ordered one truckload of explosives, even through there was substantial stock at Kalay.

At 08:00 on Thursday, April 15, 1965, I did my first of a series of visits to actual operating mines in the Bicholim area, in the hinterland of Goa. Compared to roads in the rest of India, Goa's mining roads were in good condition, and with the Simca provided the driver kept to an average speed of 100 km/hour.

On the route I got a chance of meeting our staff at the Ponda showroom. They gave me the names of persons in various mines who would be interested in our explosives as well as other engineering products.

My driver, himself, was a mine of information. I visited about twelve mining offices, including our own mines in that area, and was able to secure firm orders for almost all the explosives we had in stock as well as for various lengths of different diameters of GI pipes. Since mining offices closed at 16:30, I instructed the driver to reach me to Nachinola so that I could spend Good Friday and Easter at home and return to Vasco on Sunday on my own steam.

I got back to Vasco on Easter Sunday early evening and typed my report on my own typewriter at home. On Monday morning, I was in office before 09:00 and left the original of my report for my boss with duplicates for V.M. Salgaocar and R.M. Salgaocar.

R.M. Salgaocar, who was already in his office, read my report before Mr. Mascarenhas came into office. He immediately called me into his office (he seemed fully informed on my movements that Thursday) and asked me how I proposed to have the ordered goods delivered. I informed him that we would send delivery orders for the explosives to the nearest showroom, from where the customer would collect the delivery order against full payment by cheque, and then the customer would arrange to collect the specified goods from our Kalay godown.

He remonstrated with me that some of these customers were our regular customers, with whom we had long standing credit business. I explained that according to the Indian Explosives Act, the person transporting explosives had necessarily to be the owner and this would not be so if these goods were sold on credit. After some discussion, he finally agreed and volunteered to inform these old customers of this government requirement.

He also raised the question of selling our stock of GI pipes, since our mines regularly required large quantities of these pipes.

Fortunately, I had checked with our mines and ascertained the sizes and maximum quantity they would require. Since we were also selling agents for Tata pipes, the best Indian grade of GI and other pipes, there was no danger of our mines being deprived of their own requirements.

Plus there were large quantities of half-inch pipes, which are largely used in domestic water pipelines and these could be sold for all the new buildings – industrial, commercial and residential – now coming up in Goa.

RMS subsequently called in Mr. Mascarenhas and informed him that all orders booked by me should be executed without any delay. Since virtually all ready stocks of explosives had been booked, he was instructed to place an order for another truck-load, even though one was already on order and expected shortly.

That was my baptism of fire. After that, every Thursday I visited mining areas as well as other areas where I felt there existed a demand for our range of products, and always made it possible to visit the showrooms and inform them of customers whom I had met and who might call for various products. These showrooms were ecstatic as they had never seen such large sales before.

An interesting aspect very different from that experienced in Bombay and other parts of India, was that a 'vegetarian' *thali* meal in all restaurants in Goa at that time would contain a piece of fried fish or piece of chicken or mutton – *pure* vegetarians could not find appropriate food, the only exceptions being Satkar at Ponda and Gujarat Lodge at Panjim.

Since my driver would per force have to eat in the same restaurant, I always invited him (whether Hindu or Christian) to sit at the same table with me and paid for his meal. We ate the same food, except that I would prefer *chapattis* (if available), whereas he would eat a good helping of rice. At Satkar, Ponda I enjoyed the first real vegetarian meal since leaving Bombay but my Hindu driver was not impressed as he said *"Kai nishtem ya mas na"* (No fish or meat).

As a consequence to my regular visits to the mines, the sales of explosives reached almost one truckload each month. Prices of explosives was fixed and we were entitled to 10% discount on the selling price. Suppliers' payment terms were 10% of the invoice against delivery and balance 90% against a three month *hundi,* i.e. we actually paid for the explosives three months after the truck load was delivered to our Kalay magazine.

R.M. Salgaocar asked our accounts department to work out the profitability of this explosives business. A fresh chartered accountant had just joined our company and was assigned this evaluation. His reply to RMS was that since we received 10% discount from Indian Detonators and Cissy but paid interest to Bank of India @ 9% p.a., we were earning 1% profit. I had to sit and explain to him that actually we were saving the company a considerable amount by reducing the overdraft. We received 100% payment for these explosives within at most one week from date of arrival in our magazine, whereas we paid 90% three months after receipt of the goods.

I suggested that the company open a separate account for this explosives business and it would then be very obvious how much profit was actually being earned.

Sales of all agency products were now well organized. My colleague, Mr. Henriques, was fully briefed on how to proceed. But there was no progress on development of Salgaocar's new manufacturing industries. I decided that there was no real future for me with them.

Moving on from Salgaocars

Accordingly I submitted my resignation and requested that I be relieved with effect from December 15, 1965 – exactly two years from my date of joining. Thanks to the weekly sales tours, I had visited every part of Goa. Many were areas which I did not know even existed.

On December 15, I took Mr. Henriques with me to Kalay and after carefully explaining the various procedures required for storing and delivery of stocks of explosives, handed over charge to him.

Kalay is close to the Collem Railway Station and we went there and were just in time to meet the train coming in from Pune. Hazel had written that she would join me to celebrate my birthday on the 16 and then both of us take the ship from Mormugao to Bombay.

I barged into Hazel's compartment, woke her from her sleep and rolled up her bedding and packed her and her baggage into the car. We were home long before the train reached Vasco. I had warned Iris of Hazel's arrival, so she was at home when we arrived.

I had invited my colleagues at Salgaocars and a few other friends to a farewell party on December 16. When they arrived they were surprised to find my 'fiancée' with me. It was a simple party, but a few of them were astonished to eat cheese which was soft and fresh – they usually cursed India for depriving them of Kraft cheese, the American brand available in Goa while the Portuguese were here. I served Amul cheese out of a can, as much as they could eat.

We were unable to get a cabin for travel from Mormugao to Bombay on Scindia's steamer *S.S. Mohamadi* so Hazel and I traveled on the upper deck and enjoyed the voyage. Lourdes' colleague from Nirmala Niketan, Joy Nazareth, her husband and one of Hazel's cousins, Brian Siqueira, traveled on the same voyage.

On arrival in Bombay, Hazel stayed with us at Santa Cruz and attended the various birthday parties, Christmas and New Year dances. We also visited her and my relatives and informed them of our forthcoming marriage on January 5 at Poona.

On January 1, 1966, her sisters Rozaria and Celina made their final vows as nuns of the Jesus and Mary Convent. Hazel's mother and sisters were present and my Mum and Dad were also present as they were Rozaria's godparents. Hazel returned to Pune with her Mum and sisters on the January 2.

My Mum and Dad with Amy, Tim and Mayrose joined me on

Dividing a Home, Goa-Style

W ITH no commitment from Gerry and Granny Leopoldina getting older and less capable of managing on her own, the decision of who should stay at Nachinola was becoming critical. Further, immediate repairs had to be carried out to keep the house in good condition. Who would pay for these repairs? Anju and I enquired with friends as to how this problem could be solved.

Everyone suggested that we apply for an *'iventor'* (basically an inventory of the estate) after which family members involved could decide among themselves who would take which property. Accordingly, Anju made an application in October 1965 to the *Regis Civil* (Civil Registrar), Mapuça. This was taken on account and notices were sent to all directly concerned – Granny Leopoldina, Anju, Bemvinda and Gerry. Bemvinda (with husband Salu) replied that they had received their fair share of Grandpa's and Granny's estate and had no further claim. Gerry indicated that he would be present at the *iventor* and the auction which followed. This was fixed for April 1966.

Anju and I stayed at Nachinola and were present at the *iventor*. Gerry had told Granny Leopoldina that he would be coming straight to Mapuça to attend the *iventor*.

Taking into account the estimated costs of repairs as against the cost of building a compact cottage at Defence Colony, Anju and I decided that our maximum bid for the Nachinola house would be Rs. 20,000.

On the specified date, Granny Leopoldina, Anju and I were at the *Regis Civil's* office at 09:00. While waiting for Gerry we found out from the *Regis Civil*, that only the three – Granny, Anju and Gerry – could bid for the property. No outsider could bid. Bids could be raised in increments of Re. 1.

Till 10:00 there was no sign of Gerry. Then a lawyer appeared waving a power of attorney from Gerry to attend and bid at the *iventor* on his behalf. The *Regis Civil* immediately started the process of the *iventor*. First he enumerated all the properties involved – the *moiee*, the small plot near the house and the house itself with the adjacent compound and out houses (excluding the strip of land on the right which was already in Gerry's name) – in that order.

Anju requested that the house be auctioned first and then the other two properties could be taken by the successful bidder. To this the officer would not agree.

He called for bids for the *moiee* – Anju did not bid and the lawyer also did not bid. He then called for bids for the small plot and again Anju and the lawyer both did not bid. He then put up the house for auction – Anju bid Re. 1, the lawyer raised the bid by Re. 1. This continued till the bid amount reached Rs. 9 by Anju, then the lawyer jump bid to Rs. 10,000. Anju then bid Rs. 10,001 – the lawyer bid Rs. 11,000 and Anju bid Rs. 11,001.

This bidding was too slow by the lawyer's standard so he again jump bid Rs. 15,000 and Anju countered with Rs. 15,001. The lawyer then bid Rs. 20,000 and Anju did not bid, much to the lawyer's surprise. So Gerry became the owner of the Nachinola house.

The *Regis Civil* confirmed ownership of the *moiee* and the small plot to Anju with zero payment, as no one had bid for these two properties. Gerry had to pay Anju Rs. 10,000 as Granny Leopoldina had already received the proceeds from Grandad's estate in 1946.

Gerry, Molly and the kids shifted from Sanvordem to Nachinola as soon as the school year ended in May 1966 and took up residence there. The kids got admission to schools in Aldona. Gerry bought bicycles for them to use for traveling to and from school. Gerry would work in Sanvordem during the week, returning on Saturday and going back on Monday. Granny had a house full and was no longer lonely.

Ivy and Anju continued living at Santa Cruz, Bombay. Anju was now selling LIC's life insurance policies as an agent and no longer as an inspector of agencies.

I had been allotted a small flat by CMM adjoining their flat at Colaba.

In 1966, Hazel and I, as newlyweds, were invited to lunches or dinners most weekends by various relatives and friends, which we looked forward to as Hazel's knowledge of cooking was then practically nil. We would visit Ivy and Anju at least once a month and shoot off to Poona by train to spend any extended week end with Hazel's family – Mrs. Pimenta, Jennifer and Veronica. We were fancy-free and enjoying life.

Getting replaced by indigenous Burmans

By June 1966, meanwhile, in another part of the globe, the situation in Burma went from bad to worse. Frank together with his brothers were replaced by indigenous Burmans, irrespective of their ability to handle the job. Yet they were not allowed to leave Burma, since they had been educated there and the Burmese Government felt that they owed the State the cost of their education. Finally, on payment of substantial sums of money, they were permitted to leave, but they were not allowed to carry out any valuable assets acquired in Burma.

Patrick, Frank's eldest brother's son, was not permitted to leave as he had qualified as a medical doctor and Burma was woefully short of doctors. Patrick, his wife and daughters were left behind while the rest of the Vaz clan of Taunggyi left Burma more than eighty years after Mr. Vaz had originally gone there. Mr. Vaz himself never left Burma, he died before the family was forced to leave and was buried at Taunggyi.

Iza was lucky, since she had been wise to keep the list of jewelry and wedding presents which she had taken with her into Burma in 1957, and was permitted to bring back all these items, together with her five children (her own personal art works) whom she had acquired in Burma.

Vanessa, the youngest and only a few months old, developed a sort of tangled intestine while waiting in Rangoon for the various government clearances, and had to have a fairly serious abdominal operation. They reached Bombay in August 1966 and settled in with Ivy and Anju. Ivy was able to organize admissions for them in Santa Cruz – at Sacred Heart School for the three boys and St Theresa's Convent for Noella. Vanessa was still a baby.

Frank was fortunate to get a job with an agricultural development organization working in Central India. This involved considerable traveling from one project site to another. On one of his trips by bus, while he was asleep in his seat, someone unloaded his suitcase containing all his clothes from the luggage rack on top of the bus and carried it away.

It was really tough going for Frank and Iza. Later Frank was transferred to Bangalore to supervise agricultural projects in Anantapur, Cuddapah and other places in South India. Instead of shifting the family to Bangalore, they preferred to make Goa their base, and shifted into Frank's aunt's house in Saligao in May 1968. The boys were admitted to St Britto High School at Mapuça and both the girls were admitted to Lourdes Convent, Saligao.

Their cousin, Jose Cordeiro, who had left Burma much earlier when the situation was better, had been able to send out all his furniture and other assets by ship direct from Rangoon to Mormugao. He was already employed with the Goa PWD (Public Works Department). Frank's brothers, Sonny and Peter, who had worked with the PWD in Burma were able to get jobs with the PWD in Goa. Robert, the doctor, was inducted into Goa's health services.

Getting going at the Defence Colony

Within about a year after settling in Saligao, Iza and Frank bought a small plot of land on the *bandh* in Sonarbhat, Saligao, and built a small cottage.

After they built their house, Anju started building his own house at the Defence Colony, Alto Porvorim. Frank and his brother, Sonny, were a great help to Anju in getting this house constructed. Anju supervised the actual construction of the house as designed by Sonny.

Water had to be brought up to Defence Colony for construction as well as for drinking and washing. This came from wells down the hill in Socorro/ Torda. Each bullock cart would bring up two 200 litre barrels, out of which quite an amount spilled on the way up the hill over the rutted road. In the adjoining plot owned by Capt. Pat Tellis, there was a huge banyan tree, under the shade of which Anju set up camp, where he could sit while supervising the work.

Anju completed the building of the house in 1970. Ivy shifted all the furniture and household effects from the Santa Cruz house to 75, Defence Colony in May 1970. Ivy and Anju were the first to build and occupy their home at the Defence Colony in Alto Porvorim. Other members who were building their homes in Defence Colony would come to Ivy and Anju for help and guidance and many of them would stay with Ivy and Anju while supervising construction of their new homes.

As a consequence, Anju is treated as a founder member of Defence Colony and till date his birthday, November 10, is celebrated with a thanksgiving Mass and a get-together at our house.

A Devotee... and a Chapel

I vy had been keeping indifferent health in Goa, but she kept herself busy with tutoring Iza's kids and other children in the neighbourhood. She became the moving spirit behind activities at Holy Family Chapel, Alto Porvorim and the upgradation of this chapel into a parish church. Here she found herself up against her own cousin, Fr. Antonio Athaide Lobo, who was the parish priest of the Porvorim Church.

The Redemptorists Priests had their house at Alto Porvorim and one or other of them, particularly Fr Antonio Rodrigues, CSsR, would very happily conduct Sunday and week day services at the chapel, which Fr. Athaide Lobo was not too happy about.

For people from Defence Colony and other residents of Alto Porvorim, this was a boon as the alternative was to go down the hill to the Porvorim Church and climb up the hill again after services. After strenuous efforts by Ivy and others, Archbishop Raul Gonsalves appointed Redemptorist Fr. Antonio Rodrigues as *pro-tem* chaplain, and subsequently appointed a diocesan priest as chaplain. Holy Family Chapel was finally upgraded to a parish church in January 2009 with Fr Anand Pais of Moira as the first parish priest.

Ivy was also largely responsible for getting the comunidade to allot a plot for a cemetery for Alto Porvorim but she died before it could be fully developed. She was buried at the Saligao cemetery. However, when Anju's remains had to be dis-interred, we placed them in a niche at the Alto Porvorim cemetery and on the memorial plaque inscribed both Ivy's and Anju's names.

Water carted in

For quite some time after shifting into their house at 75, Defence Colony, Ivy and Anju were dependent on water brought up in bullock carts from the nearby village of Soccoro-Torda, located at the foot of the hill. Anju investigated the possibility of getting a bore-well so as to have his own source of water, but the rock was too hard and solid for the drilling machine to bore through to the ground water level. The costs were also very substantial and since municipal water supply was imminently promised he did not proceed with the bore-well.

Anju, in spite of the area around being solid rock, decided to have a garden. He planted various fruit trees and also some flowers. He succeeded in growing three mango trees, one coconut and one jackfruit tree. These mango trees nurtured by the output from the septic tank produce large numbers of fruit. Unfortunately one of them was blown down by cyclonic winds sometime in the early 1990s.

Anju was most particular to ensure that sea-salt and manure were put at the base of each tree in early June. This made sure that level of nutrients in the soil around these plants was maintained. After Anju's death, I had not been putting sea salt around the mango trees and discovered that white ants were eating into the bark of these two trees. I treated them with some specific chemical and the white ants seem to have disappeared, but I plan to continue Anju's schedule of placing sea salt around the base of these trees just before the monsoons in addition to organic fertilizers.

However, Anju's front garden did not yield many flowers – a few rose trees did bloom, but the evergreens he planted really flourished. One particular evergreen which had grown into quite a dense bush just in front of the verandah became the home of two tiny birds. They built their nest in the middle of the bush, visible only if you knew it was there and was looking for it. This bird would stay in its nest until no predators were visible, then it would dart out and its partner would take its place within the twinkling of an eye. After some time the change over would be repeated. I noticed that the birds usually emerged if Anju was in the verandah reading his newspapers. They knew that no crows or kites would attempt to harm them or their nest when Anju was near. Unfortunately, after some years this evergreen died and others that have come up do not provide such dense cover. We lost these lovely unconventional pets.

Never lacking in company

While Ivy was busy with housekeeping, the kitchen and giving tuitions to various children, Anju never lacked company. His best friends were usually the little ones, who when passing on the road. Seeing him in the garden, they would call out and he would invite them in. He usually kept a bottle full of sweets and toffees, which he was ever willing to distribute to these little friends. Plus he still kept his bottles of *channa* and peanuts ready for those who preferred these to sweets.

In addition to neighbours of Defence Colony, Ivy and Anju usually had as house-guests friends from Bombay, Calcutta and Burma who either stayed with them or dropped in when on holiday in Goa. Cousins, whom I have rarely, if ever, met, tell me of the enjoyable holidays they have spent with Ivy and Anju at Porvorim. My cousin, Raymond Nogueira, was with the Indian Navy, Submarines. Whenever his submarine visited Mormugao port, he would somehow manage to get a couple of days off and spend them at Porvorim. He tells of Anju buying *bangdas* (mackerels) and, because Ivy was allergic to fish, clean these fish outside the house and cook them on a fireplace in the compound. Ivy did not react to the smell of cooked fish, so they enjoyed the roasted fish at the dining table, with an appropriate appetizer-cum-digestive – *feni*.

Our next door neighbour from Santa Cruz, Bombay, Philip de Souza, has his ancestral home in Porvorim village. When Valerie, Michael and Andrea were in Goa for their holidays, instead of spending time with their grand-aunts, early morning they would come running up the hill, spend the day with Ivy and Anju and go back in time for dinner. Years later, Michael arrived late one night – his grand-aunts had died and their ancestral home was closed – so he checked into a hotel midway up Porvorim hill and got quite a talking to from Anju for not coming straight to 75, Defence Colony.

Defence Colony amenities

As the earliest resident of Defence Colony and the senior most in age, Anju's opinion carried considerable weight in the deliberation at the general body meetings of the society. Anju was particularly vociferous in respect of the *Sainik* Gymkhana.

The Services Welfare Fund had allocated some considerable fund for development of recreation facilities for ex-servicemen. A playground and gymkhana had been included in the plans of Defence Colony, Alto Porvorim.

Some of the members kept opposing the building of this gymkhana on the ground that it could become a centre for card-playing and gambling. At one meeting, Anju was furious with these gentlemen and asked them what was there to prevent people interested in card-playing or gambling from doing the same in their own homes, if they so desired. He questioned the idea that they would wait for the gymkhana to be built to start card-playing or gambling. With that he carried the house and the gymkhana is now built, though members do not as yet take full advantage of it.

Another project which he strongly supported was the establishment of the *Sainik* Co-operative Stores. I seem to remember that he was called upon to inaugurate these stores. Membership of the co-operative is open to everybody. Most utility items and a wide range of provisions, including liquors, are available. The staff is very friendly and helpful. These stores have proved very popular with residents of virtually the whole of Alto Porvorim and many people from distant areas also doing their shopping here.

The Ex-Servicemen's Welfare Fund which promoted Defence Colony did so to provide decent and quiet retirement homes for ex-servicemen. This colony has become a haven of peace among the new housing projects coming up all over Goa including Alto Porvorim.

Consequently, demand for land has very substantially increased and prices have sky rocketed. Some members, seeing this as a huge commercial gold mine, proposed that members be allowed to build multi-storeyed buildings with flats on their plots and give these flats on rent. Anju was one of those who vehemently opposed this motion. He pointed out that Defence Colony in Delhi, sponsored for the benefit of ex-servicemen, has hardly any ex-servicemen residing therein as most of the plots have been taken over by rich people or corporates for residential and commercial purposes.

Fortunately, other like-minded members supported him and single or at most double storied houses are the norm. Even renting of houses is strictly controlled and permitted only while the member remains in service. An owner-member is expected to retire to his home at Defence Colony.

Anju, without Ivy

On April 9, 1981, Anju was shocked when he discovered that Ivy had died in her sleep. Mayrose, Ivy's youngest sister, and I flew down that afternoon for Ivy's funeral. Indian Arlines, in spite of heavy bookings and long waiting lists, gave us tickets on the strength of a phone call from me without any documentary proof. Hazel followed the next day after arranging for her younger sister,

Veronica, to come down from Pune and stay with Deepika. Ivy was buried at Saligao cemetery on April 10. Mayrose, Hazel and I could not get return bookings by air on April 11, and had to travel by bus to Bombay. Anju was left alone at his house in Defence Colony.

We decided that we should visit him and spend at least a week each time as often as we could. It was difficult for him to come up to Bombay as he could not leave the house locked. Also someone had to be there to look after Chicko.

Defence Colony members took it upon themselves to ensure that Anju did not suffer too much from loneliness after Ivy died. One or the other of his neighbours made it possible to drop in to meet him morning and evening. Most evenings, Noel Kelman or Pat Tellis would sit with him chatting over a drink till it was time for dinner. Anju's little friends made sure he remembered them and would call out to him as they passed the house.

On his birthday, November 10, 1981, the ladies got together and planned a celebration. Among themselves they each prepared a dish and then everyone came over to wish Anju. Anju had only to provide the liquid refreshments – even these appeared in the form of birthday presents.

My sister Iza and her family were also present to wish Anju. Deepika, Hazel and myself went down for his birthday, since Deepika had her Diwali holidays. John Gomes's son, Anil, had his birthday on the same day, so this was a joint celebration. Young ladies of the colony, many of whom had been tutored by Ivy, were willing hostesses. Anju was pleasantly surprised. This became a yearly celebration.

Four-wheel drive to Porvorim

Our first major long distance trip in my Mahindra Jeep station wagon was to be with Anju at Porvorim for Christmas 1982. Hazel, Deepika and I drove up to Pune on December 23 afternoon, and left early morning on December 24 to travel through Belgaum to

Goa. I had convinced Lloyd Vaz, who was working in Pune, to drive down with me and spell me out on this long drive. Lloyd still had his Burmese driving licence but had no Indian driving licence. The road was in fairly good condition with relatively light traffic and we were in Belgaum for lunch. After lunch and a short rest we drove on.

As we were approaching the Banastarim Bridge, I spotted a man carrying a string of large crabs walking along the road. I immediately braked and simultaneously called out to this guy. Seeing what he assumed was a military vehicle, he started to run away. I called out in Konkani and that stopped him and he came back, but could not decide what to make of us. I was dressed in a kurta-pyjama, Hazel in a sari. Only Lloyd looked Goan. He was so confused that instead of quoting a high price and then bargaining down, he quoted Rs. 20 for the lot and then decided to quote Rs. 30. I gave him the polishing cloth from the car and when he put the crabs down on the ground to tie them they started to run away with the cloth with Deepika and the seller running after them. Finally he tied the crabs in the cloth and put them into the car. I paid the man Rs. 30 which for us was still a bargain. We now had to decide what to do with them. Arriving unannounced at Porvorim on Christmas eve was enough to get Anju excited, but with a load of large crabs, he might have thrown me and the crabs out. So we first delivered the crabs to Hazel's sister, Veronica, at Merces, with the request that she cook them and we would come for lunch on Boxing Day to eat them.

From Panjim, Lloyd took a taxi to Saligao and we drove home. Anju was indeed excited at our arrival, but he appeared a little subdued, not his usual exuberant self. After dinner and a short nap, we all went for Midnight Mass.

At Mass the priest requested everyone to pray for Carl D'Souza, who had met with an accident and was seriously injured. After Mass, Anju told us that Carl (Gerry's youngest son) while riding a scooter near Mapuça had collided with a truck on December 23 and had a serious head injury. He was then at the

Salgaocar's SMRC hospital hanging on to life by a thread. This news put a pall over Christmas. We could only pray. On December 27, Carl died and was buried at the Nachinola cemetery. Carl's loss was keenly felt by the whole family particularly since Carl was the baby and Gerry's favourite.

Other events that we recall from the time include the inauguration of our new factory in New Bombay on December 8, 1984, which Anju attended. Then there were Anju's sunset years in Goa when, besides being fiercely independent and managing, he showed surprising resilience and good naturedness when he had to recover with the occasional bout in hospital.

On June 17, 2000, Anju was up as usual and after breakfast set about preparing to make pork vindaloo for Sunday lunch. At about 11 a.m., the house help Keshav poured his bath water and Anju proceeded to his bed room. Suddenly he fell forward on to his walker, which collapsed under him and on to the ground. He fell on his face and broke his nose. There was a large pool of blood around his head when Keshav went to lift him. Keshav ran across the road and called a neighbour, Mr. Karpe, to give him a helping hand to lift Anju, but when they reached him, Anju was dead.

Spouse-Hunting...
or Being Hunted

I N Goa, a girl aged over sixteen and a boy over twenty were considered ready for marriage. No one really bothered whether they were mentally or financially ready. Possibly since these marriages were arranged taking into account the families from which these young people came most of them were successful. The girl shifted from her maternal home to her husband's home to live more or less the same type of lifestyle, with only the additional prospect of child-bearing to worry about.

She would be expected to take instructions from her mother-in-law instead of her mother and be guided by her. Since most girls in Goa in Anju's time were not highly educated, but were trained in home-craft, they adapted to their new life quite well. In short they were expected to 'lay the table and fill the cradle'.

However, when men and later girls lived and worked outside Goa, the question of finding a suitable partner kept his or her relatives in Goa constantly on the look out for a good match. After you had crossed the threshold age and you went to Goa, most of the older lady relatives would be in a frenzy to get you hitched before you went back. If not actually married, they wanted you at least engaged with a promise to marry within at most a year.

A bride for Anju

Anju had gone home to Goa in 1930, after being away for more than ten years. He was, by Granny's standard, successful, since he had been supporting the family with his earnings. Granny was naturally very keen that she find him a suitable bride. Long before he actually arrived she had lined up families with eligible daughters to come visiting.

Anju, in no uncertain words, told Granny Leopoldina that he was not interested in seeing anyone. When the first young lady, accompanied by her parents, walked in the front door, Anju disappeared out the back door and through the jungle behind on a long walk. After waiting for some time, the young lady and her parents finally left, with Granny making various excuses for her absent son. Reluctantly Granny called off visits by other mothers with gleaming eyes with their eligible daughters.

Then Granny decided to go for her annual dip in the sea at Calangute. Anju happily accompanied her. While there, Granny was told about a very eligible young lady who was also on holiday in Calangute. Anju initially refused to see this young lady, but when Granny pleaded, he decided to humour her, so a meeting was organized three evenings later.

Anju found out from Granny where this family was staying. Next afternoon, without shaving, unkempt, dressed in an old singlet and shorts (not very clean) with a dirty towel wrapped around his head he presented himself before that house. The young lady was sitting in the front *balcao* dressed in her finery to entertain guests who might drop by.

He approached her and in the Konkani dialect spoken by labourers, he said, "*Baiee, maka udic di, maka taan laglea*" (Lady, give me water, I am thirsty). She looked at him and shouted that he should go to the back door, but he persisted that he was very thirsty and would appreciate having water to drink right away.

With very bad grace she got up and from inside brought a *chimboo* (small brass vessel) of water and held it out to him. But he then asked for a cup from which to drink. This was too much for her and she shouted at him and shooed him off.

The next evening clean-shaven, hair well-groomed and dressed in fine clothes, together with Granny Leopoldina, Anju walked into that house. Her parents greeted them very profusely and promptly brought out drinks and eats. After they had been chatting for some time, the young lady was called forth. She came, took one look at Anju and disappeared back into the house. Her parents could not fathom what had gone wrong with her.

When after all persuasion failed to get her to come out and meet the boy, they reluctantly had to wish Granny and Anju "Good night" and apologize for the bad behaviour of their daughter. When they got back Anju told Granny of his experiment of the previous day and confirmed that he did not want to have anything to do with someone who did not have basic courtesy.

Anju returned to Burma and married Ivy on December 28, 1932.

Gerry, a different story

Gerry was working at Dandeli and came to Goa fairly frequently. Granny informed him that a young lady from a very good family in Secunderabad was coming to Goa in May and would be staying in Saligao. Gerry and Granny went to Saligao to meet Great-Granny and were there informed that the young lady concerned had arrived and had planned to visit Nachinola that very day.

They promptly got into a Mapuça-bound bus at Arrarim. At the junction with the Pilerne road two ladies got onto the same bus. With true Goan style the conductor told Granny and Gerry to move over to allow these ladies to sit alongside. This was an old *caminho* – and Gerry in a stage whisper in Konkani asked Granny why people with such large backsides traveled by bus and made other people uncomfortable.

On reaching Mapuça, they went promptly to the Aldona bus stop and got into a car for home. Quite some time after they got home, Gerry saw the same two ladies walking up the driveway. One of them became our Aunt Molly on December 27, 1947.

Our cousin Bella

In 1951, while I was in my final year at SMHS, Mount Abu, Ivy, Anju and Iza took a holiday in Goa. They hired a house in Calangute. Our cousin, Bella, joined them there.

Granny Leopoldina wanted Bella to meet some eligible young man in Nachinola, so she asked Ivy and Anju to send Bella to Nachinola without telling her why she was wanted. Dutifully Bella went to meet Granny, but was most annoyed when Granny literally dragged her to meet this young man and his family.

The next day she told Granny she was going back to Calangute and not to arrange any other meetings for her. Granny gave her a large jackfruit to take with her. Bella arrived back in Calangute and threw the jackfruit down and burst into tears. Fortunately, they had a large number of friends from Saligao who came to Calangute every evening, including Molly's brother, Jerry, and their cousin, Nita. They enjoyed the rest of this holiday.

And my own experiences

My own experience is quite an illustration. I had gone down to Goa in November 1963 to investigate the possibility of taking up a job in Goa, and had met various Goan businessmen. Having accepted a job with Salgaocars in Vasco I started work on December 14, 1963.

The following February, my Rh-negative blood was urgently required for a patient in Goa and I gladly donated 300 ml. of my blood. A few week ends later, Granny Leopoldina informed me that our neighbour, Mrs. Fermina D'Souza, who was also a neighbour in Santa Cruz, Bombay, wanted to meet me.

I met this lady at the village *ladain* a couple of week ends later and was requested to reach her home. She informed me that she had a marriage proposal for me, but since it was obvious that I had already found my partner in life (Eslinda, whom we called Hazel, had come over to our place that week end) she was not proceeding in the matter.

However, at various dances that year at Panjim and Margao, Leslie Britto (a Salgaocar colleague) and I were the only bachelors in our group from Vasco. We were the target for many of the prospective mothers-in-law. One particularly well-endowed young lady was pointed out to me and efforts repeatedly made to ensure that I danced with her. On enquiring, I found out that she was the daughter on one of the businessmen whom I had approached for a job.

Fortunately, since I had more or less decided that my life partner was to be Eslinda, I was not entrapped, as was a class-mate of mine. After marriage he had as his boss at work his father-in-law and at home his wife's confidant, his mother-in-law, was his boss's wife.

While a lot has to be said in favour of arranged marriages, however just because the young man or the young lady come from a *boa família* (good family) the marriage may not be successful. It is essential that the girl and boy get to know each other pretty well before they decide to venture into marriage and do not rely totally on their parents' or other relatives' recommendations.

Our Near and Dear Ones

The Cheron Family and Bakery

M Y maternal grandfather Domingo Xavier de Souza (born in Sangolda, Goa on July 16, 1852) came to Rangoon from Goa around 1880 and had bought the Cheron Bakery from a French *chef de partie* (pastry chef).

Domingo's first wife had presented him with three daughters, Flory, Bella and Stella. To ensure that he had an heir who would run Cheron Bakery, Domingo married his second wife, Euphemia Athaide (born in Salvador do Mundo on September 3, 1882) in 1908. He was extremely happy when his son, Diego, was born on November 13, 1909. They subsequently had four more daughters.

Ivy, my mother, was the first of these four. She was born on September 30, 1911 in Rangoon, Burma (now Myanmar). She was christened Ivy Victoria de Souza. Her three younger sisters were Clare, Amy, and Mayrose. I called them Aunty *Kela*, Aunty *Amlu*, and Aunty *Muchu* respectively. Goans in Rangoon were quite progressive; many of the young ladies of her age, including Ivy, were graduates of Rangoon University.

When Domingo died on March 31, 1918, Grandma, known to everyone as Mrs. Cheron, took on and ran the bakery single-handed until son Diego could take charge in 1927. Ivy helped with the accounts till her marriage in 1932.

Cheron Bakery consisted of a ground floor shop on the corner of 49th Street with the bakery just behind this building. The brick and earth ovens were wood fired. Kneading of flour for bread started in the afternoon in a large wooden trough. With the men (mostly Muslims) dressed only in *loungyis* going around in a circular motion kneading the flour with their hands, and their perspiration pouring into the dough, there was no need for added salt. The dough was left to rise for a few hours, with a wet cloth spread over the mass. Meantime, the wood fire was lit as the oven had to be at the right temperature when the moulds were inserted for baking. The dough was then divided up in to moulds of various sizes, weighed and inserted into the oven with long handled 'oars'. Large loaves went first, then smaller loaves and when these had all been baked, cakes and pastries were baked in the cooling oven. Diego, who had quite some artistic skill, would decorate the cakes and pastries.

In addition to cakes baked for sale through their own shop, Cheron Bakery also baked cakes, particularly at Christmas time, for neighbours, friends and relatives. Each of these believed that their cake recipe was special and jealously guarded that recipe. Not only in terms of ingredients used but also how the batter was mixed and stirred – by hand, no electrical mixers.

Cheron Bakery shop was manned by Diego. Since he was up the better part of the night supervising the baking of bread, which had to go out early in the morning, he usually caught up on his sleep in the afternoons on a camp-cot in the shop just behind the counter. He had no fear of robbers since he had two huge dogs (short haired, buff coloured and bigger than today's Labradors) who sat on the platforms on either side of the shop's entrance. They were so big that I would ride on their backs. When I visited the shop on my way back from school, Diego would be asleep and I could help myself to whatever pastry I felt like eating without the dogs raising an alarm. My favourites were the crisp and crunchy coconut cookies and macaroons, which even today I prefer over soft pastries.

Flory (Ivy's eldest sister) married Jose Marie Xavier Menezes. He was over 6'5" tall and proportionally broad, while she was just about 4' tall. In a photograph he is sitting on a chair and she is standing next to him – her head just about level with his head. He used to call her *Babine*.

Their only son, Albert, was older than Ivy. Albert (although our first cousin, we called him Uncle since he was older than Ivy and bigger) married Mary, who had beautiful eyes. They had three sons, Damas, Eugene and Dennis. He was big and solid. He worked as a forest conservator and lived most of his life in the Burmese jungles, safeguarding the forests from poachers and robbers of teak and other valuable timber. He always carried a revolver. Mary, his wife, told us a story of how one night in his sleep, during a nightmare, he grabbed his loaded revolver from under his pillow and pointing it at her, shouted in Burmese that he would shoot. Mary very slowly calmed him down and thereafter kept the revolver under her pillow.

Albert, Mary and their three sons trekked out of Burma after the Japanese invasion. They must have had a horrible journey, since neither Damas nor Eugene like to be reminded of it. They lived in Quitula, Aldona, until WWII ended, when Albert returned with his family to resume his work with the Burmese Government. The boys completed their education in Burma. Albert died in Burma. Mary and the boys had to leave Burma in 1970 when jobs were only being given to 'true Burmans'. They settled in Delhi. I have enjoyed authentic Burmese food made by Mary in Delhi.

(In 1994, while working on forming the alumni association of St Mary's High School, Mount Abu, I visited the Christian Brothers at Salvation School, Dadar. Bro. Adrian Noronha, another SMHS alumnus, helped me to set up the database of students of various years. He introduced me to Bro. Gerry Menezes, principal of this school. I assumed that Bro. Gerry was one of the Menezes clan from Santa Cruz, Bombay. When he said that his family was from Delhi, I asked him if he was the son of Martha and Eugene. He was taken totally by surprise. I told him that his grand-father, Albert, and I were first cousins. He was astounded as he knew none of his father's relatives. Subsequently I introduced him to Celine and Raymond Nogueira, who like me were his grand-father's first cousins.)

Bella (Ivy's step-sister) married Raymond Lobo from Karachi. Their children are Fr. Joe, Bro. Gus (both Jesuits), Marie and Edmond. We only got to know them after being forced to leave Burma in 1942. Grandma Cheron with Aunts Clare, Amy and Mayrose lived with them in Karachi for some months immediately after the evacuation. Their daughter, Marie, is one year older than her 'Aunt' Mayrose. Marie, Amy and Mayrose really enjoyed each other's company at Karachi, Ajmer and Mount Abu. Clare stayed with Grandma and took orders for stitching ladies clothes in Karachi.

Both Amy and Mayrose were appointed as resident teachers at St Mary of the Angels Convent Girls' School. In addition Mayrose was appointed music teacher at St Mary's (Boys'). They started work in March 1942.

The Resident for Rajputana came to his summer headquarters at Mount Abu (away from the heat of Ajmer) in May 1942 as usual. Young and handsome John Nogueira, P.A. to the Inspector General of Police, also moved with his boss to Mount Abu for the duration. At Sunday Mass at St Anne's Church he met Mayrose, who played the organ and conducted the choir of girls from the convent. He promptly started escorting her and her sister, Amy, for walks and to the weekly pictures at the Rajputana Club. The convent girls, ever ready for romance, matched John with Amy. However, John had set his sights on Mayrose or, as he began to call her, 'Ma-Rose'. He had to go back to Ajmer in June, but he found many opportunities to come up to Mount Abu to meet these two sisters. We in Goa received news that John and Mayrose were to be married, the wedding was fixed for December 30, 1942, at Ajmer, where John's elder sister, Lina, and her husband, Alex Pinto, lived.

Ivy, Agnes, Noellyn, Iza and I left Goa to reach Ajmer on Christmas Eve. In Bombay we stayed one day with the Feraz family (Grandma Cheron's neighbours in Rangoon) at Lower Parel. Our train reached Ajmer late at night. We got into a *tonga* (an open carriage drawn by one horse) and gave the driver the address. He knew the area, but did not know the exact house. We arrived to find the whole area in darkness. It was bitterly cold and all the houses were tightly shut. How to find the house was a problem we solved by loudly talking and mentioning the names – Alex, Lina, John, Mayrose. Our voices carried in that quiet night and finally one door opened and someone came out to enquire whom we wanted. He then directed us to Alex and Lina's house. Lina had arranged for us to use the house next to theirs for the duration of our stay.

We all needed baths after the long journey. But, being a cold night, we left it for the next morning – early so as to get to Christmas Mass. An early morning bath was some experience. We came out shivering. Our clothes were totally inadequate for the cold. Fortunately, Lina's son, Fred, and daughter, Marianne, could loan us some warm clothes. So, in this borrowed finery we went for Mass at St Anslem's.

The next few days were spent preparing for the wedding. I did get a chance to go out with Freddy (Pinto) and see some of the surrounding countryside but all I remember is the sand with some date palms and camels. After celebrating their wedding and bringing in New Year 1943, we returned to Goa.

Grandma Cheron and Amy came to Goa in May 1943 and went to live at Salvador do Mundo (*Saloi*), in Bardez. During the school holidays from April to June 1943, we visited Agnes in Quitula and Grandma, Aunty Umbelina (Grandma's spinster sister) and Amy in *Saloi*. Amy joined St Xavier's School, Moira, as a teacher from June 1943 and stayed with us at the house we had rented in Moira.

After a few months, we were visited by Fr. Damas D'Lima from Sangolda. He had met Grandma and had discussed the possibility of his brother, Timothy, marrying Amy. He invited us to Sangolda, for the feast at Livrament Chapel, where he was chaplain. We were able to visit my Grandfather's (Domingo Xavier de Souza) house. It was in fairly good condition, with basic furniture and there was crockery and glassware in the wall-cupboards. However, no one was staying in the house. The neighbours looked after the place. (When I went back to this house in 1960, the basic structure was still standing, but doors, windows, roof and the wall cupboards with their contents were missing. When I again visited in 1973, there was not even the stone foundation to show where the house had stood.)

Even though Amy had never met Timothy D'Lima, the marriage was arranged by Grandma and Fr, Damas, both of whom were in Goa. Photographs must have been exchanged, but I am sure no one checked on their respective heights. The wedding was scheduled for December 26, 1943 at Dohad (also called Dahod, today lying in Gujarat, on the boundaries with Rajasthan and MP, known as the birthplace of Mughal emperor Aurangzeb), where Tim D'Lima was posted by the then Bombay Baroda and Central India (BB&CI) Railway.

Immediately after school closed for the Christmas vacation all of us – Grandma, Ivy, Amy, Agnes, Iza, Noellyn and myself – left for Dohad together with Fr. Damas. In Bombay we stayed a day with Gabriel and Theresa Sequeira, Fr Damas' relatives, at their flat at Arthur Bunder Road, Colaba. Their son, Allan, a year younger than me, took me to Cuffe Parade through the Brady Flats area, through a gap in the fence, across the BB&CI Railway line (an area now occupied by Badhwar Park, the residential complex of the Central Railway and Western Railway officers). He also showed me how to hold one of my palms over the other hand and wiggle my thumbs. For some reason unknown to me, this amounted to some sort of insult to the young Chinese boy who lived downstairs, who promptly came to fight me.

The train journey (from Goa to Bombay and then to Dohad) in the company of Fr. Damas was painful to me, as he expected me to sit still all the way and not jump around or play with Iza and Noellyn. If I jumped up and moved about, he would catch my ear, twist it and make me sit down. Fortunately, he did not accompany us back to Goa.

We reached Dohad on December 24 morning and Tim took us to stay with a Goan family, where he was staying as a boarder even though he had been allotted his own quarters in 'D' Site of the Railway Colony. This boarding house consisted of a series of rooms around a central courtyard on the main Dohad–Godhra Road, just outside the Railway Colony. They had volunteered to carry out all the arrangements for Tim's and Amy's wedding, including the catering. We went for Midnight Mass and had a grand Christmas lunch.

Their marriage was blessed in St Joseph's Church, Dohad. After the wedding when photographs were being taken in the compound of the church, Amy, in her high heeled shoes, towered above Tim. So Amy took off her shoes, kept them with the toes just visible under her long wedding gown, and stood behind them. Even then she was taller than Tim, but not too much taller.

The reception was held in the school hall, attached to the church. At the reception, Tim noticed that his landlord and his family were not present, though their servants were there to serve the food and drink. He then remembered that he had forgotten to give them an invitation to his wedding. John and Mayrose were not present at Amy's wedding because Mayrose's baby was due any day; their son Philip was born at Ajmer on January 1, 1944. Amy and Tim's son, Noel, arrived on December 25, 1944 – two cousins born in the same calendar year yet with almost one year's difference in age.

Bella entered our house in Bandra early one evening in 1954, and without introducing herself asked to meet Ivy. Ivy was inside and when she came out she was confronted with Bella, her husband Raymond and another gentleman, who had brought them to our house. As far as I am aware, Ivy had never met Bella, but somehow she recognised her elder sister. That was quite a meeting and they carried on chatting well into the night, till their escort reminded them that the last bus to Bandra Station was at 10 p.m. and they had to race off. Ivy and Bella did not meet again.

Marie, Albert and their four children migrated to Canada.

Marie kept up a regular correspondence with Anju. Unfortunately I was not able to meet them on any of my visits to Toronto while Albert was alive. He died a short while before Anju. I did not know how to send the news of Anju's death to Marie. I found their phone number and address in Anju's diary. I e-mailed Paddy D'Souza, another ex-Karachi-ite who was residing in New Jersey, USA and requested him to phone Marie and inform her of Anju's death, but only after he felt confident that the news would not be too much of a shock to her. Paddy had a long and very interesting chat with Marie, so much so that he worked up quite a big trunk-call bill, which I still have to settle. Marie immediately wrote me a letter (by snail mail) and on the following week end when Bertie, her son (Anju's godson) came home she got him to send the same letter by e-mail. Both the original letter and the e-mail arrived on the same day. Thereafter Marie learnt to use her own computer and has kept in e-mail contact till about a few years back when she could not sit up long at the computer. I met Marie, her sons, daughters, son-in-law and grand children when I visited Toronto in 2001. Her daughters, Marilynn and Corinne, keep up a regular e-mail correspondence.

The third sister, Stella, remained a spinster and lived with Flory in Rangoon. She kept house for the boys, Damas, Eugene and Dennis, who were at school in Rangoon, since Albert and Mary were most of the time in the jungles up-country. One rainy Saturday evening, she went to St Mary's Cathedral for service. She slipped and fell, probably banged her head and remained where she had fallen. Because of the heavy rains, no one passed that way and only after she was missed at dinner did anyone go searching for her. She was found and taken to hospital where she was declared dead. The following night, her body, laid in a coffin, was kept in their sitting room with only candles burning. Young men took turns keeping the wake. Anju and a friend were sitting on benches on either side of the coffin. Both must have dozed off. Suddenly both came awake and sat up simultaneously. Seeing each other get up, they both imagined that it was a person sitting up in the coffin. They both charged out of the room.

Diego had to stay on in Rangoon until virtually all civilians had left as he was supplying bread to the army, hospitals and other essential services. Fortunately, the army ensured that he got out on one of the last steamers leaving Rangoon just before the Japanese occupied the city on March 8, 1942. He arrived in Goa a few days after Anju.

He went back after the war in October 1945, to find that the building and the ovens, which Cheron Bakery had earlier occupied, had received direct hits during the Japanese bombing. It was reduced to rubble. But Grandma Cheron's house on 50th Street was still standing – just the shell – all furniture and even doors and windows had been removed. He repaired this house and lived on the ground floor, using the front room as the retail outlet for bread and confectionery that he was producing in a small oven in the backyard. But he was not able to attain the standard and turnover that Cheron Bakery had commanded before the war. He was finally forced to close down and return to India in 1965.

Diego and his family settled in Calcutta after returning from Burma. He worked in bakeries and confectioners in Calcutta, but being an employee after having run your own business is not very easy. When last I met him in 1971 he was extremely unwell, more or less bed-ridden. After his death, four of his children, one after the other, migrated to Australia, except for Noellyn (Rosalyn) and Robert. Agnes also migrated to Australia subsequently. Agnes came for Michele's (Noellyn's daughter) wedding in 1990 in Goa. Anju and Agnes spent most of the reception chatting, catching up on old times.

Gerry, a mischievous younger brother

Anju's younger brother, Gerald, was very mischievous. He attended the church school at Nachinola. While Granny had her hands full with her agricultural and other work, he was proving too much of a handful for her.

After some feast or celebration, he went around collecting all the crackers that had not burst. These he broke in half and collected the gun-powder in a saucer. He imagined that this would result in a fountain of fire. Instead it just burst into flames and burnt his face. Fortunately his eyes were saved. Granny Leopoldina applied her home remedies and managed to heal all the burns without heavy scarring. This was the last straw. She packed him off to Burma so that Anju, who was twelve years older, could impose some discipline and give him a proper education. Anju admitted him as a boarder at St Peter's, Mandalay, together with the Vaz boys. Gerry spent his holidays in Taunggyi.

Gerry, after completing his secondary education at Mandalay, came down to Rangoon and stayed with Ivy and Anju. Anju, through the good offices of Mr. (Syriam) Lobo, got him an apprenticeship at Dhala Boat Building Yard. It built and maintained all the boats for the Irrawaddy Flotilla Company, a Scottish-owned passenger and ferry company that at its peak in the late 1920s had the largest fleet of riverboats in the world, some 600 vessels. He was given a ground floor room with attached bath-toilet in the company's quarters and had to manage for himself. He learnt to cook his own meals. When he came home for one week-end each month, he would learn some new dishes from our cook. His standard meal was *dal* and rice and later he learnt to make *chapattis*. (I do not remember eating *chapattis* at home in Rangoon. Our standard lunch was rice and curry while dinner was soup, a side-dish of meat or fish, salad or some vegetable with bread and a pudding.) His cooking was done on a kerosene pressure stove. I remember that he used an ICMIC cooker – in which rice, pulses, and vegetables could all be cooked together and fast. I suppose he and other apprentices shared their food, so he thus picked up dishes not usually prepared by Goans.

Being an apprentice at Dhala was a lonely life. When Salu took over the Maxim's night club, and wanted someone reliable to look after cash receipts, Gerry was easily convinced to give up his apprenticeship and shift to Rangoon. He normally spent his holidays with Ivy and Anju, but while working at Maxim's he stayed with Salu and Bemvinda. Neither Salu nor Gerry thought it necessary to inform Anju.

Anju was on tour when this occurred, but Ivy heard about it and informed Anju immediately when he got back. Anju was very angry with Salu for spoiling Gerry's future career and exposing him at his young age to the pleasures of night life.

After evacuation from Rangoon and a short stay in Goa, Gerry was the first to land a good job, with Killick Nixon at their Western Indian Plywood factory at Dandeli. We visited Gerry at Dandeli in April 1946 as I have recounted elsewhere. In April-May 1947, Gerry was on holiday in Goa, when Granny took him along to Saligao to meet a prospective bride. This has been recounted earlier, in the chapter on 'Spouse Hunting or Being Hunted'.

Sometime thereafter, Gerry was transferred to the Shivrajpur manganese mines, also belonging to the Killick Nixon Group. This place, like Dandeli, was in the middle of a jungle, on a branch line off the main Bombay–Delhi route. You had to change at a small station, Champaner Road, where the main line trains stopped for all of two minutes. Ivy, Iza and I went to Shivrajpur on December 20 and with Gerry left for Secunderabad on December 22.

At Champaner Road, Gerry made sure that Ivy and the two of us got on to the train. As he was about to climb aboard with his steel trunk in hand, the train started moving. Ivy promptly pulled the emergency chain, the train stopped and Gerry and his luggage got onto the train safely. When asked by the railway authorities why she had pulled the emergency chain, Ivy replied that we were going for a wedding and we could not possibly leave the bridegroom behind. From Bombay Central, the next morning, we went to Victoria Terminus for the train to Secunderabad, which left that afternoon. The journey to Secunderabad was uneventful but I was surprised when for the last part of the journey we appeared to be going backwards. We were met and transported to the new house that Mr. A L D'Souza, Molly's father, had just completed at Marredpally, a residential suburb. The family was living in the house behind and above the shop on Market Street.

The firms F X D'Souza & Co and A L D'Souza & Sons were the main importers of foreign liquors in Hyderabad State. Surprisingly though, Mr. A L D'Souza was a teetotaler and his sons Francis and Jerry would at most drink a glass of beer. Mr. A L D'Souza demonstrated how accurately he could pour out a peg of whisky, without a peg measure.

We celebrated Christmas lunch with their family. They gave me a wonderful book on the monuments of India, which I treasured. Molly's youngest sister, Wynnie, was a few years older than us and she appointed herself our guide. The wedding on December 27, 1947 was a grand affair what with the amount of liquor that flowed.

Their first child, Sylvester Philip (SP), named after our grand--father, was born in Secunderabad on January 26, 1949. Molly's two elder sisters, Irene and Lyra, who are doctors, gave her detailed instructions on how to bring up her son.

When she returned to Shivrajpur in April, she demanded a thermometer to check the temperature of Sylvester's bath water. Gerry jokingly told her to dip Sylvester in the water. If he turned blue, the water was too cold, and if he turned red it was too hot. More seriously, he suggested that she check the temperature with her own hand first, before dipping SP into the bath. She, however, insisted on a thermometer. In that jungle there was no possibility of getting a thermometer, so Gerry borrowed the huge $0 - 300^\circ$ C thermometer (mercury in glass type), which was used to measure steam temperature at the boiler. All spoons and utensils used for his food had to be boiled. When SP began to crawl, he picked up something from the floor and put it into his mouth. Molly panicked and asked Gerry what to do. He advised her to put her fingers into his mouth and pull out whatever he had put there before he swallowed it. Molly looked shocked at the thought of putting her fingers into the little fellow's mouth, so he told her, "First boil your fingers". Thereafter, SP was allowed to grow without too many don'ts.

About a year later, Lea was born, and probably another year later, Michael came along. Molly with SP, Lea and Michael spent a short holiday with us at our Bandra house in 1952, when Michael was about nine or ten months old. Michael, Fr. Theophilus's dog, would spend the day with us and go home to St Anne's Church for his dinner and spend the night there. To persuade her Michael to eat, Molly pretended to feed one spoonful to Michael, the dog, and then give one spoonful to her son. Some time later, Ivy gave Michael, the dog, the soup bones. Little Michael crawled over to him, and decided with no objection from the other Michael, to each take alternative licks of the same bone. We watched for Molly's reaction. She just looked on and smiled. This was quite some change from how particular she had been with SP.

In 1950 Gerry gave up his job at Shivrajpur and shifted to Secunderabad to set up Espee Diesel Engineers. His specialty was calibration of fuel injection systems of diesel engines, mostly of trucks. He undertook the complete overhaul of diesel engines and the older heavy oil engines. These were used by farmers for pumping water in to their fields and would arrive covered with mud and looking like scrap. After an overhaul, they looked as though they had just come out of the showroom. In these heavy oil engines, you had to actually put a burning piece of cloth or a burning cigar butt into the firing chamber to start the ignition.

In the following years, Gerry would come into Bombay off and on when he needed some special spares or tools, and each time would spend a couple of days with us. Once, Gerry flew back to Secunderabad and when seeing him off at Santa Cruz airport, I got my first chance to see aircrafts at close quarters. In those days, you could go right up to the plane to see someone off – no security checks and barriers – at the Kalina terminal. The Juhu aerodrome was not used for commercial flights.

Gerry came for Iza's wedding and stayed with us. After the

wedding mass, he changed into comfortable clothes and left his suit and formal shirt with gold cuff links hanging in Ivy and Anju's bedroom. When he dressed for the reception that evening, he found that his gold cuff links were missing. Who among guests or servants (the house was crowded) had swiped them? He told no one of this until after the reception.

Gerry came up for Bella's wedding in 1960. Granny Leopoldina also came for this wedding; she stayed with us for a couple of weeks and then she stayed with Bemvinda for the week prior to the wedding. Gerry insisted that Granny visit him in Secunderabad and took her with him. Granny's return to Goa with me as escort is recounted elsewhere.

In 1963, after Goa was liberated, Gerry closed down his business, Espee Diesel Engineers, in Secunderabad. He packed and despatched all his machines to Goa and set up his new workshop, G D'Souza & Sons, at Sanvordem. Initially, Molly and the kids stayed with him at Sanvordem, but shifted to the Nachinola house in May-June 1966.

Gerry's business prospered. Sylvester was trained to handle the overhauling of diesel fuel pumps. Gerry later set up a second workshop at Bicholim, but subsequently shifted this to Mapuça under the the name of Espee Diesel Engineers.

The other kids continued their schooling at Aldona. When Michael finished his schooling, he was entrusted with the workshop at Mapuça. Joseph did not have an aptitude for things mechanical but was more interested in agriculture. Gerry set him up in a shop at Aldona with agencies for seeds, fertilizers and pesticides. Lea, after completing her BA at St Xavier's College at Bastora and Mapuça, took up a job with State Bank of India, Mapuça. Goiya, who resembled Bemvinda and had beautiful red-gold hair, completed her college at Mapuça and proceeded to New York for further study. Gemma, after her graduation, took up teaching at Guirim. Carl, the baby of the family, died before he finished his schooling.

Bemvinda and Salu

Salu (Vincent Salvador Rodrigues) and Bemvinda (Anju's sister) were married in Goa in 1930. Because their grand-mothers were sisters, prior to the marriage both had to do penance – kneel for two hours each day for a whole week in the sanctuary of their respective churches holding a lighted candle. When they came to Rangoon they rented a flat in Lewis Street, the same street as Balbino and Mr. M. C. Pinto. Mrs. Pinto was Salu's sister. (Mr. Pinto, in addition to playing the cello, had a tailoring shop. After Anju died and I had to dispose of his clothes, I discovered one suit jacket which had the label 'M C Pinto, Tailors & Outfitters, Rangoon', which must have been bought by Anju well before WWII.)

Salu was a wonderful pianist. But to really get in the mood he had to have two or three strong drinks. Then he would play all the old sing-along favourites and slowly switch over to *mandos* and *dulpods* (our Goan folk music) which he would sing. He had a good singing voice. (As to be expected, his hearing was acute. When visiting him I whispered to Deepika to wait till he has a few drinks and then she would hear him play and sing mandos and dulpods, he was quite annoyed.)

As accompaniment for silent movies in Rangoon in the 1920s, he would play Western music including the classical overtures. I marvelled at his wide repertoire. I do not remember him reading music, but his son, Alex, confirms that he not only could read music but he used to compose music for Hindi films when working with S.D. Burman, the famous music director of Indian films in Bombay. I remember seeing some Indian films where the hero plays the piano; but if watched closely one would recognise Salu's wrist and fingers complete with the special ring he wore.

(In the book *Behind The Curtain*, by Gregory D. Booth, published in 2008, which tells the story of music in Indian films, there is no mention of Salu, while a number of Goan musicians are featured. I also checked in books about S.D. Burman, but could find no reference to Salu. Very surprising! More so when we are forced to watch the lengthy list of credits when any film is screened. I suspect even the janitor is now given due credit for his contribution.)

Salu's nephew and son-in-law, Eddie D'Cruz, sent me the following e-mail message on March 27, 2009:

> On the topic of whether V.S. Rodrigues knew to read/write music, I have heard him say on several occasions how he learnt music the hard way. He went on foot to the distant village of Bodiem to learn music. He never mentioned any instrument – violin or piano. He always said 'music'. By the way, to reach Bodiem he had to go (walk) from Olaulim to Aldona to Quitula to the river side, cross the sluice gate and walk along the *bund* along the river, then cross the river by country boat (there used to be a boatman) then walk through fields to reach the Bodiem village. My estimate of time taken to walk there and back is about 3-1/2 hours. In the monsoons at least 4 hours.

> When I was a teenager I spent many holidays and weekends in Olaulim. There, I often heard that when 'Coruc Caru' (Salu's father) walked to the chapel for Sunday Mass along the narrow road (path) – not the motorable road – and when youngsters saw him from a distance, they would jump over the stone boundary wall *(dhurig)* and hide in the bushes until he was gone. Reason: he was a terror to them.

> During the village family functions such as *ladainha* (litany) after the drinks were served and the usual village politics started to be discussed among the menfolk, *Coruc Caru* would lose his temper on those who did not agree with him, pull up his sleeves and challenge the strongest among them or even more than one. I do not think it ever ended with a fight. In contrast his brother Joaquim (Jackie Rodrigues), my

grandfather, would sit quietly in one corner, not a *boo* or a *baa* coming out from him.

Sometimes, when I was at Fair Haven (Salu's house at Bandra, Bombay), I would see him in a pensive mood. Suddenly he would get up and write a few lines of music. This I believe was some tune from Goan folk songs which he would incorporate in some of the songs he would play for Hindi films. No wonder S.D. Burman was fond of V.S. because he could adapt impromptu when they were stuck up in the middle of a tune.

When certain topics came up, he would get sentimental and would even shed a few tears.

However, being a good musician has its drawbacks. His eldest daughter, Bella, learnt to play the piano, but would never practice when her father was home. If he heard her strike a wrong note he would work himself into a temper.

Her younger brother, Alex, jogged his memory and on January 28, 2009, sent me an e-mail message, saying: "An incident I'll remember to my dying day was when I happened to be practising the piano in Bandra not realizing that Dad was present. Not being gifted with the art of playing music, I inadvertently hit a wrong note. The next thing I remember was coming to my senses after blacking out on the floor with my mother hovering above me. Apparently, Dad came around from the bedrooms and smacked me one around my head and ears in particular. That was the last time I ever touched a piano."

In this message, Alex also mentioned that Leo, the eldest brother, had a good ear for music and learned to play the violin in Belgaum (Salu was in Bombay) and also the piano. He would play whenever the mood took him, but never when Salu was anywhere around. (Leo's daughter, Ulrike, mentioned that among Leo's possessions after his death they found a clarinet, which Leo had probably also learnt to play.)

The characteristic hot temper exhibited by Salu, Bemvinda, Anju and Gerry, was possibly inherited from their grandmothers. Bella, Leo and Alex also threw temper tantrums. Once while confessing my sins to Father Miranda at St Anne's Church, Pali, Bandra I said, "I lost my temper" and Fr. Miranda replied "Did you find it?" This was a question I could not answer. As an employee and later when I started my own business, I perforce learnt to control my temper.

When talkies replaced silent movies, Salu, like all Goan musicians in Rangoon, had to find alternative sources of income. With his temper and inability to hear wrong notes being played, I do not think Salu did any teaching of music. Instead he purchased or leased Maxims – a nightclub where people could spend an evening, with drinks, food and hostesses. There might also have been a cabaret. As all payments were in cash – there were no credit cards in those days – he needed a reliable person to look after cash receipts.

When we visited Bemvinda at the Dufferin Hospital, Rangoon when her third child, Louis, was born. I, all of two years of age, discovered that by turning the handles at the foot of her bed, I could raise and lower either the front end or the back end of the bed and I kept doing this alternatively which must have irritated Bemvinda though she did not shout at me. After all that exercise, I was hungry and finished the lovely green soup that was part of her dinner.

Louis was a beautiful baby. At the Well-Baby Parade sponsored by the UK-based baby food production company Cow & Gate he was judged the winner. But he was disqualified, because when asked if he had been fed on Cow & Gate milk food, Bemvinda truthfully replied that he was breast-fed but she herself regularly took the company's milk food.

After we arrived at Nachinola in February 1942, Bemvinda, Salu with Bella, Leo, Louis and Alex went to live in their ancestral home in Olaulim. This was very small and with all of them was very crowded. They later shifted to D'Abreu's house on the hill overlooking both their ancestral house and the plot of land in which Salu built his new house in 1945. Abreu's house was much larger and had very large grounds – actually the whole hill covered mostly with caju trees. From Olaulim Bella and Leo walked to and from St. Thomas School (then co-ed) in Aldona.

Within about a week of our return from Mayrose's wedding in Ajmer, Bemvinda had to go to Dr. Correa's (later Remanso) Hospital at Mapuça to deliver Allan, born on January 16, 1943. Granny Leopoldina went to Olaulim to help Bemvinda get off to hospital. After Bella and Leo returned from St Thomas School, Aldona, Granny brought them together with Louis and Alex to Nachinola to stay till Bemvinda could return to Olaulim.

While staying at Abreu's house, Salu built a new house on a family owned property – next to his sister's (Mrs. M C Pinto) house. I remember that there was a mango tree in her part of the property, whose fruit laden branches were within easy reach from windows in Salu's house. But we were warned not to pluck any fruit as she would vociferously object.

This house was occupied by the family in 1945 and we visited them there when we came on holiday from Calcutta in May 1946. There was a loft or attic over the central corridor with wooden plank flooring. This was where all the boys slept. Bemvinda and the children lived in Olaulim, while Salu stayed in Bombay as he was working for Hindi films. (This house, now occupied by a Hindu family who bought it in the 1960s, is as Salu built it and is very well maintained. They had promised to retain the cross that Salu had installed on the front compound wall and when Ulrike – Leo's daughter – and I visited Olaulim in November 2008 this cross and house were well looked after. In contrast M.C. Pinto's house in the next compound is in very poor condition.)

Bollywood Blues

Salu and three of his musician friends had a chummery in a flat just opposite Liberty Cinema. Salu told us a couple of interesting stories of his time at this flat.

Every morning Salu and one of his friends would walk to Chowpatty beach and have a swim and return in time for breakfast. This was the only exercise they got as the whole day while at the studios they just sat around trying out various musical passages and then recording it if everyone agreed. One day as usual they stripped off their outer clothes and dived in and enjoyed their swim. When they came ashore there were no clothes to be seen; someone had walked off with them. There was no possibility of phoning someone to bring them fresh clothes, so in their swimming trunks pretending to be jogging they ran all the way back to their flat. At the corner of their street, the owner of the Irani restaurant, where they often had meals and snacks, thinking that something had happened at the beach, ran after them together with a couple of his waiters offering his help. With this retinue, a number of other people joined the procession. Salu, naturally embarrassed, had quite a job convincing them that nothing untoward had happened to any of them.

Another incident was when Salu and his musician friends were returning late at night by local train from Andheri, where the film studios were located. The train was more or less empty and each of them stretched out and promptly fell asleep. Fortunately one of them woke in time to alert them that the train was approaching Marine Lines Station. Every one woke up and discovered that their shoes had all been taken away while they slept. They walked home – the road and pavement were in relatively good condition in those days – without further problems.

A couple of years later, Bemvinda shifted to Belgaum where St Paul's School was just a short walk from their rented house. Aunty Ancy with Irene and Mrs. Manuel Machado with Joyce, Lyra and Maurice had also shifted to Belgaum, the cost of living was much lower and the climate was bracing. Living in Belgaum eliminated the problem of getting money from British India to Goa, since all earning members were employed in British India. Leo and Bella completed their school education in Belgaum. Bella came to Bombay for training as a secondary school and physical education teacher.

Leo joined the Victoria Jubilee Technical Institute (VJTI), Bombay and trained as an electrical engineer. With further training in the UK he became an expert in the new field of electronics.

In 1951, Bemvinda shifted to a rented house in Bandra, near the Bandra Talkies. The family was all together since leaving Burma in 1942. Later in 1954 Salu bought a plot of land in TPS III, Bandra and built their own single storied bungalow. At that time there were few houses in this new scheme and so they kept a huge dog, Bingo, as watch dog. His bark was really frightening, but when either Anju or I came over he greeted us as though we were his best friends. I do not know how effective he was as a watch dog, but probably his size alone would have kept potential thieves away.

In 1955 Leo left for the UK to work and study there and Alex followed within about a year. Both boys married European girls, without Salu's approval. Consequently, he would not speak of these two sons. I met Leo, Alex and their wives and families when I visited Canada in 1972.

In 1960, Bella married Eddie D'Cruz, who was employed at Dunlop's factory at Shahganj, near Calcutta. On one of my tours to Calcutta, I managed to visit them at Shahganj – a beautiful colony with all facilities. Bella had taken up a teaching job at the neighbouring girls' convent where her three daughters were students.

Allan, Ronnie and Rudy spent a couple of years as boarders in the Salesian school at Nagpur, where they discovered that if they said they were considering joining the seminary they got special food. Allan later went on to the U K, but his two brothers had meanwhile migrated to Canada. He followed them to Canada a couple of years later.

Ronnie took up a job in the Middle East and married Freda, who was working in that same town. They had a son, Jason. But disaster struck when Ronnie suddenly died of a ruptured stomach ulcer. His wife, Freda, and son subsequently migrated to Canada.

Rudi, who is a good artist, worked as a commercial artist in Bombay for a while and migrated to Canada in 1974 and there married his Bombay sweetheart, Christine. He tells me that his migration to Canada was sponsored by the advertising agency with whom he worked after migration. The agency's directors were very impressed with work he carried out for them while he was on holiday there and for which he refused to accept any payment.

About two years later, Bemvinda died. Salu rebuilt his single storied house into a four storied building and retained two flats – one for his own use and one for Collette, who had married Leslie Andrade. Salu died in 1984. Within a couple of years Collette's family migrated to Canada.

After retiring from Dunlop, Eddie and Bella settled in a flat in Panjim, Goa. Their daughters one by one migrated to Canada and she and Eddie spent summers with them. During one of these visits Bella died in Canada. Eddie returned alone to their flat in Goa. Each year he would go to Canada in the summer and return by late October, until travelling became difficult. He later settled in Canada.

When Anju died I received an e-mail message from someone who said that she thinks she is part of 'Uncle Anju's family', but did not know how she was related. She signed off as 'Ulrike Bemvinda Rodrigues'. I immediately replied that she must be Bemvinda's first grand-daughter, since she bore her name and her German first name meant that she was Leo's daughter, since his wife was German. She regularly corresponds with me and in 2009 spent quite some time in Goa and Bombay to trace her roots.

Bemvinda's children and grand-children are now all in Canada.

Balbino's music and Annie's secret

Balbino de Athaide (Grandma Cheron's brother) left Burma to go back to Bombay to find his bride, Annie D'Sa (of Sangolda) in Santa Cruz, Bombay. She was naturally left handed, but, because people believed that a left handed girl was unlucky, she did most of her work with her right hand. Once Ivy stepped into their home unannounced and found Annie cutting meat with the knife in her left hand. She was most worried that Ivy would spread the word, but Ivy did not believe in this nonsense and Annie's left handedness remained a secret.

Balbino, being a musical man, wanted a musical family, and like a good musician he started with the scale: A - Annie; B – Balbino; C - Cissy; D – Doris; E – Ernest; F – Felix. But the scale was not complete until G – Gloria appeared ten years after Felix.

This was told to me by Shalini, Balbino's grand-daughter. After Felix was born, Annie was very weak and so Balbino sent her to Panchgani (known then as the best place for recouping from weakness especially for those suffering from TB). When she returned she is supposed to have told Doris, "He is all the time after me". And thus Gloria was born ten years later and Balbino completed his musical scale.

Annie was a good cook, particularly of Goan food, so Ivy used to learn from her and wrote down the recipes as 'Aunty Annie's....' (In 1957 when Iza was getting married, she got Gloria, a proficient secretary, to type out all the recipes from Ivy's hand-written cook book. Gloria decided to take an extra copy for herself and I requested another copy for myself. When I got my copy, I was surprised to find that Gloria had typed out 'Aunty Annie's....' recipes. She was not aware that these were her own mother's recipes.)

Balbino's house in Lewis Street in Rangoon was a flat on an upper floor of a brick and cement building. On the right of the landing was the family's residence with kitchen and dining room with a half loft (the girls' bed room). The boys, Ernest and Felix, slept in the flat on the left of the landing, which was also the workshop where Balbino repaired pianos, violins and other string instruments. Since Balbino and Annie slept below them, the girls could not go out at nights unless they had advance permission and return time was noted. The boys were locked into the flat every night after dinner. They had found a way of opening the door and relocking it, after they had left, so that Balbino when checking from the opposite flat found the door locked and assumed that the boys were fast asleep, when in actuality they were out having a good time with their friends.

Each of the children learnt to play a musical instrument – Cissy the cello, Doris the piano, Ernest the violin and subsequently saxophone, clarinet and most important 'the fool'. He was an ace entertainer, way before such an activity was appreciated as a full-time, much envied and highly paid career option. Felix, I think, did learn the violin, but never persevered. Gloria learnt the piano. Balbino's family *ensemble* gave recitals at the Portuguese Club, over Rangoon radio and other venues. They also performed regularly for all religious functions at St Mary's Cathedral. (He continued this tradition at Sacred Heart Church, Dharmatala, Calcutta right up to his death, initially with his children and later with his grand-children.)

Miss Strong, our landlady, gave piano lessons to a number of children, including Cissy and Doris. To take maximum benefit of being away from their father's strict surveillance, they would come much ahead of the time scheduled for their lessons, spend time with us and then go upstairs one at a time for their lessons. After their lesson they would come down to our place. If Anju was home he would entertain them with his stories and they would forget all about going home, until Ivy returned and reminded them. Then they would race off home thinking up some excuse to explain the delay to their father. Cissy, as soon as she encountered her father, would burst into tears and would be told to go in; Doris, being the bold one, would explain that they were at Ivy's place. She would end up getting a scolding.

Gloria, being her father's pet, learnt to twist him around her little finger as is evidenced by this anecdote related by Shalini, Gloria's daughter.

Annie needed Rs. 12 to buy new curtains for the Wellesley Street, Calcutta flat. Balbino asked her if it was essential, but did not give her the money. Annie told Gloria about this. Gloria promptly spoke to her father: "Papa, these curtains are old and we must get new curtains before Christmas."

"How much will it cost to get new curtains?" was his reply

Gloria: "Only Rs. 15, Papa."

He put his hand into his pocket and gave her Rs. 15. Annie received the Rs. 12 she needed for the new curtains plus an extra Rs. 3 for lace.

Not all his music pupils were very successful. Diego was sent to him to learn the violin. Either he did not have the talent or he just did not have time to practice, but when he went back for his next lesson, his efforts were so dismal that Balbino hit him with the violin and broke it. He sent Diego home with another violin and told him to practise and come back after a week when his violin would be repaired. Much against his inclination, Diego went for his music lesson a week later, only to have the violin broken over him a second time. That was the end of Diego's violin lessons.

We had holidays for Easter (1943), from Palm Sunday to Easter Sunday. Balbino invited us to spend this week with them at Salvador do Mundo (Saloi), where they had special services for Palm Sunday and Good Friday. Grace Antunis and her family had also come down to Goa because of the bombing by the Japanese of Kidderpore (Khidirpur) Docks in Calcutta. We went to Saloi on Saturday evening to be there for Palm Sunday, Holy Week and Easter services. All the villagers cut their own palms and brought them in procession to be blessed. Palm Sunday Mass was very, very long. Since all the prayers were in Latin and the sermon in Konkani, we understood nothing.

Early Monday morning, Ernest and Felix suggested that we go up the hill to the top where there was a statue of Jesus Christ, Salvation of the World. Felix had gone ahead, wrapped himself in a white sheet and stood at a strategic place. With Ernest leading and Freddy Antunis just behind him, Gloria, Iza and I took the path from just opposite their house straight up the hill – pretty steep and fairly densely wooded. Ernest pretended to be tired. Freddy took over the lead saying that Ernest had no stamina and he would show us how to climb. As he got out of the densely wooded area to a more open area, he saw what he thought was a ghost flit across the path. He turned and came charging back really frightened. Ernest placated him saying that it must have been his imagination as a result of getting out from a dark area into bright daylight. So after a little rest we again resumed the climb with Ernest again in the lead. A little later Ernest began to pant and struggle to continue climbing and Freddy again laughing at Ernest took over the lead.

Meantime, Felix had gone and taken up a new position further up the hill and as Freddy emerged from the bushes, he suddenly shot across in front of him. Freddy really got a fright and charged back to where we were all 'struggling' to climb. Ernest placated him and since we had almost reached the top of the hill he persuaded Freddy to continue the climb. Felix took off the sheet and joined in behind all of us, panting as though he had really had a hard time climbing. At the top of the hill we saw the statue and then came down by the regular pathway of steps. When Freddy told the folks at home about seeing a ghost, someone said that they had heard that there were ghosts on that hill. After that we could not get Freddy to climb the hill by the short cut through the wooded area.

There is a large expanse of relatively shallow water between Britona and Saloi, really an inlet of the sea. There were sluice gates along the road to Britonna, which allowed water to enter this area when the tide was flowing and were closed when the tide started to ebb. These protected waters were ideal breeding areas for prawns and fish. The sluice keepers would open one of the gates during ebb tide, across which they fitted a fishing net and caught quite large quantities of prawns and fish, which they then sold at site or their wives took the catch around the village for sale.

Ernest and Felix, as *gaonkars* (members of the village clan) of Saloi, were permitted to fish in this backwater. They took Freddy and me fishing there. Gloria and Iza accompanied us. Felix and Ernest used a long fishing net – four feet wide – which they stretched across from one bank to the other and Freddy and I had to splash around and drive the prawns and fish towards the net. It was great fun swimming or rather pretending to swim in water just about four feet deep. It was lovely playing in the warm water wearing only a pair of shorts. Iza and Gloria sitting on the bank envied us as they were really feeling the heat of the sun in spite of their parasols. We took back quite a lot of prawns and fish for lunch and dinner. These prawns taste completely different from any prawns I have tasted in the best of restaurants, far more tasty.

Cissy and Doris had learnt the art of weaving grass – plenty grew on the hill side – and shaped them into bags, hats and belts.

Good Friday service at Salvador do Mundo consisted of the Way of the Cross – up the hill from the Church to the statue of Our Lord – 'Saviour of the World' – on the summit. This was in the middle of the afternoon and was real penance. This was followed by the Adoration of the Cross and then the lowering of the body of Jesus from the cross. All the hymns like *Stabat Mater* were sung in Latin.

Easter Sunday Mass was quite a celebration. The Church had all the candles on the altar lit and its bells ringing out their joy. Everyone wore new clothes. The choir was in full voice singing 'Alleluia' with a brass band in attendance. This was in total contrast to dirge like songs after Maundy Thursday service and only clappers for Good Friday. At his home, Balbino insisted that there was no singing of secular music during Holy Week.

The late breakfast got extended into lunch. Almost immediately after lunch we had to leave to get back to Nachinola. The transport was a *machila* (a brightly coloured closed box with two parallel seats made to accommodate four persons) drawn by a couple of bullocks. Over the uneven and rutted roads travel in this 'coach' was far from comfortable. Your head was continually being banged against the back wall or you were thrown forward to crash into the person opposite.

Balbino, as a refugee from Burma, had put in his claim for a residential flat to the Government Accommodation Controller, Calcutta. In 1945, he was allotted flat No.7 D in the building at the junction of Wellesley (now Rafi Ahmed Kidwai) Street and Corporation Street. After he was handed the keys of the flat, he went to see it. While inspecting the flat, a well-dressed gentleman approached him, saying that he was the building's owner and he had come to take down the ceiling fans. Balbino allowed him to do so and this gentleman had the fans loaded on a handcart and disappeared. When thanking the Accommodation Controller and confirming that his family would occupy this flat, Balbino mentioned that the landlord had come and taken all the fans. He was dismayed to find that actually these fans had been stolen by that sweet talking gentleman and he was required to replace them at his cost. This flat is now occupied by his granddaughter, Aruna, and her family.

Earnest had taken up a job playing the violin, clarinet and saxophone with the band at Grand Hotel on Chowringhee Road. He would tell us of the antics the soldiers, particularly the Americans, got up to after a few drinks. Some of them, real tough guys, would hire a rickshaw, put the rickshaw puller on the seat as passenger and pull the vehicle themselves, racing down Chowringhee Road. Then they would pay the rickshaw puller an amount in Rupees that to him was a small fortune. Another set of guys whose behaviour raised numerous questions were the guys from Military Intelligence. They were on duty all night and would turn up in the hotel early in the morning for breakfast and then let their spirits loose. Young urchins on Chowringhee Road soon learnt to speak English with an American twang and acquired the habit of chewing gum, with hand outs received from these GIs.

Ivy and probably most mothers in Calcutta at that time were afraid that these American soldiers, with plenty of money and time, would harm their daughters. Surprisingly the coloured American soldier seemed to inspire greater fear than their White colleagues.

Balbino's grand-children are also musically talented and Christina, Cissy's eldest daughter, is a world-famous pianist and pipe-organist. She has given pipe-organ recitals at churches in Germany, Scotland, Canada (Toronto) and Switzerland. Her three daughters are talented musicians. Christina and her daughters have been regular visitors to Bombay to help train young Indian musicians at the Sangath Music Festival organized by the NCPA and the Mehli Mehta Music Foundation.

Christina's love for India, and Goa, specially, is very obvious and they spend a couple of months each year at their home in Aldona. Her German husband is possibly an even more ardent lover of Goa.

One of their daughters, Renee, and her bridegroom, both working in Hong Kong, consecrated their marriage on January 1, 2000 at St Thomas Church, Aldona – their respective families and many friends came from Switzerland and USA.

The Pimentas (Hazel's family)

Mrs. and Mr. Pimenta lived in a large flat above the Oriental Insurance office, Rangoon. Once when visiting them, we children, Johnny, Helmana, Lourdes, Jimmy, Edigio, Iza and I, played hide and seek. We all hid and Johnny had to search for us. To make it more interesting someone put off the lights in that part of the flat. We were surprised that Johnny, the oldest among us, got quite a fright and insisted that the lights be switched back on.

Their twin sisters, Rozaria and Celina, were born on October 19, 1940. Ivy and Anju are the god-parents of Rozaria. Helmana, as the eldest sister, was the stand-in mother to these two and I remember her carrying both of them, one under each arm.

As stated earlier, Mrs. Pimenta with seven children and Ivy with Iza and Aloysius left Rangoon by *SS Chilka* on February 6, 1942 and arrived safely in Calcutta seven days later. From there we travelled together to Goa. Mr. Pimenta who was forced to trek out from Burma arrived about two months later. Eslinda, the fifth daughter, was born while Mrs. Pimenta was staying at her father's house in Consua. By eastern tradition she is a native Burman, since she was conceived in Burma.

Mr. Pimenta was appointed Branch Manager, Poona, by Oriental Insurance Co Ltd. He hired a large double storied house in the Poona Cantonment. Mrs. Pimenta and all the children joined him in Poona. We visited and stayed with them at this house fairly regularly and it became almost a home away from home for Iza and myself.

John, the eldest, had completed his SSC exams at Loyola School, Margao, Goa. He qualified as a Civil Engineer at Government Engineering College, Poona. After getting his engineering degree he worked for a while at Alcock Ashdown, Byculla, Bombay. In 1952 he went by ship to the USA for further studies. To earn extra money he took up a job as janitor of an office building near his college which entitled him to a room of his own in that building. His ability to play the piano and guitar and sing Western music proved a great social asset. He was responsible for various prestigious construction projects in the USA and Brazil and finally settled in the USA. His wife, Lira Costa, is from Goa. His four daughters have married and are raising their families in the USA.

Helmana, the eldest daughter, joined the Daughters of the Cross religious order in 1952. She was put in charge of the abandoned babies at St Joseph's Foundling Home, Byculla, Bombay. Her experience of handling her own younger brothers and sisters equipped her very well for a job she remained at for almost 25 years. Subsequently she was transferred to St Joseph's Convent School at Bandra and later to St Joseph's Convent School at Panchgani, where she tends to the well being of the girls in this

boarding school. Sister Mary Adelia, as she is now called, celebrated her Golden Jubilee as a nun on April 19, 2002.

In August 1957, Lourdes informed us that she had won a scholarship in child development at Montreal University, Canada. She
came down from Poona with four suitcases. I reminded her that
she had only two hands and once she left India there were no
coolies to carry her baggage. She had to repack her things into
two suitcases. We reached her to the airport. Fortunately, Anju
found that Julian Collaco of Killick Nixon, which manufactured
construction equipment, was traveling on the same flight to New
York. He helped her reach Montreal safely.

She returned in 1959 and took up a teaching post at Nirmala
Niketan, Bombay. In 1962 she married Tony Pinto, then a Captain
in the Indian Army. On his retirement as a Lieutenant-Colonel
they settled in his ancestral home at Candolim, Goa. Their eldest
son, Lester, works with a company headquartered in Goa. Their
daughter, Ruth, is married to a Swiss gentleman and settled near
Zurich. Their third child, Neil, is unmarried and lives with them.

Jimmy, after completing his M.Sc. at Poona University, went
to Germany in 1957 for specialised training in bio-chemistry. In
1965 he made an attempt to find a suitable job in India, but
his level of specialisation was way above the standard reached
by Indian industry at that time. He returned to Germany, married his German girlfriend and migrated to Canada in 1966. He
was largely responsible for setting standards for clean air and
clean water in Ontario and for designing the procedure for en-
forcing these standards. He is now retired and continues to live in
Toronto. His wife suffered from the after-effects of living in Germany through WW II and the years immediately thereafter and
passed away in 1984 in spite of the best efforts of the Canadian
medical service. His three daughters are married, two in Canada
and one in Australia.

The twins, Rozaria and Celina, one after the other in 1960,
joined the Convent of Jesus and Mary. They opted for working
in the Gujarat Mission with their HQ in Baroda. Recently this

province has been extended to include Goa and Mangalore. Sister Rozaria, now Provincial, and Sister Celina celebrated their Golden Jubilee as nuns on October 17, 2010 followed two days later by their 70th birthday.

Mr. Pimenta, who had developed various physical problems after his traumatic trek out of Burma, died in 1965.

A wedding, Pune and 1966

Eslinda (Hazel) became my wife on January 5, 1966. Her patience and ability to cope with events as they came up has been a great help in our life together and in my work particularly after we started our own business.

Unfortunately cancer took her from my side in January 2003. Our daughter, Deepika has to some extent tried to take over her mother's responsibilities. But now, since she is married, she has her own family to look after. Her son, Raphael, is a perfect little bundle of joy tied up with mischief and keeps me fully occupied whenever he comes over to my place.

Jennifer lived in Pune with Mrs. Pimenta until the latter's death in 1991. She devoted her life to teaching at Hutchings School, Pune. She also trained children in singing and piano playing. She had earned a scholarship for study at the Orff Schule in Austria, where teaching children through music is the main subject. She is now retired and continues to live in Pune. She is a great favourite with my grandson, Raphael. She is now married to Jamshed (Jimmy) Boga.

Veronica married Antonio Cardoz and is settled in Goa. They have two daughters, one of whom is married. They now have two grand-daughters.

The Lobo and Fernandez families of Syriam

Pedro Jeronimo Lobo (Anne's father) of Paliem, Uccassim and Antonio Caitano Fernandez (Peter's father) of Aldona had together attended engineering college at Poona, India and were very good friends.

Mr. Lobo had trained as a draftsman and Mr. Fernandez as a mechanical engineer. They were working for the railways and were posted at Hubli. When one of his colleagues, also a Goan, was promoted out of turn, not due to his merit, but because he used to wine and dine the boss, Mr. Fernandez decided to quit the railways in India and seek his future in Burma, where there were good jobs for the asking. When he mentioned his decision to Mr. Lobo, the latter decided to join him in seeking a future in Burma. Accordingly, in 1906, they came to Madras and boarded a ship for Rangoon. On enquiry, they were directed to the Burma Oil Company (BOC), which was recruiting staff for the new refinery being built at Syriam[12], across the river from Rangoon.

Syriam had been a Portuguese trading station in the 16th Century and an old church, now in ruins, still stood with old graves of Portuguese who had worked and died at this station. Portuguese sailing ships would come from Goa to Syriam and travel on to the Malaccas to collect teak, spices, silks, silver and gemstones traded against European products. (Descendants of Portuguese adventurers were to be found in villages in Shwebo and Sagaing districts. These Portuguese–Burmese people had become gunners for various Burmese kings in their wars with one another and with the British and French.)

Mr. Lobo was a very religious man and found it very difficult to contemplate having to go all the way to Rangoon for Mass only on Sundays and major feasts, especially since there was the old Portuguese church at Syriam. He approached Fr St Guilly at St Mary's Cathedral, Rangoon, but the priest did not think it was necessary to have a church at Syriam, which at that time had only about thirty Christians. Mr. Lobo took the rebuilding of this Church as his personal project.

---

[12] Thanlyin (formerly, Syriam) is today a major port city of Burma, located across Bago River from the city of Yangon. Thanlyin Township now comprises 17 quarters and 28 village tracts. It is home to the largest port in the country, Thilawa port.

(Annie, when shown the photograph of the old ruined church at Syriam, remembered that that was the church which her father had got rebuilt.)

He was able to get the Government of (British) Burma to allot land for this church. BOC together with Christian residents of Syriam contributed money to build this church. Each resident Christian family contributed Rs.2 per head. With this money they were able to buy bricks @ Rs.18 per thousand and employ a labour contractor to construct the building. The Church was completed in 1935.

Both built their own houses using the locally available black stone with similar architectural features.

Because of their work experience, knowledge of English and dedicated service, both rose to high positions second only to the European, mostly Scottish, officers. After thirty years of dedicated service both retired in 1936 and stayed on at Syriam as their sons and daughters were now part of the BOC employee family.

Mr. Lobo's son, Frank Vincent, after completing his education, joined BOC as a chemist. Mr. Lobo had a second son, Aloysius, who died on January 26, 1933 aged 18 years in a drowning accident when crossing from Rangoon to Syriam. Mr. Lobo's daughter, Anne, married Peter Fernandez.

Mr. Fernandez's two sons, Peter and Tom, who after completing their education, joined the refinery – Peter as a process engineer and Tom as maintenance engineer. Mr. Fernandez's daughter married Mr. Lynch, who was also employed at the refinery. His other son, Joe, became a priest and has remained in Burma to date – rising to be a Monsignor. (Monsignor Joe Fernandez subsequently lived in the old-age home at Prome and writes fairly regularly to Peter. All letters to Msgr Joe and by him were censored by the Myanmar Government.)

When Anju was travelling from Calcutta to Rangoon in 1919 on the ship he sat listening to an older lady talking in Konkani to other people around her, all obviously Goans, and discovered that she was related to him. He went up to her and said "*Tu am-*

chi!" (You are ours). She was Mrs. Lobo's sister, Ida de Menezes, who was going to live with them at Syriam. Mrs. Lobo's mother and Anju's grandmother were sisters. Anju visited them whenever he was in Rangoon.

I remember visiting the Lobo family at Syriam when I was about two years old. The whole family would say their night prayers on their knees; fifteen decades of the Rosary, litany of Our Lady, the Sacred Heart rosary and litany and one Our Father, three Hail Marys and Glory Be for the intercession of a large number of saints and for various members of the family and various intentions. I think all this took more than an hour, I obviously could not stay that long on my knees and must have been carried by Ivy and fell asleep, I think, to the annoyance of Mr. Lobo.

A well-remembered wedding was that of Annie (Lobo) and Peter (Fernandez) on May 12, 1936 at Syriam at which I was page boy and Iza, my sister, was the flower girl. As to be expected, I managed to drop the wedding rings – which rolled under the pews and had most of the small congregation on all fours searching for the rings.

My being christened 'Aloysius' may have been partly due to the fact that I arrived soon after Mr. Lobo's son, Aloysius, had died. But Peter's and Anne's elder son, Aloysius, was definitely named after his late Uncle.

When the Japanese bombed Rangoon on December 23, 1941 and it became evident that the British were not able to prevent the Japanese from over-running Burma, the Portuguese Consul in Rangoon informed all Goans that their women and children should be sent out as early as possible, preferably on the British India Steam Navigation Co. (BISN) steamer, *S.S. Chilka*, due out on January 16, 1942. Since the Lobo-Fernandez families were the most prominent Goans in Syriam, the message was sent to them through the Goan branch manager of the Imperial Bank in Syriam. This gentleman forwarded the message in an envelope through his own nephew, also employed at the refinery, to Peter. This message reached Peter around 10.30 hours on January

14 and he had to make a dash to the BISN office, buy the tickets and be back for his shift at 14:30.

On reaching the BISN office, he found thousands of people milling around trying to buy tickets. He approached the ticket window and fortunately saw that his college professor, Mr. Gibson, was in charge. He approached him and was asked to state his business. When he told him he had come to buy six tickets to India, Mr. Gibson asked him why he had delayed so long and that he would be lucky to get even one ticket. Then Mr. Gibson called him to another window, to which Peter was followed by lots of other people just waiting for a chance to get tickets. Mr. Gibson told him to put the ticket money in his handkerchief and give it to him at the booking window.

Peter put the money in his handkerchief, made it into a roll and threw it to Mr. Gibson saying "Take – this is your handkerchief." Mr. Gibson returned the rolled up handkerchief to him saying "Hey! This is not my handkerchief." But after going away from the crowds at the booking window Peter discovered that six tickets were wrapped in the handkerchief. He headed back to Syriam with the six tickets for Mr. and Mrs. Fernandez, Mr. and Mrs. Lobo, Aunty Ida and Annie. No tickets were required for the children, Aloysius and Rita (Mr. Lobo's adopted daughter). With considerable persuasion he managed to get them ready to leave for India on January 16.

Annie took up the story of their voyage from Rangoon to Calcutta. They had to manage on deck, but food, while not a wide selection, was adequate – just fish curry and rice – Goan style, as cooks on BISN ships were all Goans. They had a few anxious moments when they spotted a torpedo heading for their ship, but fortunately their captain was able to take corrective action and avoid the torpedo. They reached Calcutta safely and were welcomed by friends and volunteers who gave them food and tea and coffee at the dockside. They stayed a few days at Edward Martyres' boarding house at Dharmatala. They went on by train to Bombay, where Mr. Lobo's brother lived.

They were able to deposit all their bank drafts and deposit certificates with the Imperial Bank in Bombay and this account was credited with 100% of the amount with no commission deducted. Having permanently settled in Syriam, Mr. Lobo had given up his right to his ancestral home at Paliem, Ucassim in favour of his brother. Consequently, they went to Mrs. Lobo's ancestral home near the Uccassim church.

Whenever we went to Aldona, we would meet Peter's mother sitting on her door-step awaiting news of her three sons, left behind in Burma. Mrs. Lynch was able to hire a house just across the road from Peter's ancestral home in Aldona.

British hopes of safeguarding Singapore, Malaya and Burma against Japanese invasion were dashed with the sinking of the battleship, *Prince of Wales,* and the battle cruiser, *Repulse,* by Japanese dive bombers on December 10, 1941 on their first venture out of Singapore. Japanese radio broadcast this news accompanied by the tune of 'Run Rabbit Run' with fresh lyrics:

Run British, run, run, run,
Prince of Wales *and* Repulse
Now at bottom of the sea
Run British, run, run, run.

Meanwhile in Burma, the Japanese were advancing with little effective opposition from the British and Indian armies. BOC decided to blow up the refinery when there was absolutely no chance of the British pushing the Japanese back. When the Japanese reached about 25 miles from Syriam, the officers were instructed to stand-by to blow up the refinery. Fifteen men were selected for the demolition team – eight Europeans and seven Indians, one of whom was Peter – with a Romanian, an expert demolition engineer, in charge. These men were instructed to pack one suitcase and report to the main control room and be ready to leave immediately the demolition was complete. Either by steamer from Rangoon or trekking to Assam.

The night before, when it was confirmed that the Japanese could not be repulsed, the General Manager opened the club's liquor storage and told everyone to take whatever they liked. The rest would be blown up with the buildings. After quite a few drinks, there was a competition to hit the large wall clock about ten feet above the floor. Everyone tried with billiard and snooker balls, but no one succeeded thanks to the quantum of alcohol imbibed and also to the stress of that time. Finally the Refinery Manager himself took up a cue-support and hooking it onto the clock pulled it down to crash on the General Manager's shoulder, who at that moment entered through that door.

All fifteen men slept on the floor – Indians in the club room and the Europeans in the main office. Early next morning they went about getting the demolition completed. A box had been designed and filled with cotton wool. There were three holes in the lid to accept three sixteen ounce sample bottles. Two bottles were filled with kerosene and the third was three-quarters full of H_2SO_4 (concentrated sulphuric acid). To prime this 'fire bomb' all three bottles were inverted. The kerosene soaked the cotton wool. Into the cork of the H_2SO_4 bottle a metal capsule had been inserted, when the bottle was inverted the acid would eat through the metal capsule and the heat generated would ignite the kerosene soaked cotton wool.

Peter was assigned the job of placing one box at the outlet valve of the main crude oil storage tank (containing over two million tons of crude oil mixed with discarded refinery products). Another engineer was assigned the job of setting up a similar box below the outlet valve on the other side of this huge tank. They were given five minutes to complete their respective tasks and run back to the bus, about five hundred yards away, that would take them to the jetty. They were warned that if they were late they would miss the bus and probably die in the fire and explosions that would follow.

Peter placed his box of tricks after emptying the kerosene into the cotton wool, inverting the acid bottle and opening the outlet valve. He then discovered that the other engineer had got cold feet, left the box and ran away. He picked up this box, ran to the other valve and after priming it, opened the second outlet valve. By the time he got back to the bus seven minutes had elapsed and he got a shout from the Romanian that he was late and they were just about to leave without him. Peter did not mention to anyone that his colleague had left him to set off both ignition boxes. The contents of this tank took seven days to burn and the dense black smoke made it impossible to see the sky. Peter was given a merit award and a service medal for a job well done.

While they were setting up the demolition boxes there were Burmese with bows and arrows trying to stop them from their work. They had been given a Gurkha escort to guard them during the demolition. These soldiers had been instructed by their commander to shoot if the Burmans loosed their arrows, but the soldiers were warned by the refinery staff that if they started shooting they could set off explosions in the refinery and tank yard.

At the jetty they got into small boats to go out to two British Naval ships which were anchored at the mouth of the river. When their small boat reached the ships, they found the sea quite rough and they had to clamber onto the ship using a rope ladder. Each man, in addition to his suitcase, had a number of bottles of whisky, brandy and other liquors in pockets or inside their shirts. While climbing the rope ladder many bottles were lost. Another boat came alongside with the Gurkha escort, who were also being repatriated to India. The Navy accommodated the Europeans in the officers' quarters, leaving the upper deck for the Indians and the lower deck for the Gurkhas.

The bottles, which had survived, were too much of a temptation and all the BOC officers (Indian and European) broached their bottles to recover from the stress of the last few days. One of the oil drillers, an American, was so drunk that he fell through the hatch down to the lower deck where the Gurkhas were quartered, and was injured. The Gurkhas raised quite some noise and the ship's doctor was called. When he approached the American, the latter refused to let him attend to his injuries, but insisted that only the company's doctor should attend to him. The General Manager sent Peter to call the company's doctor though he knew fully well that the doctor was also drunk. When Peter tried to wake the company's doctor and told him that the General Manager was calling for him he turned over and said "Tell so and so to go to hell." Turned over and went back to sleep. When Peter shook him again, he turned over and said "You too go to hell" and went back to sleep. When Peter reported this to the General Manager, the ship's Captain gave an order that there would be no drinking from now on and called for all liquor bottles to be brought to him. Some of the men tried to hide their bottles in their pillows and among their clothes but to no avail – all bottles, full or half empty, were brought to the Captain and he ordered them thrown over the side. After that everyone had nothing to do but sleep and eat – they were really well fed by the Navy.

The two ships carrying them were escorted by a small destroyer – which had to keep circling them as these ships were too slow. Suddenly a Japanese midget submarine was spotted and a torpedo was aimed at one of the ships. The two ships were immediately told to scatter – that is head in different directions, while the destroyer dropped a number of depth charges where the submarine had been spotted. Peter does not know if the Japanese submarine survived the depth charge attack, but their ship went well out to sea while the other continued to hug the coast, with the destroyer zigzagging between them. They reached Calcutta after five days and were immediately put up in a hotel.

One of the passengers on the ship with them was the Post Master from Syriam, together with his ten year old son. He was sitting on a small tin trunk from between the lid and the base of which some ten Rupee notes were peeping. They suspected that he had all the cash from the Post Office in that trunk. For the entire journey he sat on that trunk, not joining them for meals in the dining room, but getting his son to bring him his meal on a plate. When they reached Calcutta, he and his son took the trunk and quickly disappeared among the crowd at the docks.

In Goa their families first heard over the radio that BOC demolition team was missing, this started them all crying and offering Masses for the repose of their souls. After a few days, a further news bulletin announced that BOC demolition team traced and safe and on their way to India. *Laudinho* was organised in thanksgiving.

Annie continued their story. Life in Goa, while quite different from life in Syriam, was pleasant – paddy (rice), fruits and vegetables were available from their own fields. But cash for other necessities was a problem. There was no bank in Goa through which they could draw money from their account in Imperial Bank in Bombay. Money from British India to Goa could only be remitted through British Indian postal money orders. The alternative was to get cheques cashed through the *soucar* (local money lender), who charged 40% commission – i.e. you received only Rs. 60 for each Rs. 100 of your cheque. Mr. Lobo would therefore travel to Bombay to draw the cash required, send fifty to one hundred money orders (maximum in each money order was then Rs. 75) to himself, but these money orders would not be delivered to Ucassaim – one had to go to Mapuça to collect them. En route he would visit his professors and friends at Poona Engineering College and come back after a pleasant holiday of a week. On his return he would go to Mapuça and collect all the money remitted by money order.

Repeated trips were tiresome and after two years, they decided to shift to some place in British India. One of their neighbours in Goa mentioned Belgaum as a very healthy and inexpensive place. Annie and her mother went to Belgaum and fortunately at the station met Grace Stevens, a neighbour from Syriam. She and her family were staying at Kirkee (near Poona) but she was just returning from Kolar Gold Fields, where she had found a beautiful house in wonderful surroundings with good neighbours. She suggested that the Lobos come to KGF. She gave them both addresses – Kirkee and KGF. On returning to Ucassaim they were able to convince Mr. Lobo to shift base to KGF and sent off a letter to Grace Stevens in KGF asking her to confirm when it would be convenient to visit with a view to choosing a house and arranging to shift from Goa. Anne addressed the letter to 'Bowringpet' – the industrial township of K G F, instead of 'Robert-sonpet' – the residential area, but the KGF Post Master personally re-addressed the letter. Annie believes that the letter reached because she had written 'SAG' (St Anthony Guide) on the envelope. Grace received the letter and replied immediately. They found KGF a very pleasant place and lived there till 1966.

The morning after arrival at Calcutta the seven Indian employees of BOC, including Peter, his brother, Tom, and brother-in-law, Frank, received instructions to appear for an interview, as they were to be transferred to the Anglo-Iranian Oil Company at Abadan, Persian Gulf. They were called according to alphabetic order of their names and Peter was first on the list. The General Manager from AIOC in the presence of the General Manager of BOC, interviewed him. They already had before them the bio-data of each of these seven persons. He was told that they were classified as essential staff and if they did not follow orders they could be arrested. He was instructed to immediately proceed to AIOC to take up the same position as he had held at Syriam on the same salary. This Peter refused, as he was aware that at Abadan the clerks were drawing salaries much higher than what he was being offered – and he was an experienced process engineer with experience of commissioning various petroleum refining plants. He was asked to go into a separate room while the other six were interviewed. These six agreed to the terms offered. Peter was called in again and told that he must think over his decision and next morning return to confirm that he would proceed to AIOC.

Next morning Peter met these two officers and confirmed his decision not to accept this job on their terms. While leaving the room the AIOC General Manager requested him to meet him next morning, Saturday, at the Grand Hotel. When he called there, he was not granted admission by the police who were stopping anyone who was not a resident. He spotted the AIOC G M and on waving to him, this gentleman came to the main door and took him inside. They sat at a table in the garden and the GM called for a beer for each of them. He then explained that he had read through his bio-data and his experience and definitely wanted him to join AIOC. He offered him twice his BOC salary after six months. Peter responded that in the meantime his wife and son would starve in Goa. Finally, the GM offered him twice his BOC salary immediately with an increase to three times that salary after three months if he was able to successfully bring the various plants to full production. To this Peter agreed.

They were told to immediately proceed to Bombay, where their passports would be made, and then they could take a week off to meet their families in Goa before joining ship to Abadan.

On route to Abadan, their ship met an Arab *dhow* with a large number of passengers, some of whom were speaking Konkani. They explained that they were from Zanzibar and not being able to get passage on any steamer had decided to travel in this Arab dhow to Bombay, but the Arab crew had apparently lost the way and after so many days at sea they had no food. Fish they could catch but they had no rice. Peter appealed to the Captain of their ship to give them a bag of rice and sailing directions for Bombay. The Captain very generously gave them three bags of rice, but while letting the cargo net down to the dhow, one bag fell into the sea. With this rice and the necessary sailing instructions the dhow proceeded to Bombay.

Peter's ship went on to Karachi. They were allowed to go ashore and, seeing the lovely Karachi beach, were tempted to go in for a dip. They were warned that while they were in the sea their clothes could be stolen.

After about seven days sailing from Bombay they reached Abadan. AIOC had instructed their manager to meet the ship and bring these seven men to the refinery. This gentleman met the ship, but saw only people in khakhi clothes, unshaven and decrepit – he concluded that the seven "gentleman" he was sup-

posed to meet were not on this boat. The boat moved on to its final destination, Koramshahr, from where Peter phoned the General Manager, who had interviewed him in Calcutta. It was late
evening and the AIOC telephone operator did not want to put the
call through as the GM was at his residence. On Peter's insistence,
the call was put through and the same manager, who had been
deputed to meet them at Abadan, was instructed to immediately
proceed by road to Koramshahr and pick up these gentlemen. He
met them at 23.00 hours and took them to Hotel Iran in Abadan
for the night. Next morning this manager picked them up and
took them to their quarters – which turned out to be small single
rooms with common facilities – these they rejected. They were
taken to slightly better quarters, which too they rejected. Finally,
they were shown individual bungalows – one for three and the
other for four of them. These they accepted and Peter, his brother,
Tom, and his brother-in-law, Frank, occupied one of them. *(AIOC
in those days offered no accommodation for families. Annie did
join Peter in Abadan in 1944, when family quarters were made
available.)*

The next day they were back at their own familiar jobs within
less than a month of demolishing BOC refinery at Syriam.

They did not have their own cooking facilities and used to take
their meals at the company's officers' mess. On one occasion
when the mess cooks were on strike, they had to do their own
cooking. Peter recounts his contribution to cooking. He went to
the local market and picked up a large leg of mutton, cut it and applied *masala* as suggested by one of his colleagues. He had then
to fry the lamb pieces with the *masala* in oil, but there was no
cooking oil. Frank, being a chemist, had samples of various oils in
his room. Peter took a bottle of "vegetable oil" from this stock and
poured it into the dish. He noticed that this oil was very viscous –
it turned out to be castor oil. He went back to the colleague who
had advised him about the *masala* and was told to add plenty of
water and then skim off the oil. He skimmed off as much as he
could. When the other two got home for lunch, he served up his

masala ghosh with lovely chilled beer. The food smelled good so the others said "Today must be Pedro's birthday!" and promptly started eating the food washed down with beer. Peter was careful to take only a small helping. After this heavy lunch with beer, each retired to his room for a *siesta*. After some time he heard one of the guys say "Hey! I have a stomach ache!" and rushed off to the toilet. About half an hour later the second guy and subsequently the third had the same complaint. That evening, Peter did not trust his own cooking and went off to the company clubhouse where some food would be available. His experiment with cooking had already been broadcast among employees of AIOC and he was welcomed with loud praise for his culinary expertise.

Peter was the Chief Process Engineer (the only Indian process engineer) of the two largest petroleum cracking units at AIOC. He was awarded by the British Government for remaining on duty at this plant under attack from German aircraft.

AIOC was supposed to be increasing the number of local employees in their staff, gradually repatriating Europeans. The Shah of Iran decided to visit the refinery to check progress on this indigenisation programme. On the day of the Shah's visit, all Europeans did not come into the refinery. In the main control room only Iranian staff was left to operate the refinery. Peter had to stay to deal with any emergency, but remained hidden behind one of the control panels. When the Shah entered the main control room he saw a large number of red lights on the panel and asked the Iranian operators why there were so many red lights. They could not explain nor did they know what action to take to correct whatever was causing the red lights. On the Shah's insistence, they finally called Peter from his hiding place and within a few minutes he was able to restore normality. He then explained to the Shah what had happened and how he had corrected the faults. The Shah was quite impressed and invited him to his palace for a dinner dance that same evening – an official invitation was immediately issued by an aide.

Fortunately, Peter had packed his dress suit in the one suit case he had brought out from Syriam. He attended the dinner dance. The only other Indian present was the Indian Consul General. The Shah, in military uniform, with his American wife sat on a sort of dais and watched the dancing. After some time he disappeared and re-appeared in civvies and then joined in the dancing and mixed with the invitees.

Among the guests there were a number of Polish girls – some with crosses around their necks. Peter spoke to them and they informed him that when Poland was overrun by the Germans, they had escaped and some of them reached Iran. Here they were employed as dancing partners to teach Iranians ball-room dancing. Some had married Iranians.

They worked at AIOC at Abadan till 1949 coming to India every second year for two months' holiday. When the political situation in Iran deteriorated and AIOC was nationalised, Peter was transferred to Assam Oil Company at Digboi, Assam. Frank was transferred to British Petroleum Refinery at Aden.

Oil in Assam was discovered not by men but by elephants – who would go off to places where oil was oozing out of the ground and roll in the gooey stuff – this would keep off ticks and other parasites. These wild elephants when tamed for logging work remembered these "medicinal" spas and thus guided humans to these deposits of mineral oil. The name Digboi is said to have originated from the American oil drillers, who kept continuously admonishing the labourers to "Dig boy, dig!"

At Digboi Peter had a very comfortable cottage and life was good. With the war over, Anne joined him in Assam. Peter enjoyed his tennis, cricket and golf. Regular tournaments were organised between refinery staff teams and various teams from tea gardens. The staff club also had numerous activities where Annie could participate. Their second son, Raymond, was born here.

Their elder son, Aloysius, remained at KGF with his grand parents to finish his schooling and then joined the seminary. I met him at the Papal Seminary when with a group of friends from Santa Cruz, Bombay, we enjoyed a Diwali holiday at Poona in

1961. Aloysius was ordained at Poona in 1962. Fr. Joe Fernandez, Peter's brother, from Rangoon came for his ordination.

Time and motion study was a new management tool. While at Digboi, one of his colleagues, a specialist time and motion study engineer, was assigned the task of improving the efficiency of local labour. Digboi crude oil has very high wax content. This molten wax is released into huge vats, where, after it cools, it is cut into blocks of 50 lbs. each. Each block is packed into gunny (jute) sheeting and then loaded into railway wagons, in layers up to about five feet height. This packing and loading of wax blocks was handled by local labourers, mostly of Nepali origin with height not exceeding five feet. This engineer, complete with stop watch, started observing and noting the time taken for various operations. In his preliminary report he pointed out that quite often the labourers just sat around chatting – he did not note that this happened while the men were waiting for the loaded wagons to be shunted away and empty wagons brought into position for loading. He showed this preliminary report to Peter and suggested that he talk to these labourers to improve their efficiency. Peter told the workmen what the learned engineer had reported, they just nodded and went back to work. The next morning when the learned engineer came with his stop watch for further observations, two of the workers quietly slipped away, each got a bucket of crude oil, which they then emptied into this engineer's new car – one bucket over the front seat and the second over the rear seat. Peter and the General Manager, from their respective office windows, watched this happening. When everyone went off for lunch, the engineer returned to his car and was appalled at what had happened to his new car and new upholstery. He rectified his report and the General Manager arranged to have his car cleaned and new upholstery fitted.

Peter had gone for a check-up to the old company doctor, who advised that he be given an injection. He loaded the syringe with the requisite medicine and kept it on his table. He turned to talk to Peter. At the same time his junior colleague was treating a pregnant Nepali lady and filled and kept on the table a second syringe with the medicine for her. Without looking too carefully, the old doctor picked up a syringe and injected the contents into Peter's buttock. The junior doctor suddenly discovered that the medicine meant for the pregnant lady had been injected into Peter. That evening at the club, Peter was quizzed as to when he was going to deliver his baby.

The company policy was that everyone had to retire at age 55 years. In 1961, when he completed his 55th year, Peter retired and arranged to shift back to KGF and Bangalore. They had packed and sent off whatever they were taking with them and sold off the balance, when suddenly the assistant general manager called at their bungalow to tell him that the general manager wanted him to report immediately at his office. When he went there, Peter was informed that he should cancel his departure as he had been given a five year extension. He was required to commission the new refinery being set up at Duliajan – no one had ever been given such an extension before.

While working at Duliajan, the Chinese invaded India in 1962 and Peter felt that history was repeating itself and he would have to set demolition charges for this new refinery if the Chinese moved closer. Fortunately, this did not become necessary. He finally retired from Duliajan Refinery in 1966.

Peter had invested in two and a half acres of land in Whitefield on the outskirts of Bangalore and built a small cottage on this property. When he finally retired in 1966 they shifted from KGF to Whitefield. However, Whitefield was not too well developed and for virtually everything they had to come to Bangalore. For Raymond, now in college in Bangalore, commuting was quite a problem.

Living at Whitefield became particularly difficult when Annie developed breast cancer – she was given a course of cobalt isotope radiation. It was impossible to commute from Whitefield for this treatment, so she stayed at St Martha's Hospital and was well looked after by Sister Ignatius. She was not given any chemotherapy. She has had no relapse and only suffered from 'heart trouble', as her husband and companion of many years jokingly put it.

They therefore decided to shift to Bangalore. Aloysius approached Mr. George DaCosta, who owned DaCosta Square, for a plot on which they could construct a house. Only one small plot, No. 75, was left and this they purchased. Fortunately, this plot was up against Plot No.1 on which Annie's brother, Frank, had built his house. Aloysius was able to convince Vijay Construction to work immediately after the plot was allotted and he completed construction of the house within three months, much to George DaCosta's surprise.

(Anju told me that when he visited Frank and Anne, he would bang on both their gates – next to each other – and wait. Whoever answered first, he would visit first. Frank, usually pottering around in his garden, ended up being the first whom Anju would visit. Then he would visit Anne and, as she later told me, always teased her and told her a number of jokes, some of which were not "nice" and she would hide her face. When I visited them subsequently I followed Anju's advice, thus ensuring that I did not upset either Anne or Frank.)

Frank was transferred to BP Aden from AIOC, Abadan. He became a regular visitor to us at Bombay every two years, on his journeys to and from KGF / Bangalore. He married late and initially we two Aloysius were the beneficiaries of his generosity. I received my first LP record player from him and every subsequent trip he would enlarge my library of beautiful music. He also brought a portable typewriter, for which I paid him his cost of Rs.200, and then discovered that a similar model in Bombay would have cost over Rs.800. Aloysius was the recipient of a Horner piano-accordion – he was musically talented and already played the violin and the guitar. In the last trip he made by ship from Aden in 1965 he brought me a Baby Belling oven with hot plates. When my brother-in-law, Frank (Vaz), was passing through Aden on his return to Burma from U K after his training at Kew Gardens, Frank Lobo gave Iza and Frank a present of an electrical hand mixer for cake mixing.

One incident I remember very well was when all of us were getting ready to leave for St Francis Xavier's Exposition, Old Goa in December 1954. Frank had reached Bombay a few days earlier and was scheduled to fly on to Bangalore a couple of days later. Bemvinda with Bella, Alex, Allan, Ronnie, Rudy and baby Collette were to come directly to the docks latest by 09:00 to board the ship for Goa – scheduled departure 10:00. Salu and Leo had already gone to Goa to manage their hotel at Margao. Frank volunteered to help Bemvinda get the kids ready for the journey. He went to their house at 07:00 and found everything at sixes and sevens – no one ready and packing still to be done. He gave them one shout and got the boys organised, while Bella helped her mother to get the packing completed. She also got baby Collette ready for the journey. With his assistance they were able to leave their home at Bandra and be at the docks well in time. I am sure, if left to themselves, they would have missed the boat.

Frank married Lira D'Souza of Saligao and settled in his house at No.1, D'Costa Square, Bangalore. They have three sons – I remember the eldest, Mario, because he was allergic to nuts – the first such person I had ever come across – and consequently was allergic to *Ovaltine*, which most of us considered a very safe product to supplement one's diet. As the boys grew, he added two more floors to his cottage so that each son would have his own residence.

After his ordination in Poona, Aloysius returned to Bangalore and was appointed secretary to the Bishop. Aloysius proved himself an effective administrator of various diocesan projects. He started the Young Christian Workers' and Young Christian Students' movements. On his own scooter with his piano accordion, he would organise the youth from various parishes for picnics, parties and a number of social projects.

In spite of his several duties and extra-curricular activities, he studied for and passed his M.A. After four years his parents sent him for further studies to Oxford University, UK. He specialised in economics and went on to Louvain University in Belgium for further studies in Sociology.

On his return Cardinal Gracias deputed him to Delhi to work with Caritas India, where there were much larger projects which would benefit from Aloysius' expertise. He tried to professionalize the organisation but was not successful and in 1975 resigned from Caritas India and left the priesthood – which entailed giving up his accommodation in the church's hostel for priests in Delhi. Thanks to the generosity of a friend, Aloysius stayed in a *barsathi* (the top room on the terrace of a Delhi house) and managed for himself.

(It is noteworthy that Caritas India in 2000 in appreciation of Aloysius' very successful, effective and lasting development work awarded him the Caritas Millenium Award. This award consisted of a silver plaque together with Rupees one lakh, which Aloysius donated to MYRADA to construct schools in Veerapan's (the infamous dacoit of Tamil Nadu) forest area and a township, called Srinivasnagar named after Srinivasan, the forest officer, killed by Veerapan.)

Fortunately, his abilities had been very well appreciated by Canadian International Development Agency (CIDA) which appointed him their consultant for various development projects in India. During his "exile" Dipika came into his life as a housekeeper, who ensured that he did not neglect his health and cooked for him. After he was finally released from his priestly vows, he married Dipika.

The news that Aloysius had left the priesthood and shortly thereafter the news that he had married Dipika, came as a double shock to Anne and to Ivy, who felt that he should have put up with all the problems at Caritas, but definitely not have left the priesthood.

Aloysius subsequently went on to work for the World Bank in Washington and to tutor in Selly Oak College, Birmingham, U K. He returned to Bangalore in 1982 with the objective of raising one million poor people above the poverty line.

With this objective in view he revived MYRADA (Mysore Rural Agricultural Development Association) which has been hugely successful in improving the living conditions of numerous villagers in Karnatak, Andhra Pradesh and Tamil Nadu. MYRADA project villagers have earned the reputation of repaying 99% of all loans on time – taken for agricultural or household or educational purposes. His target of one million people being raised above the poverty line has long been passed. MYRADA projects have been visited by prominent people from around the world, including the Prince of Wales, Rahul Gandhi and Queen Beatrix of the Netherlands.

MYRADA has set up similar development projects in Meghalaya, Haryana, Orissa, Chattisgarh, and Jharkhand, plus jointly with UNDP in Myanmar (Burma) and with IFAD (International Fund for Agricultural Development) in Indonesia.

Government of India, in appreciation of his work awarded Aloysius the Padmashree in 2000.

The fact that my daughter is named, Deepika, adds quite some spice to this family history. When I visit Bangalore, I telephone and say "Hi Dipika, Aloysius here – but not your Aloysius!" Similarly when she phones me she announces herself "Dipika here" and then giggles. A few years back all of us were present in Goa for Leon's (Iza's son) wedding. At one large table were Anju, Aloysius, Dipika and Niharika (their daughter), my cousin, Celine, her husband, Dudley, their two daughters, Gisele and Karen, myself and Deepika, and other friends. We were laughing and joking among ourselves, when we heard my sister, Iza, talking to someone at the adjoining table – she said:

"My brother, Aloysius, yes he's here at this very next table."

Then a male voice speaking softly: "Please introduce me, I'd like him to meet my daughters."

Then Iza: "Meet Aloysius? But he is married – there with him is his daughter, Deepika."

Then she brought this gentleman across to meet us and we thoroughly confused him with the two Aloysius and two

Deepikas – poor man – his two beautiful, well qualified and very successful daughters could not find suitable husbands in the U K and he was now looking around in Goa. He had seen me a couple of weeks earlier at Vanessa's (Iza's daughter) wedding when I came down alone – I do not wear a wedding ring.

In my opinion, our loss of Aloysius, the priest, has benefited thousands in their daily lives. I personally believe that Aloysius is a better Christian today than he might have been if he had continued as a frustrated priest. I also believe that his ordination has made him "a priest forever" and when I am dying, in case there is no other priest nearby, I will expect him to hear my confession and give me the last rites.

After Anju died in 2000, Deepika insisted that I seriously write the story of their lives in Burma and through India to Goa. The only people of their generation were Peter, Anne and Hugh Nazareth all living in Bangalore. So we decided in March 2005 to drive from Goa to Bangalore in the new car she had presented me for my birthday and record how Anju and they had interacted over the years. We were to leave on March 26, but the driver whom we had appointed did not turn up and we almost decided against the trip. But on the March 27, I decided that since I had driven from Bombay to and from Goa a number of times, the drive to Bangalore should be much less tiring being only six to eight hours. We set out at 06:00 via the Anmod Ghat towards Belgaum. The road was in very poor condition. It took us over eight hours before we finally reached the Bombay-Bangalore Highway, after which driving was comfortable. We stopped for lunch at a wayside restaurant and realising that we would not be reaching Bangalore before nightfall, Deepika asked the restaurant keeper if he knew of anyone, preferably a driver, who could travel with us to Bangalore. Fortunately, an experienced driver, working with one of the engineering companies building the Bombay-Bangalore Highway was from Bangalore and he had just come off duty. He was happy to drive to Bangalore and receive payment in addition. We reached Bangalore around 19:00 and

Dipika guided us over the mobile telephone to a land mark near their house from where Aloysius met us and personally piloted us to his home. We reached their home around 20:00 and were royally welcomed.

After chatting with Peter, Anne and Hugh Nazareth and making notes and an audio recording, we left Bangalore on March 31 after celebrating Peter's 99th birthday in advance. We promised to return that Christmas to make a video CD of Peter's, Annie's and Hugh Nazareth's stories.

On December 28-29 that year, Deepika got in touch with friends, who video-recorded our interview with Peter and Anne, and subsequently with Hugh Nazareth. Much of the above account of Syriam Lobo and Fernandez families is based on these video-recordings.

On April 4, 2006 Deepika and I went down specially for the double celebration – Peter's 100th birthday and his and Anne's 70th Wedding Anniversary. There was a Eucharistic Celebration at the church followed by a formal reception and *burra khana* at the club. They produced an impressive brochure to record this occasion. We were made very welcome particularly with Anne telling everyone that I was the page boy at their wedding.

Age has not much dimmed Peter's capabilities – just two years earlier he was walking from his house to the neighbouring club for his usual game of bridge. He is hard of hearing and did not hear the motor cyclist approaching from the rear until he was knocked down. Fortunately he was not hurt as the motor cyclist was a learner and was driving very slow – but Peter promptly got up and boxed the guy and asked "You do not know how to drive?" He informed nobody at home of this incident, until his son Ray on his way home the next day was asked by a neighbour "How is your father?" and when Ray asked "Why?" He was told about this incident.

Peter celebrated his 105th birthday on April 4, 2011. Till shortly before then, he did all his own banking work. I had met them July 7, 2009 to check the draft of this chapter. At that time, Annie was looking forward to her 99th birthday on August 31, 2011. Peter unfortunately broke his hip, and was admitted to hospital around that time. Annie, while fretting being alone at home, was also admitted to the same hospital, and to the same room. Peter died on January 30, 2012, but Annie was not informed because of her state of health. She herself passed away a few days later, on February 20, 2012.

The Vazes of Taunggyi

W HILE touring the Shan States, Anju reached Taunggyi. Since there was no hotel or *dak* bungalow, he was directed to the residence of Louis Jose Vaz (of Saligao) who welcomed Anju and made him very much at home. Anju stayed overnight at Mr. Vaz's home and was awakened by male voices singing the *Kyrie Eleison* and other Mass prayers in Latin.

On investigating he found Mr. Vaz's sons making *chapattis* for breakfast and practicing their Mass prayers. There was no church in Taunggyi and whenever a priest visited, he would offer Mass at Mr. Vaz's house for the benefit of the few Shan, Goan, Indian and Chinese Catholics. Anju was intrigued that Mrs. Vaz spoke only Konkani and would never address her husband by name or call him directly – she would say to one of the boys "Go call your father". Or, if none of the boys was close at hand, she would loudly exclaim in Konkani, "You asked for your dinner (or lunch...) and it's now getting cold. Where are you?" She normally did not sit with her husband at the table for meals.

After the incident with the crackers when he got his face burnt, Granny packed Gerry off to Burma with instructions to Anju to ensure that he was properly disciplined and also got a good education. Anju admitted Gerry as a boarder at St Peter's, Mandalay. Mr. Vaz's sons were also boarders there. Since Anju had no fixed residence at that time, Gerry would go to Taunggyi and spend time with the Vaz boys for the holidays. Anju would try to spend a few days with Mrs. and Mr. Vaz to be with Gerry during his holidays.

During one such Christmas holiday, while Anju was at Taunggyi, Mrs. Vaz went into labour. As there was no hospital in Taunggyi, Anju and the elder boys were sent post haste to call the midwife, an Anglo-Burman lady. She came immediately.

Anju and the Vaz boys carried various equipment, including a bed pan, which she would require. Mr. Vaz, his sons, Gerry and Anju waited anxiously in the freezing cold while Mrs. Vaz was delivering her baby – a girl – the first after seven boys, who was promptly christened Queenie. Anju was made the god-father. Anju never forgot this experience when ten of them were striding about to keep warm while waiting for Mrs. Vaz to deliver her baby, and the relief and rejoicing when Queenie arrived safely and Mrs. Vaz was all right. I am sure Mr. Vaz and Anju must have had a celebratory drink and, if I remember Anju with my daughter, Deepika, he would have dipped his finger and wet Queenie's lips with Scotch whisky.

Anju visited St Peter's, whenever he was passing through Mandalay, to meet Gerry and the Vaz boys.

Next to St. Peter's was the girls' convent where many Goan girls were boarders. So Anju became a regular carrier of parcels of tuck for his friends' sons and daughters at St. Peter's and the convent. These boarders eagerly looked forward to his visits.

One of the boarders at the convent was Joyce Athaide, whose father was with Burma Railways. Her son, Noel, an alumnus of St Mary's at Mount Abu, is now a Christian Brother. Some time in 1992, Arun Jeyasinghe and I (both SMHS alumni) visited Noel at his home in Bombay. His mother recalled one of Anju's visits to the convent at Mandalay. To show off to her class-mates that she knew this handsome young gentleman, she approached him and asked, "Do you remember me?" Anju looked her up and down and replied in a voice loud enough for all the girls to hear, "Sure! I used to change your nappies." Joyce was thoroughly embarrassed.

After my bouts of convulsions, Anju took the three of us together with Mayrose to Taunggyi, where we stayed with Mrs. & Mr. Vaz.

One morning, Mr. Vaz took Queenie, Iza and me to a neighbouring *kawshwe* shop run by a Chinese gentleman who was well known to Mr. Vaz. Mr. Vaz ordered a bowl of *kaukswe* costing four *annas* (quarter Rupee) for each of us and went off to attend to his work. Iza and Queenie ate as much as they could and pushed their bowls away. For me however, this *kawshwe* was too good to waste. I kept on eating it slowly. When Mr. Vaz returned, I was still struggling to put down the *kaukswe*. Finally, when I could not possibly eat any more, I told Mr. Vaz: "Uncle, please tell this gentleman to keep this for me. I shall come tomorrow to finish it."

(Mr. Vaz did not forget this incident, and in 1955, when he visited us in Bandra, he asked me whether I would like to return with him to Taunggyi to finish my bowl of *kawshwe*.)

With plenty of room to run and plenty of playmates, I was soon perfectly healthy. All of us thoroughly enjoyed this holiday in Taunggyi.

Mr. Vaz and his family were unable to leave Shan States and were forced to stay there during the Japanese occupation of Burma. Their house had a direct hit and they more or less lived in the trench they had dug beneath the fowl coop. After the war they came to India in 1947, when Peter and Joe visited Goa and found their wives and returned. Joe Cordeiro (their first cousin) and his wife returned with them to Burma. (The detailed story is published in the book *Songs of the Survivors* edited by Mr. Vaz's grand-daughter, Yvonne Ezdani and published by Goa,1556 in 2007. It has since gone into a new edition called *The New Songs of the Survivors*, published by Speaking Tiger in 2015.)

The youngest son, Frank, married my sister, Iza, on Feb 2, 1957 and took her back to the Shan States. Because of Burma's policy of reservation of all jobs for Burmans, all of them were forced to come to India in 1966 and have all settled in Goa. Mr.

Vaz died and was buried in the Taunggyi he loved.

Anju's other relatives in Burma

Myingyan Uncle Hippolito (Great Granny's brother) and Aunty Ancy D'Souza owned a two-storey brick and concrete house in a corner plot next to a beautiful park with a small lake in Rangoon.

I do not remember much of Uncle Hippolito, since he was always seated in an easy chair during our many visits to their home. Aunty Ancy, who stayed with us for some time in Bandra, is a beautiful memory. Arist, Hilda (my god-mother), Irene, George and Alphonse are their children whom I remember. Their eldest daughter, Tiny, was married much earlier to a doctor in Colombo. She and her husband did visit us once in Bandra, when Aunty Ancy was staying with us.

Beautiful Isabelle (also D'Souza) was being courted by George. As her family lived up-country, she stayed at our house to complete all the wedding arrangements. I fell in love with her and told George that I was going to marry Isabelle and I would not allow him to marry her. Finally I relented, and was appointed page boy with Iza as flower girl for their wedding at St Mary's Cathedral, Rangoon. Having learnt from my previous performance, the rings were stitched onto the cushion.

Arist was a civil engineer, who qualified from Government Engineering College, Poona and was working with the Rangoon Development Authority. George and Alphonse, if one recalls right, were employed with foreign embassies in Rangoon. Hilda trained as a seamstress and later trained other young aspiring seamstresses. Isabelle's brother, Walter, was very jovial and whenever he visited us in Rangoon he kept us thoroughly entertained. (Hilda's Singer sewing machine was later gifted to me by Arist.)

Uncle (Myitkyina) Sequeira's (Granny Leopoldina's brother) family included Fr. Vally, Germaine, Josie, Ada and Laura. As to be expected there was not much of coming and going with this family, though I do remember visiting Aunty Ismen and the girls in their ground floor flat at Parel, Bombay and visiting Josie and her husband, Richard Duarte, at their Mahim flat. Fr Vally remained in Burma and was subsequently elevated to Bishop. Germaine married very late and lives in Bandra. (My one regret is that our Great Granny's house in Arrarim was sold, hardly maintained and is now a total ruin.)

Hugh Nazareth of Toungoo: 'You must have luck!'

Hugh Nazareth is a good friend of Ivy and Anju. He took the trouble of coming from Bangalore to Goa to meet Anju at Mandovi Clinic in July 1998 after Anju fell and broke his hip joint. When I walked into the hospital Hugh stood up and asked me to guess who he was. With his *"do Burma"* accent and Shanbag on his shoulder, I knew it could be nobody else but Hugh even though it must have been at least twenty years since I had last met him.

When Deepika and I called on him on December 28-29, 2005 to help us with his memories for my book on Ivy and Anju we were greeted as friends and Hugh and his sister, Theresa, agreed to video recording an interview regarding his life in Burma and in India after leaving Burma. This is Hugh's story, as recorded.

Hugh's father, Salvador Nazareth of Candolim, Goa, used to travel by *patmari* (sail boat) from Goa with coconuts, copra and coir rope to Burma for trading against rice. On the last trip in 1901, their boat ran aground at Monkey Point and was wrecked. He went ashore to investigate the possibility of doing business in Burma. He found Rangoon full of competitors and decided to go up country to Toungoo, about 170 miles from Rangoon, which was a fairly important district town. He bought a plot of land in the better part of town and built a house, the ground floor was for the shop and the upper floor for his residence.

He started business in Toungoo as a small provision store and gradually grew. He visited all the surrounding areas including the oil fields at Yenang Yaung and made friends with the officers and got himself appointed as distributor for Toungoo and surrounding areas for BOC's (Burmah Oil Company) petrol. In those days petrol was packed in one-gallon cans. These cans were despatched to him in rail wagon loads.

As business grew he called for his brother, Candido Nazareth, from Goa to join him. The business was called Nazareth Brothers. He expanded into medicines, learning some simple remedies which he used to compound, plus a range of patent medicines, which were imported. He recruited a Portuguese doctor from Goa to help in this medicine business. This doctor made friends with the Government Civil Surgeon and their friendship greatly helped the medical business. Unfortunately the Portuguese doctor had a fall and being unable to continue work returned to Goa. He appointed an Indian doctor to take his place. The latter worked with him for a couple of years and then left to set up his own medical practice.

Growth of their distributorship required efficient transport. So they expanded into transport business and their trucks used to ply to and from Rangoon and neighbouring towns.

Being from an agricultural background, he acquired about 10 acres agricultural land on which he cultivated sugar cane. The sugar cane produced in his field would not measure up to one wagon load, so he persuaded his neighbours to plant sugar cane and their joint produce, in wagon loads, was sent to Zeyawadi Sugar Factory, the largest sugar factory in Burma. Their own trucks proving useful to get the sugar cane to the railway wagon.

They set up a bakery and confectionery, since Toungoo was now a military base and had quite a high population of British officers with their families and other ranks. They were producing up to 6,000 loaves of bread per day.

They acquired all-Burma distributorship for arms and ammunition, which they imported from manufacturers in England. They supplied guns and ammunition directly to the police and the army and sold to various shops in different parts of Burma for sale to individuals. At that time there was no restriction on the sale of guns and ammunition to civilians.

In 1910, he went home to Goa and married Aurora Colaco, a girl from Ribandar. The normal route was by steamship from Rangoon to Madras and then by train to Goa. Their eldest daughter, Sophie, was born in 1911, followed by Hugh on September 4, 1913 and two more daughters, Theresa and Bertha. Hugh attended primary school in Toungoo, which by then had a convent for girls, run by Italian Catholic nuns. He finished his schooling as a boarder at the Christian Brothers school at Moulmein[13]. He graduated from Judson College in Moulmein and Rangoon.

Hugh's father died in 1935. His brother, Candido, had returned to Goa earlier in 1933. Hugh had to take over the running of the business, when they were having a really bad time because of the world depression of 1933-35. People would accept their stores but were unable to pay the bills. To increase income during this bad time, he got himself appointed as collection agent of insurance premia on behalf of the Oriental Insurance Co. This involved considerable travelling and thus fitted in with his distributorship businesses. He was also required to visit Rangoon frequently. Business began to pick up by 1939. Burma was unaffected by WW II (in Europe), until the Japanese bombed Rangoon in December 1941.

Hugh, now 28 years of age, was in Pyinmina, north of Toungoo, when the Sittang Bridge[14] was demolished and the Japanese crossed the river Sittang and advanced northwards and westwards. He was forced to keep going north. At Mandalay he met Mr. Pimenta, who with all the records and substantial cash of Oriental Insurance Co., was trying to make his way back to India.

Hugh and Mr. Pimenta went to the Imperial Bank in Man-

---

[13] Mawlamyine, formerly Moulmein, is the fourth largest city of Burma, 300 km south east of Yangon and 70 km south of Thaton, at the mouth of the Thanlwin River.

[14] The Battle of Sittang Bridge was part of the Burma campaign during the Second World War. Fought between February 19-23, 1942, the battle was a decisive victory for Japan, with heavy losses for the British Indian Army, which was forced to retreat in disarray. Brigadier Sir John George Smyth, V.C.—who commanded the British Indian Army at Sittang Bridge—called it "the Sittang disaster"

dalay and though it was April 3, 1942 – Good Friday – they were able to deposit the cash and obtain drafts payable in Bombay. Hugh was promised a flight to India from Shwebo (a city in Sagaing Region, 110 km north-west of Mandalay between the Irrawaddy and the Mu rivers), provided he had no baggage. He offered the same to Mr. Pimenta, but the latter preferred to take a boat up the Chindwin to the closest point for crossing into India, as he could not leave Oriental records behind. At Shwebo, even though there was a seat for him, he still hesitated, until finally the pilot, Mr. Adam, said, "If you are coming, jump in". So Hugh jumped in and the plane flew him to Calcutta. Hugh could not return to Toungoo as he had been acting as liaison officer for the British Government in Burma, and if caught by the Japanese would surely have been executed. He went on by rail to Bombay to his mother's brother's house and then to Goa, stopping for a day at Belgaum.

Toungoo was bombed shortly after Rangoon, so Hugh's mother and sisters shifted to Tandaung, a hill station. Hugh's sister, Sophie, and Manager, Peter Stevens, were with Hugh at Mandalay. They managed to return to Toungoo and then joined the family at Tangaung. They lived through the war with the Karens, in a thatched hut and wearing the same type of clothes. They thus survived Japanese occupation.

Constance Diniz was their manager at Toungoo till WW II.

After re-occupation by the British, Constance returned to Goa and then joined Vinayalaya, the formation-retreat house in Andheri, as a Jesuit Brother. He was in charge of manufacture of Mass wine. When Anju and I visited him at Vinayalaya in 1949-50, Anju tried without success to persuade Constance to give him a taste of the wine he manufactured.

After a short stay in Goa, Hugh came back to Bombay and got into a 'holy' mood. He joined the Jesuit Seminary at Vinayalaya, Andheri (which had just been started) to train to become a priest. After studying theology and other subjects for one year (1942-1943) his novice master had different ideas. Taking the novice master's advice, Hugh moved on and set about searching for a wife. He went to Our Lady's shrine at Karjat to seek her advice. He felt that Our Lady was advising him that he would find his wife over the mountain. He took this to mean Belgaum.

On his trip from Burma to Goa in 1942, he had stopped over at Belgaum. There he met a family who were related to him. He remembered their daughter, Mary Fernandes, and decided to go and seek her hand in marriage. When he reached her home in Belgaum, the family told him that she was making a retreat in the convent, where he went. After three days she accepted his proposal and they were engaged. They were married on February 11, 1944 at the Pro-Cathedral of the Holy Name in Bombay. After marriage they lived at the Great Punjab Hotel at Dhobi Talao (just opposite Metro Cinema). With the war on, he was undecided over what to do next; his plan was to join his mother and sisters in Burma as soon as it became possible.

After some time his wife started vomiting every morning. He sent a telegram to his mother-in-law requesting her to help him. She came and gave him quite a lecture for not realising that she had morning sickness. His mother-in-law also scolded him for continuing to live in a hotel. She asked him if he planned to bring up his baby in a hotel. He immediately set out to find a flat.

Some years earlier in Burma he had met a gentleman, Mr. Tiwari, the President of the Bullion Market of Bombay. He helped him to purchase one ton of silver and arranged for shipment of this valuable cargo to Habib Bank, Bombay. At that time Mr. Tiwari had introduced Hugh to the Manager of Habib Bank who was travelling with him. He approached Mr. Tiwari with his problem. This gentleman directed him to the General Manager of Habib Bank, which had flats in Habib Park at Clare Road, Byculla.

Hugh went to the office of Habib Bank and sent in his visiting card to the General Manager. The card was sent back, but there was no invitation to enter. Hugh opened the door slightly, peeped in and discovered that this was the same gentleman he had met in Burma. The GM remembered him from his Burma trip and invited him in. He asked "Are you a Jew?" Hugh, for the first time, realised that Nazareth was also a Jewish name. He assured the General Manager that he was not a Jew but a Goan Catholic. On explaining his need for a flat, the GM called in an assistant and told him to give Hugh the keys to a flat on the second floor of Habib Park. Hugh's luck had again come to his aid. Their first child, Maureen, was born at Habib Park. All assets of Habib Bank, including this flat, were declared "enemy property" in 1947 since Habib Bank was a Pakistani bank. Hugh, as a legal tenant, was able to purchase this flat at a very nominal price.

Early in 1945, allied forces were moving into Burma and driving the Japanese before them. In May 1945, Rangoon was re-occupied. Leaving his wife and baby in Habib Park, Hugh immediately made efforts to get back into Burma.

At this stage only army personnel were being permitted entry into Burma. He went to Chittagong (in today's Bangladesh), where Anju was posted, and pleaded that Anju find some way for him to go to Burma. The Canteen Stores Department was sending ship loads of provisions to the troops and other personnel in Burma. They recruited local labour to load the goods onto the ship, travel with the ship and unload the goods at Rangoon. Anju got a *kalasi's* uniform for Hugh, taught him how to march and salute, and got him into the gang of *kalasis* going on the next ship to Rangoon.

While at sea, they were attacked by a Japanese submarine, in spite of the ship being a hospital ship painted white with a red cross. Fortunately the torpedo went wide. This was after August 6, 1945 when the first atomic bomb had already been dropped on Hiroshima and Japan had capitulated. The ship's captain signalled to the submarine that the war was over. The commander of the Japanese submarine cautiously came to the surface and exchanged signals. Then, when he was convinced, he came aboard and had some refreshments with the captain of the ship. He too was apparently happy that the war was over and he could return home. With no further incidents the ship sailed up the Rangoon river and started unloading. As the *kalasis* were moving to and fro between ship and dock, Hugh found an opportunity to disappear in the dockside crowd. He then went to Toungoo to search for his mother and sisters, from whom he had no news since the Japanese occupation of Burma.

On reaching Toungoo there was no sign of their house, just rubble. Hugh was not even able to exactly locate where their house had stood. He asked an old *rickshaw* puller and he was surprised when this man was able to direct him to the site of their old home and also take him to where his family was living. Hugh was thus re-united with his mother and sisters.

He re-built their house and re-started his business, initially as a British army contractor. When travel to and from Burma was opened to the general public, he went back to Bombay and brought his wife and daughter to Toungoo. His next child, Hubert, was born at home as the hospital at Toungoo had not yet started functioning, though the building was complete. With the local midwife in attendance Hugh also called in a doctor. By the time he arrived Hubert was born and the doctor was greeted by the cry of the baby.

As he was born and educated in Burma, Hugh knew many of the senior people in independent Burma's new government. Using all his old contacts, he built up the business with his office in Phayre Street (now Pansodan), Rangoon. He bought a house on 49th Street in Rangoon and shifted his wife and children there, while his mother and sisters remained at Toungoo. His sister, Theresa, who had completed B.A. and B.Ed. at Rangoon University, was teaching at the local convent. His mother died in Toungoo in 1945 and was buried next to his father at the local cemetery.

He bought another house on the outskirts of Rangoon, but did not occupy it. An American gentleman approached him to rent this house for his own residence. This American had established good contacts with the Chinese Government of Generalissimo Chiang Kai-shek, whose wife was American-educated.

He had been the manager of Firestone in Bombay and had organised the import of tyres for China from South Africa through Rangoon. These tyres were landed at Rangoon and the Chinese would take them to Kunming – the capital and largest city in Yunnan Province, Southwest China – in their own trucks.

He suggested that Hugh take up the handling of this business for which he would receive a substantial fee. All that was needed was a godown in which to store the tyres after being unloaded from the ship. There was no investment required; again Hugh's lady luck was at work. Gradually, in addition to supplying tyres for the Chinese, Hugh started importing tyres on his own account for sale in Burma. The railway was still not organised and most transport of goods was by trucks. Roads were in poor condition which increased the demand for tyres. Tyres commanded a very high premium and Hugh made really good money.

When his next child was due, the Government hospital in Rangoon was functioning. His wife was admitted and allotted bed No.13. She refused to occupy this bed and instead accepted bed No. 14. During that night the patient who had been placed in bed No.13 died. His wife successfully delivered his second son, Terrence. Another son, Bonny, was born while they were at Rangoon.

Gradually Burmese government became dominated by Chinese atheistic communism. This resulted in fairly strong 'Burman only' policy. One day one of the senior ministers of the Burma Government asked Hugh directly in Burmese: 'Are you a Burman?' This was an indication that his days of successful business were over, so he decided to slowly wind down and get his money out.

Hugh, his family and sisters left Burma in 1957. He and his family came to Belgaum, while his sisters remained at the flat at Habib Park, Bombay. His wife, who was again expecting, delivered Noel in Belgaum.

After Noel was born, Hugh's wife found that she had a demand draft payable on Grindlays Bank for Rs.4,000 which was over six months old and could not be en-cashed by any of the local bank branches in Belgaum. One of the branch managers suggested that this DD be sent to Bangalore where Grindlays had a branch. Hugh went personally to Bangalore. On arrival at Grindlays Bank, Bangalore, Hugh found that the manager was someone whom he had known in Burma and the demand draft was immediately en-cashed. This gentleman suggested that Hugh should look into the possibility of doing business in Bangalore.

His lady luck intervened yet again. There was an Englishman who was packing up and going to U K and had put up his house for sale, right opposite Sacred Heart Church, Bangalore. Hugh met this gentleman, who quoted Rs.20,000 for the house with its large compound. He immediately bought it, using the Rs.4,000 just encashed and getting the balance as loan from this same bank manager.

While experimenting with all the electrical gadgets he had in-herited with the house, including electrical cooker, oven, etc and trying to convince his wife to start using them, he was surprised to receive a visit from a senior manager of Firestone, Acworth, USA. This gentleman, who had known Hugh in Burma and had enjoyed Mary's specially prepared dishes, having heard that he was now in Bangalore, had flown down from Bombay to meet him. He asked Mary what Hugh was doing and was told that, "He is interfering in my kitchen." This gentleman promptly told Hugh to come out of the kitchen and get back into his old business – the sale of tyres. In India distributorship of tyres did not exist, but only dealership. He told Hugh to get himself a shop and he would give him a dealership with a liberal quota of tyres. Tyres were in short supply and commanded premium prices. Hugh went down Narasimha Raja Road and found a shop whose owner wanted to sell out. He quoted Rs.10,000.

Hugh agreed to this price and immediately bought the shop – the first business deal in Bangalore done so promptly. With this shop, General Tyre Sales, and the liberal quota from Firestone, Hugh was again in business and soon came to be known as the

'Tyre King of Bangalore'.

With tyres chronically in short supply, Firestone told Hugh that he should get into tyre re-threading business. He bought a much larger premises at J.C. Road and set up his tyre re-treading business there. His daughter, Maureen, and his four sons now run both the tyre sales and tyre re-treading businesses.

His sisters lived at Habib Park. Sophie married and her only son, Leonard, now lives in Bandra, Bombay (or Mumbai). Theresa continued to teach until she left Bombay. Bertha studied to be a doctor at Nair Hospital, Bombay and did her internship at JJ Hospital. Hazel, my wife, was studying at JJ College of Nursing while Bertha was an intern. Bertha used to organise get-togethers of her colleagues at this flat. Hazel and I were invited to one of these parties; I was surprised to learn that Bertha was Hugh's sister. After Bertha died, Theresa shifted to Bangalore and Hugh received a windfall from sale of this flat – his lady luck at work again!

Hugh officially retired from the tyre business and after that has spent his time to social causes. One of these has been counselling the youth contemplating marriage. He has used his own experience to explain how and why these youngsters should prepare themselves mentally, spiritually and materially before turning their steps to the Altar. (Just short of his 102th birthday, he died in May 2015.)

Goan Friends in Burma

IVY and Anju's Goan friends in Rangoon included the Macha-dos (there were two families, all cousins – Sunny, Bertha and Julie (Mrs. R Lobo) and their cousins Neville, Bobby, Ernie, Freddy, and Cissy). Manuel Machado, who was somehow related to us, was another branch of the Machado family – his daughter, Joyce, referred to them as "Much-ado". Tony, Joe and Tessie were of another branch of the Machado family from Burma whom I got to know only in Bombay.

Sunny Machado rose to quite a high position in the British Administration of Burma and then decided to join the Seminary to become a priest. Anju tells us that as a test, his novice master gave him an old tin can filled with filth and asked him to wash it and bring it back. Sunny wondered why the novice master would want such a tin, but in spite of the stink and mess, he washed and gave the cleaned tin back. The novice master then explained that this was a final test to ascertain that Sunny, who had held such an important position in Government, would accept the rules and regulations of the seminary and, when ordained, the authority of the Church as interpreted by his Bishop. I always had a problem referring to **"Father Sunny"** Machado – the nick name "Sunny" persisted even after he was ordained. After the war he was posted at Mount Mary's Basilica, Bandra.

Another nick-name that has continued to intrigue me was

"Baby" Menezes – for a grown up lady of Ivy and Anju's age.

Mr. R Lobo, whose wife, Julie, was a Machado, settled in Poona after evacuation from Burma. On a visit to them in Rangoon his daughter, Gladys, sat like a statue of Buddha, absolutely still as though in a trance and frightened Iza and me. In India, Gladys, now a doctor, dedicated her life to help the sick and aged near Madras. Enid, another daughter, taught at Hill Grange School, Cumballa Hill. Dennis, their youngest, also a doctor, settled in California, though he did make an attempt to set himself up in practice in Margao, Goa. Bertha Machado stayed with Mr. and Mrs. R Lobo in Poona. After both died she took up residence at the Seniors' Home at Wanowrie, Poona – she died a couple of years back.

Neville Machado was with Anju in the Canteen Services Department during WW II at the Burma Front. He stayed on with CSD after the war and I remember visiting him at the Canteen in Bombay Castle (behind Town Hall), Bombay. He married Dr Patsy Fernandes, who was much younger, very late in life. He fixed a week day for their wedding "because only my real friends will definitely come on a week day". They rented a flat on Perry Road, Bandra and the wedding lunch was enjoyed there. Unfortunately, the roast pigling from Mac Ronells, which was supposed to be the central dish at the feast, did not arrive. After lunch they locked up the flat and proceeded on their honeymoon. On their return after a week, their noses twitched to a really bad smell in the flat – probably a dead rat somewhere? On investigating they could not find the source for this nasty smell – till they came to the pile of wedding presents – and there discovered the roast pigling, beautifully wrapped, which was now really smelly. After a couple of years they moved to British East Africa where Patsy had got an appointment in one of the best hospitals. Unfortunately, their marriage did not last. Patsy went off with a young doctor colleague and Neville returned to Bombay alone. I last saw him at Bombay Hospital where he died of . . . . a broken heart!!!

Ernie Machado had stayed back in Burma and was subjected

to torture by the Japs. After the war he came to Belgaum and then to Bombay, where he taught Mathematics at St Andrew's School, Bandra and stayed at Virendra Colony. He and his family migrated to Canada subsequently.

Cissy Pinto nee Machado with Celine, Kevin and Derek lived in her husband's, Tutu's, house in Moira for a few years after evacuation from Burma. Her husband lived out the war in Burma and then came to India. They shifted to Belgaum and Tutu went back to his job with Burma Railways. The last I remember is their stay at Pearl Housing Colony, next to St Paul's Church, Dadar. One by one the boys migrated to Canada and Cissy and Celine finally joined them. A few years back we were visited at our home in Bombay by Mr. & Mrs. Ian Pinto, as Mrs. Christine Pinto is a sister of my daughter's colleague, Collin Gonsalves. Mr. Ian Pinto with a full beard struck a familiar chord. Most of our conversation was about their life in Canada and their love for the outdoors. With their two sons they did regular treks and camping expeditions. Suddenly, some phrase he used must have jolted my memory and I asked him if he knew Kevin and Celine Pinto. He then confirmed that he was their youngest brother. A very small world !!!

Kevin wrote the article 'Wartime Shepherds' in *Songs of the Survivors*. Unfortunately he is no longer one of the survivors – he died on September 7th, 2008. Celine had been diagnosed as having a rheumatic heart in Rangoon and had to lead a very sheltered life. She passed away on September 27th, 2008 thanks to the very good care she received from her care givers during more that forty years in Toronto, Canada.

Another 'Sunny' was Albert Sequeira –Sunny and his wife, Olive, were very good friends – their daughter, Frances, was born on December 3, 1934 at Dufferin Hospital, Rangoon and Olive came out of hospital just as Ivy went in to deliver me. His sister, Biddy, was the owner of the house on 52nd Street where we had lived while I was small. They had another sister, Betty, who remained unmarried. Sunny stood for election to the Municipal

Corporation of Rangoon and I remember going around in a car shouting that people should vote for him. Sunny, Olive, Biddy and Betty were staying in Bandra until all the children Eleanor, Frances, Catherine and Gerard settled abroad.

Dr. Mark Lobo, known to pupils of St Paul's, Rangoon as the 'weight lifter', and his family were also good friends. After the evacuation they stayed at Pintoville, Dadar. Joyce and her husband, Joe Saldanha, rented a flat near us in Bandra. Arthur migrated to Australia and gradually they all followed – the last to do so was Dr Margaret, who had married George Pereira of Karachi. Margaret's and Joyce's sons have visited us when they each did an extended tour of India.

A musician of note was John Menezes. His elder son, Eric, was with me in class at St Paul's, Rangoon. From his very detailed story "The Story Beyond the Headlines" in *Songs of the Survivors* I discovered that we owe thanks to his father for his foresight in hiring Gardner's bungalow at Kokine Lakes, where our family and many friends took refuge immediately after the Japanese bombed Rangoon.

The Manrick brothers, Francis and Mario, were really good friends with whom we have now lost touch. Francis was a specialist piano tuner, much in demand for his fine ear. Mario was a jolly trumpeter – and played other wind instruments. I do not know how they managed to get out of Burma. In Goa Francis married Evelina Saldanha of Panjim. He and his family lived in a large flat on Arthur Bunder Road, Colaba. Their sons, Freddie and Malcolm, and daughters, Evelyn and Enid, were most happy to spend week ends with us at Bandra and have an impromptu dip in the sea at Carter' Road. The whole family migrated to Montreal, Canada.

Mario after a short spell in Bombay shifted his base to Colombo where he joined a musical ensemble at Hotel Ngbonga. He married, but we have no news of his family.

Another outstanding memory is of the Oliver triplets – all girls. It was quite a sensation and made headlines in the Rangoon newspapers. Cow & Gate sponsored these babies and their needs of baby food and other essentials were looked after. On a visit to see these babies I marvelled at the amount of attention they required – these three tiny babies were laid horizontally across the length of a bed and each was covered with a small net, of the size which most of used on our tables to keep flies off a dish of food. Mrs. Oliver would feed one baby and put her down, and the next one would start crying – either for her feed or for a change – and barely had she attended to this one the next would start crying and when she finished with the third the first would require attention. She just had no time for herself or to prepare the feeds. (Deepika and I were pleasantly surprised to discover that all three had survived childhood and the evacuation. Two had married and had children of their own and one, a nurse, remained unmarried and is now in the St Anthony's Home for the Aged near Mount Carmel Church, Bandra.)

We had other Goan friends up-country – S M Pereira, "Lumboo" D'Souza, 'Thaton' Mary D'Souza, 'Dundidaw' Lobo. One Lobo family lived at a beautiful place, high on the banks of the Rangoon River, from whose house there was a long series of steps to a small private jetty. I think he was in charge of the sewage pumping station for Rangoon and that place was 'Monkey Point'. As a small chap, I was threatened that if I was really bad, I would be flushed down the pot and come up at Monkey Point.

Other friends

Ivy and Anju had Burmese and Anglo-Burmese friends, but as I have not met them subsequently, I cannot remember their names. Ivy also had a large number of Burmese and Indian pupils, who were in and out of our home, but I cannot recall their names.

Anglo-Burman friends that I do remember were Douglas (Duggy) Dawson and Gerry Lawrence.

Duggy Dawson was a teacher at St Paul's. He continued to

teach even after the military junta had taken over the country and nationalised all schools. Medium of instruction was changed to Burmese. Duggy Dawson's son, Cyril, was based in Hong Kong in charge of a ship management company, whose specially built and equipped ships carried live buffaloes from Bombay to the Arabian Gulf ports, because these Muslim countries would only eat meat of an animal freshly killed. On an Air India flight from Hong Kong to Bombay, Cyril, normally a teetotaller, asked the air hostess for a cocktail so that he could sleep all through the flight and wake up fresh to take up his duties immediately on arrival. The air hostess did not understand what exactly he required and asked the purser within Cyril's hearing *"Is admi ko combra ka poonch chahiye"* (This person wants the tail of a cock.). Cyril, who understands Hindi very well, had a good laugh.

Gerry was a forester with BBTC (Bombay Burma Trading Company) and spent most of his time in the jungles. When he came to Rangoon for three or four days each month he was always invited for dinner. He would be telling stories of his experiences in the forests, and had not finished his soup while everyone else had finished dinner. Then looking around and seeing that everyone was waiting for him he would put all the courses, including his pudding, into his soup plate and eat the mixture with relish. He said, "It all goes into the same stomach."

From Saligao

Sequeira – father of Bishop Vally, Germaine, Josie, Laura and Ada (my grand-mother's brother – house next door to Dr Vitorin Saldanha and in front of Dr Rudolph D'Mello – now ruined)
Hipolito D'Souza (wife Ancy was sister of Miss Ethelvin D'Mello, whose school later became Lourdes Convent) – father of Arist, Alphonse, Tiny (Colombo), George, Hilda, Irene.
Manuel Machado (house where Muriel & Mario now stay) – father of Maurice (UK), Joyce Nazareth (Mahim), Lyra (UK)
Francis **Machado** – father of Neville, Bobby, Freddy, Cissy (Pinto),

Julie (Lobo), Bertha

Machado – father of Tony (of Otis), Joe and Tessie (Chembur)

Machado – father of Father Sonny (Mount Mary's) & Lily (Menezes)

Sequeira – U. Sonny, wife Olive (D'Sa) – father of Frances (wife of Orlando, Dr Willie's brother), Eleanor (wife of Oswald D'Mello)

Vaz – father of Alexander, Alex, Dr Robert, Joe, Sonny, Peter, Frank (my brother-in-law) and Queenie

Cordeiro – father of Bobby Fernandes (Bandra), Vivian (Wife of D'Lima of Chembur later posted in Washington, USA) and May (wife of Willie Mascarenhas)

Joe Cordeiro – husband of Anne and father of Eric, Allan and Chu-chu (Mr. Farmer, Guirim)

R Lobo – father of Nellie, Gladys, Dr Dennis Lobo (who tried to establish himself in Margao and then returned to California)

Joe Lobo – father of Gerard (UK) and Catherine (Germany)

D'Souza – father of Walter & Isabelle

Lobo, Dr Mark (W.L.) – father of Arthur, Dr Margaret, Joyce, Joan (all in Australia)

D'Cruz – father of Dr Victor (Bangalore), Arnould (Pune), Wynnie & Emily (Nagpur) – Grand-father of Dr. Bertram (Nagpur)

D'Souza – father of Edmund and his sisters (went to Karachi)

Saldanha – Joseph (wife Carmelina)– Customs at Rangoon / Akyab – father of Willie (Rangoon), George (US), Len (US), Alda (Calcutta), Sylvie (Calcutta) and Victor (UK)

From Sangolda

Domingo Xavier de Souza (Cheron Bakery) – my grand-father (house in ruins)

Athaide – father of Olga Nobre, Bandra

Prudencio Noronha – father of Jeanette D'Souza (Bandra)

S M Pereira – father of Bertie

D'Souza– father of Reuben (Sherley, Bandra)

From Olaulim

M C Pinto – father of Maxie, Selwyn, Angela, Agnes...

Vincent Salvador Rodrigues – married my Dad's sister, Bemvinda – father of Bella (D'Cruz), Leo, Louis, Alex, Allan, Ronnie, Rudi, & Collette (Andrade) – all in Canada

Nasciment Rodrigues – brother of Salu – his wife, Eulalia is at Olaulim, father of Dr. Agnelo, Linda (Noronha–Delhi), Melba (Remedios, Canada) & Ronnie

From Salvador do Mundo

Balbino de Athaide (brother of my Mum's mother) – wife Annie (D'Sa) – father of Cissy (D'Souza), Doris (Ghoshal – California), Earnest, Felix (IC Colony, Borivali), Gloria (Francis – Calcutta) – completed his musical scale – A to G.

Martin – father of Stella and her two sisters (from Todda)

From Curtorim, Salcette

Reginaldo Joao Pimenta – transferred to Rangoon in 1938 as branch manager of Oriental Insurance – father of John (Chicago), Helmana (Sr Mary Adelia – Panchgani), Lourdes (Pinto – Candolim), Jimmy (Toronto), late Edigio, Sr. Rosaria (Baroda), Sr Celina, Eslinda (aka Hazel, my wife), Jennifer (Pune) & Veronica (Peres Cardoza – Merces)

From Calangute (I think)

Carmo-Lobo – Father of Quentin, Prince and Veronica (beautiful young lady as per my Dad)

San Lazaro – family was in Belgaum

Salgados – Father of Dr Alwyn (Bangalore) and Tiny (married to Carvalho, RTO official who has built his house just behind O Coqueiro, Alto Porvorim)

From Candolim

Hugh de Nazareth – Tyre king of Bangalore

From Ucassim

Lobo – father of Frank (wife Lyra, sister of Fenelon D'Souza, Saligao) and Annie (Fernandez) – grand-father of Aloysius Fernandez, Bangalore (Mr. Lobo's other brother was in Africa)

From Aldona

Peter Fernandez husband of Annie Lobo and father of Aloysius & Raymond)
Monsignor Joe Fernandez (brother of Peter) still in Burma
Lynch (sister of Peter Fernandez)
Menezes – husband of Florry (my Mum's eldest sister) – father of Albert – Grand-father of Damas, Eugene, Dennis – Great-Grand-Father of Bro Gerry, Principal, Regina Mundi School, Dabolim
Dr. Menezes – father of Major Caesar (Burmese wife, Thelma, lives in Bangalore) Grand-father of Oscar (Bangalore), Bill (Australia), Lynn and Asha (Dubai)
Menezes – father of Lily – grand-father of Lenny (Nagpur)
Coutinho – father of Eremit (deceased), Felix (deceased), Lily & Mary (in home for the aged at Ucassim) and Fr Rufus (Jesuit priest in Kathmandu)

From Nachinola

Anju D'Souza – Iza's and my Dad (My Grand-dad Sylvester Philip had gone to Canada in 1918 after WW I)
Gerald D'Souza – (Dad's brother) – father of Sylvester, Eulalia (Mathias), Michael, Joseph, Goiya (Fenelly, New York), Gemma (Sequeira – Mahim) and late Carl.
(Our neighbour, Dr Jose D'Souza's brother had gone to Brazil – my Grand-Dad visited him in Brazil)

From Moira

Pinto, Tutu – husband of Cissie (Machado) – father of Celine, Kevin, Derrick, Ian (all in Canada)
Nazareth George (lighthouse keeper) & his brother

From Divar

John Menezes – father of Eric, Tony (Goa Management College) & Maria (married to my cousin Sylvester Philip D'Souza)

Goan village not known

Constance Denis – worked with Hugh Nazareth's family – became Jesuit Brother at Vinayalaya (in charge of making Mass wine)
Sylvester Castellino – brother of Castellino Bakery, Pune
Fernandes – piano tuner – family at Roselands, Santa Cruz
Manricks – Mario (Colombo)
Manricks – Francis (Canada)
[Thanks to Stanley Pinto, Asha, Paul D'Gama and Aruna Gomes, Calcutta for inputs.]

Understanding Burma

Burma and Goa – age-old links

GOA'S association with Burma goes back to the early six-teenth century. Goa was discovered and conquered for Portugal by Afonso de Albuquerque on March 3, 1510, without a shot being fired and without a man being lost. He set himself up regally in keeping with the title of Viceroy of India, endowed on him by King Manuel of Portugal before his departure from Portugal on this voyage of discovery.

However, his reign came to an end very soon. In May that same year the Sultan of Bijapur sent an army of 20,000 to re-take Goa. Albuquerque and his soldiers and sailors, in all about 1,200 men, could not face this army, so they boarded their own ships but could not sail away because of the advent of the monsoons. In addition to the sailors and soldiers, they took with them aboard the ships all the provisions and treasures they had captured from the well-stocked harems of the Sultan's administrators, which included about 300 women chosen for their sturdiness and beauty.

They waited out the monsoon rains marooned in the Mandovi Harbour. The cramped living conditions on board were aggravated by the presence of women. Surprisingly in spite of so few women compared to the number of men, there were not too many incidents and by September, when the monsoons ended, all these women had found husbands to whom they were legally married by the priest present on each ship. This priest also ensured that each woman before being married was baptised and made a Christian. By September, most of these women were pregnant and thus Albuquerque had complied with the directions of Pope Alexander VI to increase the number of Christians in India.

Rather than face this garrison immediately, Albuquerque withdrew to Anjadiv Island where his men could rest and recuperate. To his pleasant surprise he found four Portuguese warships there. These had been sent by King Manuel to take over Malacca, at that time the largest and richest port for trade in spices in the Far East. These warships carried three hundred fighting men and sailors, commanded by Diogo Mendes. Albuquerque convinced Mendes that it would be impossible with his small force to take over the well fortified forts in the Malaccas. He suggested that Mendes help him re-conquer Goa and then their joint force of over 1,500 soldiers and sailors would sail to establish Portuguese trading stations in the Malaccas. This was agreed.

On November 25, 1510, the Portuguese won a resounding victory over the Sultan's garrison in Goa. Two churches, one dedicated to Our Lady of the Rosary and the second to Our Lady of the Mount, were erected in Velha Goa in thanksgiving for this victory. The Viceroy's gate was erected to commemorate this event.

To avoid future revolts the Portuguese put to death all the Muslim men, but did spare some of the women, provided they accepted baptism, became Christians and agreed to marry a Portuguese sailor or soldier. These soldiers and sailors were rewarded with a house and a few acres of land with the right to trade and, of course, the wife he had selected together with whatever jewellery and personal property she owned.

In a few months, after organising the administration of Goa, Albuquerque together with Mendes sailed for the Malaccas and was successful in capturing and establishing a well-fortified base for trade there. He returned just in time to prevent the Sultan of Bijapur retaking Goa. After staying long enough to ensure that his administration was functioning properly, he sailed westward and was successful in establishing a trading base at Ormuz. In October 1515 he felt death approaching and, wanting to die in Goa, turned his ships back to Goa. En route they encountered another Portuguese ship whose captain informed him that his old rival at court, Lopes Soares d'Albergerial, had been appointed Viceroy of India and had arrived there two months earlier with a large number of administrators. King Manuel had not bothered to inform Albuquerque of his dismissal. Albuquerque died on December 16, 1515 just as his ship dropped anchor in the harbour at Goa.

Goa became the eastern base for Portuguese trade with the Far East. Portuguese adventurers now investigated other ports where they could establish trading bases further eastward – these included Ceylon, Nagapattinam, Porto Novo, Sao Tome de Meliapore, Pulicat, Masulipatnam, Pipli, Ugolim, Bandel, Sandwip, Chittagong, Syriam, Malacca, Moluccas, Solor.

The first trade agreement between Portugal and Burma was by Anthony Correa with the Viceroy of Martaban in 1519. However the King of Burma, Tabinshweti, did not approve of this agreement and attacked Martaban in 1541. Surprisingly 700 Portuguese mercenaries fought on the side of the King of Burma against the Viceroy of Martaban and the Portuguese garrison. Martaban's Portuguese garrison retreated to Arakan, where they continued to maintain a trading station.

In 1600 Philip de Brito y Nicote, a Portuguese cabin boy, took up a job with the King of Arakan, who had conquered Bago (Pegu) and started constructing forts in the city. De Brito took a trip to Goa, where he married the daughter of the Viceroy of India and returned to Bago with men and weapons. As a wedding present to himself, de Brito declared himself the King of Pegu and Toungoo and set up his base at Syriam. He ruled for thirteen years, but because of his brutality, the locals finally convinced the original Kings of Pegu and Toungoo to attack. They laid siege to Syriam and after 34 days the bastion fell. De Brito was impaled on a pole and placed over the city's ramparts – it took him three days to die. The Portuguese who survived the siege were sent to villages in Shwebo and Sagaing districts, where their descendants still live. These people provided a reservoir from which the King's gunners were drawn. Throughout the sixteenth and seventeenth centuries Portuguese adventurers, as mercenaries, continued to take part in local wars between various Burmese chieftains on both sides. These Portuguese adventurers brought chaplains, who engaged in mission work. Portuguese, French and Italian (Catholic) priests worked in Burma from the late 17th century onwards, without encountering any direct opposition from the Buddhists.

Portugal had a series of fortified trading bases in the Indian Ocean – Sofala, Mozambique, Mombasa, Hormuz, Bahrain, Muscat, Diu, Daman, Bassein, Bombay, Calicut and Cochin. The Viceroy's base for the administration of these areas was in Goa. With the addition of trading bases in the Bay of Bengal, Portugal was able to monopolise trade in spices, gems, gold and silks between the Far East and Europe. Portugal's declared policy was not to establish colonies, but only strongly held trading posts, each with a small garrison. When other European powers, England, France, the Dutch and to lesser extent the Danish, contested Portugal's exclusive right to trade, one by one these bases were ceded or taken over.

England contested Portugal's right to exclusive trade with India and the Far East by establishing the East India Company in 1600. E I Company, also called 'John Company', started with one trading post in Calcutta and then opened trading posts in Madras and Surat. Bombay or Bom Bahia (good harbour in Portuguese) was given by the Portuguese as part of the dowry brought by Princess Catherine de Braganza to the English King Charles II on their marriage in 1661. Bombay soon took precedence over Surat (where the harbour had silted over) as E.I. Company's main trading post. Over the years from 1600 to 1857, E I Co., using the policy of 'divide and rule', virtually took over the entire Indian subcontinent. After the Indian Mutiny in 1857 (or as we Indians now call it, The First War of Independence) Queen Victoria nominated herself Empress of India and the whole sub-continent of India including Ceylon became the 'Jewel in the Crown' (of England).

England established its first trading base in Burma, at Syriam in 1709. In October 1759, alleging that the English were secretly arming the Mons tribe, as reported to him by their French rivals, A-laung-pa-ya, King of Burma, laid siege to Syriam and massacred the English factory staff. This brought to an end trading by East India Company in Burma for the time being. The E I Co. was now looking at India and Burma as potential markets for the products of the industrial revolution in England, not merely as a source for supply of luxury articles like spices, silks and gems.

In 1784, the new King of Burma, Bo-daw-pa-ya, invaded and conquered Arakan. Most of the Arakanese did not accept his rule, revolted and fled to Chittagong, in E I Co.'s territory of Bengal. In spite of repeated diplomatic approaches between 1795 and 1811 the King of Burma and his officials remained unfriendly to the English, and were definitely pro-French.

The Anglo-Burmese Wars

There were three Burmese Wars or Anglo-Burmese Wars: between 1824 to 1826; 1852 to 1853; and 1885 to 1886. The expansion of Burma had consequences along its frontiers. As those frontiers moved ever closer to British East India Company and later British India, there were problems both with refugees and military operations spilling over ill-defined borders.

The First Anglo-Burmese War (1824–1826) ended in a British East India Company victory, and by the Treaty of Yandabo, Burma lost territory previously conquered in Assam, Manipur, and Arakan. The British also took possession of Tenasserim with the intention to use it as a bargaining chip in future negotiations with either Burma or Siam. As the century wore on, the British East India Company began to covet the resources and main part of Burma during an era of great territorial expansion.

In 1852, Commodore Lambert was dispatched to Burma by Lord Dalhousie over a number of minor issues related to the previous treaty. The Burmese immediately made concessions including the removal of a governor whom the British had made their *casus belli*. Lambert eventually provoked a naval confrontation in extremely questionable circumstances and thus started the Second Anglo-Burmese War in 1852, which ended in the British annexation of Pegu province, renamed Lower Burma. The war resulted in a palace revolution in Burma, with King Pagan Min (1846–1852) being replaced by his half brother, Mindon Min (1853–1878).

King Mindon tried to modernise the Burmese state and economy to resist British encroachments, and he established a new capital at Mandalay, which he proceeded to fortify. This was not enough to stop the British, however, who claimed that Mindon's son Thibaw Min (ruled 1878–1885) was a tyrant intending to side with the French, that he had lost control of the country, thus allowing for disorder at the frontiers, and that he was reneging on a treaty signed by his father. The British declared war once again in 1885, conquering the remainder of the country in the Third Anglo-Burmese War resulting in total annexation of Burma.

WW II and the aftermath

Burma was invaded by the Japanese from the south and the east and taken over in 1941-42. The Indian National Army (of Netaji Subhash Chandra Bose) and some Burmans joined the Japanese.

When the British got the upper hand in 1945 Burman irregulars under Aung San joined the British in mopping up operations against the Japs. In January 1947 Britain decided to give Burma Independence with Aung San as the nominated Prime Minister. However on July 19, Aung San and six of his ministers were assassinated. Independence to Burma was finally granted on January 4,, 1948.

However, the Shans, the Chins, the Kachins, the Karens and other ethnic tribes have not accepted merger with "low-land Burmese" and there continues to be insurgencies almost throughout Burma

Burma continues to be more or less run by the Military – civilian rule has been suppressed. Once a really rich country, Burma is now one of the poorest countries in Asia.

Background literature

In *The Burman – An Appreciation*, C. J. Richards (Longmans Green: 1945) speaks of his 23 years in Burma as a British government official.

George Orwell (real name Eric Blair) in *Burmese Days* (1935), now believed to be his biography, sets down his experiences as an Officer in the Indian Imperial Police in Burma from 1922 to 1927. On page 100 he describes to Elizabeth, newly arrived from Great Britain, a *pwe*, a Burmese dance drama set to music: "Every movement that girl makes has been studied and handed down through innumerable generations. Whenever you look closely at the art of these Eastern peoples you can see that – a civilization stretching back and back, practically the same, into times when we were dressed in woad (blue body paint of ancient Britons)."

In his book *Dancing in Cambodia – At Large in Burma*, Amitav Ghosh quotes his Uncle, Prince: "It was a golden land. The richest country in Asia, except for Japan. There are no people on earth to compare with the Burmese – so generous, so hospitable, so kind to strangers. No one goes hungry in Burma: you just have to ask and someone will feed you."

Some new titles

:

The Permanent Resident, short stories by Roanna Gomes (Australia)

Yesterday in Paradise. Journalist Cyprian Fernandes' take on life in East Africa.

The Salt of the Earth, stories from rustic Goa by Jayanti Naik (translated by Augusto Pinto)

Lengthening Shadows (I and II), charming Portuguese stories written by Goans, translated by Dr Paul Melo e Castro.

Preia-Mar, a posthumously-published novel in Portuguese by one of the region's finest short-story writers in that language

Feast, Feni and Firecrackers -- life of a village schoolboy in Portuguese Goa , by Mel D'Souza

Aida's Forever -- a young girl growing up in the Goa of the 1940s

Shorty Gomes, a detective novel with a Goan character. Ahmed Bunglowala.

Get in touch for how to get our books via mail-order, to all parts of the globe.

Contact us at
Goa,1556
784 Near Lourdes Convent
Sonarbhat Saligao 403511 Bardez Goa
Email goa1556@gmail.com
M 9822122436 P 9822122436
http://goa1556.in

Goa books make a great gift! Promote writing from Goa, understand your home.

Goa 1556

Interested in Goa books?

Write to us for a free Goa-related ebook
goa1556@gmail.com
SMS 91-9822122436
Include your email address